Hands-On INTERNET

A Beginning Guide for PC Users

David Sachs
Henry Stair

D1227558

P T R Prentice Hall
Englewood Cliffs, New Jersey 07632

Library of Congress Cataloging-in-Publication Data

Sachs, David,
 Hands-on Internet: a beginning guide for PC users / David Sachs,
Henry Stair.
  p. cm.
 Includes bibliographical references and index
 ISBN 0-13-056392-7
  1. Internet (Computer network)   I. Stair, Henry H.,
II. Title.
TK5105.875.I57S33 1994
004.6'7--dc20   93-40879
                                                       CIP

Editorial/production supervision: *Harriet Tellem*
Cover design: *Violet Lake*
Buyer: *Alexis Heydt*
Acquisitions editor: *Mary Franz*
Editorial assistant: *Noreen Regina*

 © 1994 by P T R Prentice Hall
Prentice-Hall, Inc.
A Paramount Communications Company
Englewood Cliffs, New Jersey 07632

The publisher offers discounts on this book when ordered in bulk quantities. For more information contact:

Corporate Sales Department
P T R Prentice Hall
113 Sylvan Avenue
Enlgewood Cliffs, NJ 07632

Phone: 201-592-2863
Fax: 201-592-2249

All product names mentioned herein are the trademarks of their respective owners.

Printed in the United States of America
10 9 8 7 6 5 4 3 2 1

ISBN 0-13-056392-7

Prentice-Hall International (UK) Limited, *London*
Prentice-Hall of Australia Pty. Limited, *Sydney*
Prentice-Hall Canada Inc., *Toronto*
Prentice-Hall Hispanoamericana, S.A., *Mexico*
Prentice-Hall of India Private Limited, *New Delhi*
Prentice-Hall of Japan, Inc., *Tokyo*
Simon & Schuster Asia Pte. Ltd., *Singapore*
Editor Prentice-Hall do Brasil, Ltda., *Rio de Janeiro*

Dedication

To Linda and Lorrine, for patience, perseverance, and perfection.

Acknowledgments

In recognizing all those who have helped us along the way, we begin with a tribute to all who have gone on ahead. The authors of many fine books on the Internet have helped us much and will later, we hope, help our readers.

At Prentice Hall, Mary Franz has been of inestimable and tireless assistance. She has both guided us and traveled with us through the thickets of text, publishing, and software acquisition.

The production has been excellently created, done, and re-done by our wonderful one-woman design company, Deane Pfeil.

Mary and Deane and others at Prentice-Hall have reviewed this book so many times with us that it is fair to say that what you see is the product of many hands. The errors and omissions, however, remain ours and ours alone.

David Sachs
Henry Stair

CONTENTS

SESSION TWO
Electronic Mail

37

SESSION THREE

57

The News

SESSION FOUR

81

Contributing to Usenet

SESSION FIVE   103

Mailing Lists

SESSION SIX   133

Other Hosts - Telnet

SESSION SEVEN   159

Getting Things: File Transfer Protocol

SESSION EIGHT 191

Finding Things

SESSION NINE 217

Quick Reference

APPENDIX A   A 229

Where to Learn More

APPENDIX B   A 235

PC Communications and The Disk

APPENDIX C

Dial-Up Internet Services

APPENDIX D

The Internet Society

INDEX

Preface

The Internet. Once only an obscure road for university researchers, it has become a worldwide electronic superhighway for everyone. Magazines, newspapers, and television programs continuously proclaim about the wonders of the Internet. They declare that millions of people are on the Internet, but they don't tell YOU how to get there and you can't find a map. You'd like to travel this highway, but you can't find an entrance. You look at all the books about the Internet and they are full of wonderful ideas. But they are also full of strange words that you don't understand. They don't tell you what to do or how to do it. You would like to learn, but you just don't know where to begin. We suggest that you begin here.

If you are a PC user, we will get you started. We will take you gently step by step. We will show you how to start, where to start, and what to do. All you need is your PC and a modem. If you don't have a modem, we will tell you how to get one. We have included a disk with the communications software you will need. We will tell you where the entrances are and show you how to enter. We will demystify the strange words and let you in on the "secrets."

Then you will begin your own hands-on practice of electronic mail and electronic news. You will subscribe to electronic mailing lists that interest you and you will learn how to leave them. You will go legally into other computers around the world and find the vast information resources there. You will learn how to find software, poems, speeches, and games along this electronic superhighway, and then you will learn how to bring them back home with you. You will become an Internaut!

Come along with us now, for your first hands-on explorations of the Internet.

About the Authors

David Sachs is professor of office information systems at Pace University's School of Computer Science and Information Systems where he has been actively involved in teaching computer science courses for the past 10 years. He has previously co-authored *Discovering Microsoft Works* and *Mastering Microsoft Works*. Dr. Sachs is particularly interested in the field of telecommunications and its impact upon our world.

Pete Stair is a senior consultant with Mycroft Information in New Canaan, Connecticut where he specializes in high performance global telecommunications and computer networking. He previously co-authored the post-graduate textbook *Megabit Data Communications*. He is a registered professional engineer (CA) and a member of the IEEE and the Internet Society. His interests include de-mystifying technology, cross-country skiing, consciousness research, and classical music.

INTRODUCTION

Before Your First Session

The Game Plan

Our game plan in this book is very simple. We want to get you started on the Internet! And we want to get you up and running as fast as possible. You can learn the fascinating histories and wonderful tales about the Internet elsewhere. Our only purpose is to teach you the basics and to do it while you are actually on the world's greatest network. You won't need to know anything about networks or communications. We will give you only what you need and only when you need it. After you are well started, you can move ahead on your own to learn the more advanced ways of doing things.

So here's the plan: in this section we tell you what we're going to do. Then we will work together to make sure you have everything you need to start. If some things are missing, we'll show you how and where to get them. Then we will get you going right away in Session One.

We call the chapters of this book "sessions" because every section (except this first one) will be done while you are connected to the Internet. Each session introduces one or, at most, two new concepts. Each session takes you step by step through what you need to learn to move on to the next session.

You can work through the sessions as quickly or as slowly as you wish. You are completely in charge of the pace and you can repeat a session if you wish.

We have developed and tested these sessions to be sure you learn things quickly, clearly, and consecutively. Each section builds on what has gone before. We want to be sure you have completed each session before you move on. Please stay with us and don't skip ahead unless you really know that section.

Start Right Away

Session One starts by getting you connected to the Internet and showing you all the things you will need for later sessions. We will also do several things to help make you feel comfortable. Learning the Internet doesn't have to be intimidating. A lot of what happens on the Internet is not all that complicated, but Internet history has created its own jargon and language. At first we will not use this jargon because you won't need it. Later in the book we will begin to introduce a few acronyms, words, and phrases because by then you will need them to understand what's really going on.

When we do have to use a new term or phrase, we will always show it in **bold**. Then we will tell you what it really means in plain English. In fact, our intent is to use plain English everywhere we possibly can. When you finish with our book, we hope you will be ready to move on to many more activities on the Internet. If we have done our job right, you will also be ready to read some of the many excellent but more advanced books about the Internet.

Many people have told us that getting started is the hardest part because of the strange acronyms and terms. We will lead you carefully to these new words so that you really understand them. But we won't start until you are ready.

Learn by Example

For each new Internet activity we describe, there will be several examples for you to work through. The examples have been carefully chosen to show you how the Internet works but also so you can have some fun while doing them. For example, in Session Two you will be able to send yourself some electronic mail. Then you will see what it looks like when someone else receives your notes, because you will have sent it to yourself. There will be many examples like this to help teach you what's happening.

For each session we will suggest other examples you can invent and try yourself. As we go through each example, we will point out the ideas and concepts behind what you are learning. In later sessions, these ideas and concepts will keep returning. We hope you will begin to build a base of real knowledge that allows you to move on far beyond this book.

Train by Doing

This is not an armchair textbook. We want to train you "on the job," and we also want that job to be fun and interesting. We want you to know how to do Internet activities AND we want you to understand why they are done that way. We are going to make a few assumptions about you. If we sometimes go over some simple things that you already know, bear with us. There may be another reader who doesn't know them. If you already know what we are covering, just skim over it. Don't go too far; we may have something you need just beyond.

The Internet

Let's look for a moment at the Internet. Let's see what it is and what it can do. Then we'll see what you can do to start.

The strangest thing about the Internet is that many people don't know or understand it at all. Some people think of it only as an electronic mail system. Others wonder if it is an information service like Prodigy or CompuServe. Yet other people know it only as a way to get to distant supercomputer centers. We need a model to think about what it is. Then we can see how it is used to carry electronic mail, information services, and many other services.

Probably the best model or analogy is that of a giant highway system that connects computers. It connects all kinds of computers, no matter who made them, what programs run on them, or who they belong to – computers as large as the biggest supercomputers in the world and as small as a laptop PC. By connecting these computers, the Internet connects the people who use the computers. It's called the Internet because it connects not only computers, but all the different kinds of regional and local networks that hook up all these computers as well. Like the highway system, the Internet consists of interstates and state highways and little roads. The number of computers and people linked by the Internet is now in the tens of millions and growing at an ever-faster rate.

Another amazing fact about the Internet is that no one is really in charge. Many experienced scientists, engineers, administrators, and technical people work hard to keep each of their road systems running. A smaller group of people devise standard ways of communicating, but there is no chief executive. It runs because a cooperative group of people from all over the world wants to keep it going. Things may change in the future, but for now this highway system works because a lot of very good people want it to work. Although it started many years ago in the United States, this cooperative effort now extends all around the globe. But what does this highway system do and why is everyone so interested?

What's Out There?

The highway system by itself is not as interesting as where it can take us. With this highway system, you can exchange nearly instant electronic mail with more than 10 million people. You can read all kinds of news and opinions you won't ever find on radio or television and find them neatly organized in thousands of topics. You can also read the opinions of people with wildly different interests. Some of this is really pretty strange, but you can follow just what interests you. Then you can share your thoughts and ideas with people who have your interests.

There are hundreds of electronic mailing lists for special interests of all kinds and you can subscribe to as many as you wish. As a PC user you can find vast libraries of free or shareware software programs. There are books and documents and pictures and maps of all kinds to be shared. There are games you can play by yourself and multiuser games you can play with others. There are things for children and things definitely not for children. Like any road system, the Internet roads lead past both the cultural and the seamy. You can find information of almost any sort. If you can't find what you are looking for, you can ask others for help. There are other computers that you can sign on to (it really is legal) and find further resources for fun or interest, work or play.

So Now Let's Get Started!

Getting you ready for the Internet really means three things. We assume that you have an IBM PC or workstation of some kind. We assume that you know how to turn it on, and how to start and run a program. If you use a computer to write letters or do your checks, you know enough to get started. We'll take you from there.

Let's begin with your PC.

We will call it a PC for short, but it could be an IBM personal computer, a more powerful workstation, or a keyboard/display terminal connected to some other computer. In any case, you will be typing things onto the keyboard and reading things on the screen. This is a beginning book and we won't talk about graphic user interfaces or window programs. That can all come later. We want to start with simple typed commands and easy-to-read text screens. First, we have to find out if your PC has a connection to other computers.

NOTE: *If you already have a "full" connection to the Internet and want to jump ahead, you should go immediately to Session One. Make sure you have more than just an electronic mail connection. If you are not sure, stay with us here for a while.*

Two Ways to Connect

There are really just two basic ways your PC can connect to other computers. The first is by a telephone connection that dials up some distant computer. This is the slower method, but it can be used from anywhere there is a telephone. The second is by direct wire connections to other nearby computers. This is the faster method, but it is usually available only on campuses or in larger businesses. If you must connect to the Internet via telephone, we will point you toward several "public" Internet access services that you can dial up. In the second case, your school or business may already have a connection that you can use.

Two Kinds of Connections

After you know you can reach another computer that is "on the Internet," you have to find out what kind of Internet connection the other computer has. It may have only an electronic mail link to send and receive notes and messages to and from others on the Internet. Or it may have what we will call "full" Internet connectivity. Here, the computer can give you access to all the worldwide resources. By the way, all the dial-up Internet access services we show later offer the "full" range of Internet functions.

If you want to take advantage of these tremendous resources, you will need this "full" connection. In a little while, we will detail exactly what we mean by "full." First you will have to help us find out what you have. Then we'll ask more questions about which way you would like to go. Ultimately you will have to decide which is best for you. We'll help you all along the way. Let's begin with your PC.

Your PC's Connections

Our first questions will tell us if you have dial-up telephone capability, wired capability, or neither of these. If you don't have either one, don't worry. We'll suggest what you need to do to get connected. Here are the first three questions:

Question A:

Do you have a PC and already use a telephone dial-up service such as Prodigy, CompuServe, MCI-Mail or America Online? If your answer is yes, then you already have a **modem** and run a PC program to use the modem. (As noted before, we will use **bold print** for terms like **modem,** that may be new to you. We will always put such terms in **bold** and explain them briefly the first time we use them.) A **modem** is just a telephone set for computers. It dials up and "talks" to other modems and computers at the far end of the telephone line.

A: Modem & Telephone? _____ Yes _____ No

Question B:

Do you have a PC, but don't have any kind of wired connection to another computer and don't have a modem to use a dial-up service?

B: No Connection? _____ Yes _____ No

In this case, you will need to get a modem. This is not difficult, and we'll lead you through how to do so step by step. Remember, this is a hands-on guide.

At this point, you should jump to **Appendix B** where we will lead you through getting a modem and a communications program. When you have them, you will be ready to start Session One.

Question C:

Do you have a PC or keyboard/display terminal that is already connected to a larger computer that serves your campus or department or company? If it is, there will a connecting wire of some kind on the back of your PC. Often these wires are called Local Area Networks **(LANs)** or **Ethernets** or **Token Rings**. These are all just different types of wires to connect local groups of computers. It is often said that your PC is "on a LAN." Here, you may already have a connection to another computer that has a connection to the Internet. We'll tell you how to find out.

C: Wire (LAN) Connection? _____ Yes _____ No

Which Way to Go?

If you answered NO to Question C, that is, you do not have a wire or LAN connection, then dial-up is probably the quickest way to get you started.

If you answered YES to Question C and don't want or need to use a dial-up service, jump ahead to our section on LAN connections in this session.

Using Dial-Up Services

If you already use dial-up services, then you recognize that many charge for their services. The same will be true for dial-up Internet access services. If this is the way you choose to go, we have listed several dial-up services in **Appendix B** at the back of the book. Through the courtesy of several of these services, we have also included some coupons at the very back of the book. These coupons give a variety of introductory offers. (The authors are not connected in any way with any of these services.)

If you decide to dial-up an Internet access service, you may be ready to jump ahead to Session One. Let's find out.

If you already use a dial-up service other than Prodigy, you have a modem and a communications program. (Prodigy supplies you with their own communications program that can talk only to Prodigy.) Your communications program may be called Telix Lite or Crosstalk or Smartcom or it may be the "Terminal" or "Communications" feature of a Microsoft Windows or Microsoft Works package. If you have these, you should review **Appendix B** to select an Internet access service and then jump to Session One.

If you have Prodigy, you may need to acquire a more general communications program. The good news is that you may already have one. If you have Microsoft Windows, it has a "Terminal" application on the Accessories window. If you have Microsoft Works or Lotus Works, each has a "Communications" function. Each of these three will work with your modem and allow you to dial-up an Internet access service right away. If you don't use these programs regularly, you will want to review the manuals for these communications functions.

You may have other programs that can communicate. Check your manuals and see if they do. If you don't find a communications program, jump to **Appendix B** where we will teach you how to use Telix Lite. After this, you will be ready for Session One.

LAN Connections

If you answered YES to Question C, you have a wired or LAN connection to your PC. To see if you can reach the Internet this way, we need to learn about the other computers on your LAN that may connect to the Internet.

The Other Computer's Connections

After we know that you can reach another computer, we have to find out if it has Internet connectivity. Then we need to know what kind of connection it has. When we know these things, we can help you decide how you would like to proceed. To do this we must ask you to ask some other people. We will give you the questions and help you interpret the answers. When we are done, we hope you will know exactly what you can do through this LAN connection.

Whom You Should Ask

When a business or campus or school has a LAN, there is usually someone who takes care of it. This person may be called a LAN Administrator or the Information Systems person or just Pat. The hardest part here may be finding this knowledgeable person. You may have to ask co-workers or managers, but we suggest you ask the person who always knows about computers. In almost every school or business there is at least one person everyone always goes to with computer questions. Hopefully, you already know who this is. If you don't, ask around until you find this person. This is quite important because we need to find real answers, not just guesses.

What You Should Ask Them

Here are the questions to ask to find out if your LAN connected PC can get to the "full" range of Internet services. The "full" range is important, as we will be introducing this range throughout the rest of this book. Don't worry if you don't fully understand the questions or the answers just yet. When you get connected and work through this book, you will understand. For now, it's important just to get the answers from a knowledgeable person.

There is going to be a pattern to our questions. The pattern is this: if any question is answered with a "no," or an "I don't know," you probably cannot use the LAN connection on your PC to get to the Internet. At least you will not be able to use the full range of services. If this is the case, you have two choices. The first is to argue with your school, campus or business that an Internet connection is really needed – needed not just for you, but to bring the whole organization into the 1990s networking world. The second is to revisit the sections above on dial-up connections and look to **Appendix C** to find a dial-up Internet service provider.

The questions to ask are:

1. *Are any of the computers on our "network" on the Internet?*

2. *Can I reach that computer from my PC or workstation?*

3. *Is it OK with our school (campus, company) if I get a connection to the Internet?*

4. *Can I send and receive Internet electronic mail?*

5. *Will I be able to use "telnet" and "FTP" and get the "Usenet newsgroups"?*

6. *Can you help me get connected or can you tell me someone who can tell me what I need to get connected?*

What the Answers Mean

1. *The local area network (LAN) probably connects many different computers. If there is an Internet connection, one of these computers may be on your "network" (LAN). If none is connected, you may have to go back to a dial-up approach.*

2. *If there is a computer connected to the Internet, do we have the software and connections on both that computer and my PC to reach it?*

3. *If all the wires and programs are there, will I be permitted to use them? That is, do we have the approvals (funding, permissions, etc.) for me to be part of it?*

4. *Electronic mail is usually the lowest common denominator of Internet access. Many places have only electronic mail access. This is a good beginning, but will not give you the richness of "full" Internet access.*

5. *Here is the real key question. If you can get these three things, you will have "full" Internet access. Later in the book, we will spend entire sessions on each of these topics. For now we just need to know whether you can reach them.*

6. *This is also a tough one. We need to find someone who can help you with the complexities of the connections and programs. Since every place is different and often*

unique, we can only help you find the local experts. If you have a LAN, they exist; you'll just have to find them.

If all the questions are answered "yes," you have the capability to connect your PC to the Internet. What you have to do now is get all the necessary things done. This may be as simple as having the knowledgeable person issue a few commands on some system. It may mean ordering and installing some programs on your PC. You may have to fill out and submit paper or electronic forms for approval of your connection and use of the Internet. Whatever is involved, you will need to get these things done before going further.

One possible outcome is that you will be given an **account** on the computer that accesses the Internet. You should also be told what you need to enter at your PC to get to that **account**. We will explain **account** as the first item in Session One.

Computers and the Internet

We are going to make a few assumptions about your PC and about the computer that connects to the Internet. We also have to talk for a moment about the programs that run both computers.

We are going to assume that your PC is running an **Operating System** called DOS or the Disk Operating System. An operating system is just a program that coordinates everything that happens on the computer. You can think of it as the program that's really in charge of everything on that computer. Almost all IBM and compatible computers now run DOS.

You may also be using Microsoft Windows to make it easier to use DOS. Once we get you connected to the Internet, some of the things going on will be happening on your PC under the control of DOS. Most of the things, however, will be happening on the computer actually connected to the Internet. That computer also has an operating system but it will most likely not be DOS.

Probably more than half of the computers that connect to the Internet run some form of an operating system called UNIX. While there are several slightly differing versions of UNIX (the name's not an acronym, just call it UNIX), you won't need to worry about the differences. UNIX also has programs, called **shells** that interpret commands. The most common shells are the "C" shell, the "Bourne" shell and the "Korn" shell. Most UNIX systems give you a choice of which shell to use, at least between the "Bourne" and "C" shells.

Although a computer doesn't have to run UNIX to be on the Internet, most of the systems you will encounter probably will use UNIX. For this book, we are going to assume that you will be connecting to a computer that runs some form of UNIX. Almost all of the dial-up services listed in Appendix C run the UNIX system. We are also going to assume that you will be given a "C" shell. Later in the book, we'll show you how to tell what you have and whom to ask if you want it changed.

You are now ready to begin Session One, which will have you using your new connection or account.

SESSION ONE

Logging In

Exploration

In our first session, we will begin our exploration of the resources of the Internet with a gentle peek. This is a vast and foreign territory for most people and we want to take it in small bite-sized chunks. During the first chunk, we will get familiar by getting in, looking around, and getting out.

Getting In

Getting in means understanding what our "account" is and how to get at it. After we are "in," we will build some confidence by doing a few simple tasks:

1. We will look around and find out who else is there;

2. We will look up a few ways the system can help us;

3. We will see how to get out gracefully.

Getting Out

We talk about getting out before logging in, just as we would show you how to use the brakes in a car before starting up. Getting out may sometimes seem tricky in this Internet world, as it can sometimes be a little difficult. We want to be sure that you have no fears in this area before we go in.

Getting out comes about in three fundamental scenarios. You will need these even after you are a real expert.

1. There is the normal or regular exit;

2. There is the exit we use after some trouble; and,

3. There is the "all else has failed and I want out" kind of exit.

We will make you an expert in all three. But first, we must begin by getting you connected to your "account."

What's an "Account"?

By now you have received your account. It may have been sent to you by your system administrator. It may have been arranged for you by your local computer expert. Or you may have signed up for a dial-up service from the instructions in **Appendix C**. One way or another, you are now the proud owner of an "account." Before we actually use the account, a few words of explanation are needed.

Your account is actually like owning or renting a timeshare or condo. You have exclusive rights to a part of a larger structure and shared rights to most of the common facilities. You have to behave by the rules set by the people who run the condo and you shouldn't become a nuisance to the others who reside there. Like a timeshare or condo, you can do whatever you like within your own space, as long as it doesn't bother or harm anyone else who lives there.

Your account comes in two parts and identifies you uniquely to the computer system.

1.   The first part may be called your **username** or **userid** or **loginname**.

2.   The second part of your account is your **password**.

Before telling you any more, we should say a little bit about the computer system "host."

What's a Host?

In specific terms, your account gives you certain rights to a portion of a computer that is somewhere else and belongs to somebody else. For historical reasons, these computers are usually called "hosts." They are, most often, not the big mainframe computers that live in big computer rooms or "glass houses." More often, they are minicomputers or powerful workstations that have the power to support a number of users (accounts) at the same time. From here on, we'll call them hosts.

Your account rights are exclusively yours, in your area, and only the computer system manager of the host can check up on you. System managers are truly busy people who won't check up on you unless someone else complains. This is why you should understand the "condo's" rules and be a good resident. Then you will be free to do what you would like to do.

Your Account or Loginname

Also like a condo, your account on the host system has a unique identifier or address and a key to get in. The account name may be one you were able to choose or it may be one you were assigned.

If you picked it, it may be your name or initials or a nickname or something about you that you wanted to be known by.

In the next session, we will introduce electronic mail, which is also known as **email**. Email is just what it sounds like; it is a way to send and receive electronic notes and messages to and from others. You will see that your account name is also what people will use to send you email. It will be the name on your electronic "mailbox." This account may be called by a number of different names on different systems.

The most common names for this new account of yours are:

1. your **loginname**;

2. your **userid**;

3. your **username**; or,

4. just your account name.

All mean the same thing. Your account or loginname is really just a string of letters (and/or numbers) that you use when you connect (or login) to the host. The host uses this string of characters to identify you uniquely.

The word **unique** is absolutely essential to assure that we don't start living in each other's condos. In this book, we will use **loginname** for this identifier, but you will see the same concept referred to by many other names.

Another small confusion has been created by the terms **login** and **logon**.

They both mean the same thing; they have different origins.

When you connect to the host where your account resides, a program usually asks you to: **Please Login:**

Other hosts may ask for your **userid**.

When we begin Session One in a moment, you will see that this is the first thing that you must type so that you may enter the shared system.

Your Key or Password

The other thing that you will need to get in is your key. On almost all computer systems, this is called a **password**.

This password is usually something you picked out when you signed up. It is also something you can change whenever you are connected to the system. Like the key to the front door of your condo, it permits access only to those who have it.

And, just like real keys, anyone who gets (or guesses) yours can use your account and run up your bill. However, unlike real keys, you can change yours whenever you are connected to the host. You don't need a locksmith.

Many hosts require you to change your password when you first connect to your account. They are concerned that just like in a real city, there may be thieves around. If you pick a simple password, the criminals can easily get into your account. If you use care in selecting your password, you make it difficult for the dishonest people to enter.

Not even the system manager can find out your password. It is kept in a file on the host in encrypted or coded form. When you change it, you will then be the only one who knows it. The administrator <u>can</u> change it for you, if you forget it.

Later in the book, we will learn that many hosts on the Internet pay important attention to the difference between lower case letters and capital letters. For now, we will point out how this becomes an advantage in selecting passwords.

In addition, many systems permit the use of numbers and punctuation marks in the password. This really makes it difficult for the password thieves to guess your password and enter your account.

Selecting a Password

It's safe to say that almost all computer systems will allow up to eight characters in your password. A few will permit more, but eight is a good number. It's not a good idea to use short passwords as this makes it easier to break into your account. We recommend that you always use eight characters to be safe.

Here are some ideas for passwords. Please don't use these specific ones, as others may read this book and try these examples. Let your imagination roam here and create your own. You may wish to create several, as it is a good idea to change your password regularly. Few people actually do this if the system doesn't insist, but it remains a very good idea. If the system does insist, by threatening to throw you off if you don't, you will need to have another password ready.

Sample Passwords

Here are a few ideas to start from, but please don't use these; build your own following these (or other) examples:

GoOd0ne5   Be$Tpa5s   #5sAliVe   9tEEntWo

There are also some not very good ideas. The reasons they are not very good is that there are a few people with access to the Internet who run programs to "crack" passwords. Most often the programs look for words found in dictionaries or common names. They also look for keyboard patterns such as:

qwerty   asdfgh   qazwsx   1q2w3e4

You may need to look at your keyboard to see why these are so simple. Be assured that simple passwords leave your account exposed.

In later sessions, we will show you how to reach other systems on the Internet. If you can reach other systems, and you will, others can reach your system.

Protecting Your Account

You can protect your account in several ways. The first and best way is to have a strong password that is changed regularly. If you suspect that someone has "cracked" your password, you should contact your system administrator right away.

Your First Real Session

You may have already been connected to your host if you signed up for your account **online**. Some others will not have done this, so we will pretend that you are starting for the first time.

Appendix B explains all about dialing up hosts and modems and communications programs. We will just put a short reminder here as a review. If you don't need to dial up a host, you may have to key in some commands given to you by the person who set up your account. For those readers, you should key in those commands and jump ahead to the section called **Logging In**.

Readers Using Dial-Up Services

1. Start your communications program.

2. Have that program dial the access telephone number of the Internet host. (Alternatively you can dial the number yourself, but most programs can do it after you set them up with the number.)

3. If your modem's speaker is turned on, you will now hear the dial tone followed by the tones of the program (and modem) calling the host.

4. When the host answers, a series of strange noises will indicate that your modem and the host's modem are exchanging some kind of information.

Explanation: The first noises sound like whistles and the later noises sound like hisses. This process is called **handshaking**. Handshaking means that the modems are negotiating to find common ground. This happens quite quickly and most modems then turn off their speakers.

Logging In

At this point, communication has been established between your program and modem and the distant host. It is now time to login. However, some systems won't respond right away. If nothing happens for more than 5 or 10 seconds, you may wish to press the **ENTER** key once. You should now see the host responding with something like:

Please Login:

Type your loginname exactly as it was given to you and press the **ENTER** key.

It's very important to type in your loginname exactly using upper and lower case letters. Remember that most hosts on the Internet treat upper and lower case letters as different symbols. Most people's loginnames consist of only lower case letters. For example, the authors use **dsachs** and **hstair** as loginnames.

The host will always respond with:

> **Password:**

Type in your password exactly, using all the correct upper and lower case letters, numbers, and any punctuation marks.

If You Make A Mistake

If you make a typing mistake here, most systems will not allow backspacing to correct errors. If you made a mistake in typing either your loginname or your password, the system will usually respond with **Login incorrect** and ask you again to login. If this happens, don't worry. Just type in your loginname again. Go slowly to be sure that you are right. Follow this with your password, when the system asks for it.

Like all computers, Internet hosts are very particular. This is also the front door to your condo and you would like it to be secure.

If You Continue To Have Trouble

If you continue to have trouble at this point, you will need to place a phone call to your service help number or call your system administrator.

Welcome Screens

Normally you will be greeted by a welcoming message that may contain important news about the system. This might include schedules or new tools available for the system's users (that now includes you!). This is called **MOTD** or the "message of the day."

Here are several sample welcome screens.

Sample login screen from The World

* To create an account on The World, login as **new**, no password.

```
SunOS UNIX (world)

login: loginname
Password: XXXXXXXX
Last login: Mon Aug 23 19:57:35 from stamford.ct.ts.p
OS/MP 4.1B Export (CREATION++/root) #1: Wed Aug 4 01:02:20 1993

Welcome to the New World!  A 4 CPU Solbourne 6E/900.
Public Access Unix -- Home of the Online Book Initiative

Type 'help' for help!  --  Stuck? Try 'help HINTS'.
Still Stuck? Send mail to 'staff'.

For complete details on recent hardware and software upgrades,
type 'help upgrade'.

TERM = (vt100)
Erase is Backspace
No new messages.
When a speaker and he to whom he is speaking do not
understand, that is metaphysics.
-- Voltaire
world%
```

Sample login screen from Alumni

```
SunOS UNIX (alumni)

login: loginname
Password: XXXXXXXX
Last login: Sun Jul 18 07:45:20 from stamford.ts.psi.
SunOS Release 4.1.3 (GENERIC) #3: Mon Jul 27 16:43:54 PDT 1992

Updates regarding problems found and fixed will be placed in
/vol/ccovol/doc/sumer-93.changes and posted to the
caltech.cco.changes newsgroup
------------------------------------------------------------
To review this message: more /etc/motd
To review announcements: "announce all" or "/ccovol/local/
bin/announce all"
For help: "help" or "/ccovol/local/bin/help"
For reporting problems: send electronic mail to "root"
```

```
For general information about the Unix cluster:  "more /
ccovol/doc/intro"
To check disk space "du -s ~/."---please keep usage under
1000.
-------------------------------------------------------------
DOWNTIME! Due to a planned power outage, Wednesday, August
25th, the Alumni computer will be unavailable from 8 am to 10
am. The CCO Unix cluster will be up and down Thursday August
26th for a few hours of hardware maintenance from 9 am to 1 pm
and some software packages will be unavailable at this time.

TERM = (vt100)
Your disk usage is 304 / 1000Kb
host%
```

Terminal Type

Usually you will be asked for your terminal type, with a suggestion such as [vt100] indicated in square brackets .

At this point, just press the **ENTER** key.

(**Appendix B** has more information about terminal types if you need it.)

You will now be told if you have any messages or mail. We will leave these alone until the next session.

Finally, you may be shown a quotation or saying or just some smart remark called a "fortune." Fortunes, which will be different every time you login, date back to the early days of computers. They are no longer necessary, but people got so used to seeing them that they won't go away. However, by now not all systems still use these "fortunes."

The Host Prompt

Next you will see a host prompt. This prompt is just like those in your PC from DOS; it says that the host is ready and waiting for a command.

Where DOS usually uses a >, Internet hosts most often show a % or a #. Here is where you can tell what UNIX shell you are using. The % indicates the "C" shell and the # indicates the "Bourne" shell. You may also see the host's name before the prompt.

The differences are not important to us yet, so we will just try a few commands and look around your new territory.

NOTE: *Some systems may present a menu type screen at this point. As the menu is somewhat easier to follow, you may wish to use that. However, we will describe the command prompt approach below. For those PC users who are familiar with DOS commands, this may be the easier approach. The menu will usually offer a command prompt as an option.*

Your Directory

First we will look at your directory. Your directory is your exclusive place in the host. This is where you put your own files and documents and programs. This is your place and it will remain yours as long as you "pay the rent;" in other words, as long as you have authorization here. On a public Internet service, that really does mean as long as you pay your fees to the service. On campus or business systems, it is yours as long as you are associated with that campus or business.

Let's see what your directory is called. At the prompt, type:

pwd

This is a command called **Print Working Directory** and it always tells you where you are in the system.

The system will respond by typing out your **home directory**. This is what the system calls your place here. You can move around in these systems and sometimes you forget where you are. You can always type:

pwd

and find where you are. The system will respond with something that looks like **/user/yourloginname**.

This is your home directory.

If you find yourself somewhere else and want to get home, just type the following command, which is an abbreviation for **change directory**:

cd

You will be returned to your home directory.

Let's try that now. At the command prompt, type:

cd

The only response will be the prompt coming back on the next line.

Now you can type:

pwd

and see where you are.

What we have done is to move you to the very top of what is called the **tree** or **root** directory.

All users have their very own directories, just as you do. Also, there are many directories that may be used by everybody. In addition, there are a few directories that are reserved for the system administrator. All the directories come together at the root. This is where you are now.

While all these other directories have names, the root is only called **/**.

NOTE: *This is a "forward" slash or stroke and not the reverse slash (\) that is used in DOS.*

Now let's go back to your home directory. Type:

cd

Again, there will be no response other than the prompt, so type

pwd

to see that you have returned home.

Looking Around

There are already some files in your directory that were put there by the system when you got your account. Let's look at some of them.

First, we will want to list them to see what they are. The command to do this **list** is:

ls

Since your account is new, it is possible that you might just get a prompt, and not a list of files. There are, however, some "hidden" files that will be there. They are not hidden in the same sense that DOS hides files. These are just administrative files that are kept out of the way. Many of them have file names that start with periods.

We will use another form of the list command to find them. This adds a dash and a letter after the command. Type:

ls -a

for a list of **all** of the files. Now you should see a few files, including one called:

.login

This file controls what happens when you login each time. We can look at it in greater detail with another command.

NOTE: *If you are not using the "C" shell, you will not see a .login file. With the "Bourne" shell, you will see a .profile file.*

Some File Commands

You may have noticed that all the commands we have typed so far have been in lower case. This is an example of "case sensitivity" and it's important to remember that for the commands to work correctly, we must type them exactly as shown.

Most commands will be in lower case, but some of their options, like **-a**, may come as a mix of upper and lower case. Commands in these systems also may sound a little strange to you, because you are used to using a PC.

Most of the hosts connected to the Internet use the same family of programs and the commands come from a long history. Don't try to understand where the funny command names come from yet. If you really have to know, we will explain many of the important commands in greater detail in **Appendix C**.

Looking At the .login File

Let's use two different commands to look at your **.login** file (or the **.profile** file).

The first will show you the file, one screen at a time. It is called **more**.

This command acts in a strange way for people who are used to PCs. When you use **more** to look at a screen, the command will indicate how much of the file you have seen as a percentage of the whole file. It shows this at the bottom of the screen and looks like this:

```
% more .login
# ^C interrupts
stty dec
# backspace deletes
stty erase ^H
# set for your terminal type . . .
# you can change "vt100" to the name of the terminal you use
set noglob; eval 'tset -s -m ':?vt100
unset noglob
#Avoid nasty core files
limitcoredumpsize 0K
# Print announcements of note,
msgs
# a random adage,
/usr/games/fortune
# show what mail you have
subj
# and whois logged in
--More-- (99%)
```

More is a handy command to keep screens from flashing by before you can read them. **More** allows just one screen of information to show at a time. It also indicates how much of the information it has shown so far. The 99% tells you that you have seen all but 1% of the file.

After you have looked at one screen, you use the **spacebar** on your keyboard to tell the **more** command to show you the next screen. If you are finished looking and want to **quit** before **more** is done, just press the letter **q** on your keyboard (you don't need to press enter) and **more** will just quit.

Let's try this now. Type:

> **more .login**

and press **ENTER**. You should see something like this:

```
host% more .login

# CCO Unix Cluster .login
################################################################
#
#.login file
#
#Read in after the .cshrc file when you log in. Not read
#in for subsequent shells. For setting up terminal and
#global environment characteristics. See the csh man page
#and CCO documentation for more information about this file.
#
#If this file becomes damaged, you can get another copy by
#running the "ccoconfig" program.
#
################################################################

if ( $CCOARCH == sol2 ) then
 set path=( /ccovol/local/bin.$CCOARCH /bin /usr/bin \
          /ccovol/X11R5/bin.$CCOARCH )
else
 set path=( /ccovol/local/bin.$CCOARCH /usr/ucb /usr/bin /bin\
          /ccovol/X11R5/bin.$CCOARCH )
endif
--More--(39%)
```

It is a strange-looking file, but don't worry about that. We're just getting our feet wet.

Now try another command that shows the whole file by letting it just roll or scroll up your screen. This command is **cat**.

Type:

> **cat .login**

and see what happens. If it is a long file, it will just roll on by, perhaps faster than you can read it.

You may be asking why you would want to use this command if you can't stop it. The answer is that you may wish to **download** some text to your PC. The file really exists on the Internet host, but most communications programs allow you to "catch" or download what goes by on the screen and store it on your PC. If you do this, the **cat** command is very handy.

NOTE: *We will cover upload and download in Session Seven, later in the book.*

Let's stop a minute and recap. So far, you have done the following:

1. You have logged in to your new account with your loginname and password.

2. You have set your terminal type and looked at the message of the day.

3. You have discovered what the system prompt looks like and learned a little about directories. (**pwd**)

4. You have moved from your home directory to the root directory and back again. (**cd**)

5. You have listed the regular files in your home directory. (**ls**)

6. You have seen some additional file names with an expanded **ls** command. (**ls -a**)

7. You have actually looked inside one of these files with two different commands.

   a. One command, **more**, showed you just one screen at a time.

   b. The other, **cat**, scrolled the file up your screen without stopping.

Congratulations! You're doing fine!

Reading Some News

Later in the book we will show you how to get access to many different kinds of files of news and opinion. We will wait until Session Three for all of the details, but now let's just look at a few for fun.

NOTE: *In Session Three we will explain much more about the newsgroups. Here, we will just try out a few without much detailed explanation.*

We will use a program called a **news reader**. This program takes you to a particular set of news (or opinions) and shows you the headlines. You mark it if you want to read it. The news reader keeps track of what you have already seen so you don't have to look at it again.

The reader we will use is called **nn**.

1. It will keep track of which news is available and see what you want to read.

2. It will hold your place if you have to leave in the middle of an article.

3. And it will remember where to start you the next time.

In the examples that follow, we will concentrate on real news. We'll leave the discussion groups to Session Three.

There are over 3,500 newsgroups and you can't expect to follow more than a small percentage of them. We will begin with real news in three different areas. As you will see in greater detail in Session Three, the names of these groups are arranged in a very logical order. Let's use one of our examples to illustrate.

news. announce. newusers

Our first example focuses on the newsgroup called **news. announce. newusers**.

The first part of the name, **news**, is the major name of the group; in this case it is a combination of news about the newsgroups.

The next part, **announce**, says what the newsgroup is about.

The last part, **newusers**, indicates something about the group.

Since you have not used the news reader before, it will provide you with the most recent news.

How To Begin Using nn

1. When you type the **nn** command, it will show you a list of lower case letters, each with a size and a headline.

2. If you want to look at a story, press the letter of that story.

    WARNING: You **DON'T** use the ENTER key here.

3. After you have pressed the letters for all of the stories you want to see, press the **spacebar**. If all of the headlines weren't shown on the first page, **nn** will show you another page before showing your stories.

4. When all articles have been selected, **nn** will display the stories in a manner that is very similar to the command **more**.

Let's try this now.

Type the following command and press **ENTER**: (don't worry about the -x)

nn -x news.announce.newusers

1. **nn** will now show you one or more screens of news headlines.

2. Select one or more of them by pressing the lower case letter at the left edge of your screen.

3. When you have done this, press the **SPACEBAR**.

You may select more news stories. The length of each story is shown by a number near the actual headline. The number is the number of lines in the article.

Here is an example:

```
Newsgroup: news.announce.newusers           Articles: 21

  a. David C Lawrenc    667  List of Active Newsgroups, Part I
  b. David C Lawrenc    667  >List of Active Newsgroups, Part II
  c. David C Lawrenc    915  Alternative Newsgroup Hierarchies,
                             Part I
  d. David C Lawrenc    735  >Alternative Newsgroup Hierarchies,
                             Part II
  e. David C Lawrenc    834  List of Moderators for Usenet
  f. David C Lawrenc    152  How to Create a New Usenet Newsgroup
  g. Stephanie Silv    1476  >Publicly Accessible Mailing Lists,
                             Part 5/5
  h. Jonathan Kamens    784  How to become a USENET site
  i. Jonathan Kamens    284  Introduction to the *.answers
                             newsgroups
  j. Jonathan Kamen    1371  List of Periodic Informational
                             Postings, Part 1/6
  k. Jonathan Kamen    1354  >List of Periodic Informational
                             Postings, Part 2/6
  l. Jonathan Kamen    1096  Changes to List of Periodic
                             Informational Postings
  m. Jonathan Kamen    1264  >List of Periodic Informational
                             Postings, Part 3/6
```

```
n. Jonathan Kamen    1239  >List of Periodic Informational
                           Postings, part 4/6
o. Jonathan Kamen    1451  >List of Periodic Informational
                           Postings, Part 5/6
p. Jonathan Kamen    1443  >List of Periodic Informational
                           Postings, Part 6/6
q. Ron Dippold        715  Usenet Newsgroup Creation Companion
r. Stephanie Silv    1024  Publicly Accessible Mailing Lists,
                           Part 1/5
s. Stephanie Silv    1395  >Publicly Accessible Mailing
                           Lists, Part 2/5

-- 09:30 -- SELECT -- help:? -----Top 90%-----
```

And here is a sample of one of the articles:

```
David C. Lawrence:  How to Create a New Usenet Newsgroup
23 Jul 1993 17:26
Archive-name: creating-newsgroups/part1
Original-author: woods@ncar.ucar.edu (Greg Woods)
Comment: enhanced & edited until 5/93 by spaf@cs.purdue.edu
(Gene Spafford)
Last-change: 23 Sep 1992 by spaf@cs.purdue.edu (Gene Spafford)

GUIDELINES FOR USENET GROUP CREATION

REQUIREMENTS FOR GROUP CREATION:

    These are guidelines that have been generally agreed upon
across USENET as appropriate for following in the creating of
new newsgroups in the "standard" USENET newsgroup hierarchy.
They are NOT intended as guidelines for setting USENET policy
other than group creations, and they are not intended to apply
to "alternate" or local news hierarchies. The part of the
namespace affected is comp, news, sci, misc, soc, talk, rec,
which are the most widely-distributed areas of the USENET
hierarchy.
    Any group creation request which follows these guidelines
to a successful result should be honored, and any request
which fails to follow these procedures or to obtain a
successful result from doing so should be dropped, except
under extraordinary circumstances. The reason these are called
guidelines and not absolute rules is that it is…
```

```
-- 09:30 --.announce.newusers-- LAST --help:?--Top 13%--
```

Notice the **?** on last line of the article. At any time in the newsreader program, you may press the question mark key and get a help screen of the most commonly used commands. Many programs contain this feature. It means that you only have to remember to use the question mark to find a brief list of the key commands.

There are a number of other ways to get help while you are connected to the host.

Finding Help Screens

Most of the systems you will be using have their computer manuals available for reading right on the screen. Since you will need only a few commands, this can be very handy. However, you will need the magic word to find these manual pages.

That word is **man**, which is an abbreviation for the word **manual**.

Let's look at a command we have already used: **pwd** for **print working directory**.

If you type **man pwd**, you will see something like this:

```
host% man pwd
PWD(1)               USER COMMANDS                   PWD(1)
NAME
   pwd - display the pathname of the current working directory
SYNOPSIS
   pwd
DESCRIPTION
    pwd prints the pathname of the working (current)
directory.
    (and so on with a lengthy description of the command...)
—More—(35%)
```

To get just the command header line, you may also use the command **whatis**.

This will provide you with just enough information about the command to use it if you have forgotten.

Try this now; type:

whatis pwd

You will get something like this:

```
host% whatis pwd
pwd - display the pathname of the current working directory
host%
```

On many systems, you can also type **:help** and get a menu of help topics.

Who Else Is On With Me?

The last thing we shall do in Session One is to look around to see who else is here. We will use two simple commands to peek around. The first will tell who is also logged on with you (including you). The second will show what programs they (and you) are using.

Here is the first for you to try. Type:

who

Can you find your name in the list, or did it go by too fast? If it scrolled off the screen before you could read it, there's a way to slow it down.

Just tell the command **who** to send its output to the command **more**. Then you can read it just as you did before, by pressing the **SPACEBAR**.

Here's how it's done. We will use a keyboard character you may not have used before. It looks like a vertical bar |. This is how to use it; type the following and then press **ENTER**:

who | more

NOTE: *On an IBM keyboard, the | may be found near the ENTER key.*

```
host% who | more
console    console       Aug 16 01:47
djf        ttyp0  Aug 16 01:47  (ussr.std.com:0.0)
user1      ttyp1  Aug 16 01:48  (visual1.std.com:)
user2      ttyp2  Aug 16 01:48  (visual1.std.com:)
user10     ttyp3  Aug 18 17:59  (std-annex.std.co)
max        ttyp4  Aug 18 17:36  (auvm.american.ed)
whobut     ttyp5  Aug 18 01:23  (std-annex.std.co)
kks        ttyp7  Aug 18 17:57  (std-annex.std.co)
pop        ttyp8  Aug 17 02:39  (ussr.std.com:0.0)
smitty     ttyp9  Aug 18 17:50  (std-annex.std.co)
user12     ttypb  Aug 18 17:58  (std-annex.std.co)
user6      ttypc  Aug 18 16:07  (std-annex.std.co)
maint      ttypf  Aug 18 17:33  (std-annex.std.co)
hbrown     ttyq0  Aug 18 17:55  (std-annex.std.co)
jonesy     ttyq1  Aug 18 17:58  (std-annex.std.co)
clinton    ttyq2  Aug 18 16:37  (std-annex-std.co)
—More—
```

Notice that in this case **more** did not tell you how much of the output you have seen.

Now the list stops for you at the end of each page.

Can you find yourself this time?

NOTE: *Remember to use the **spacebar** to move to the next page. Also, remember that you can type the letter **q** to go back to the prompt immediately.*

Next let's see what everyone is doing. To do this, we will use the command **w**.

Type the following:

w | more

You will see:

```
host% w | more
6:03pm up 2 days, 16:23, 38 users, load average: 4.50,4.13,4.02
User       tty      login@  idle  JCPU   PCPU   what
console    console  Fri1am  2days                -csh
djf        ttyp0    Fri1am     14 34:13  26:32   emacs
user1      ttyp1    Fri1am  2days  4:27     17   -tcsh
```

user2	ttyp2	Fri1am	2days	1:13	11	xarchie
user10	ttyp3	1:23am	14:12	50	6	ftp ftp.nevada.edu
max	ttyp4	5:57pm		5	1	more legends .info.IIIa
whobut	ttyp5	Sat2am	13:08	17		-sh
kks	ttyp7	5:50pm		1		telnet x25.bix.com
pop	ttyp8	5:58pm		4	2	nn
smitty	ttyp9	4:07pm		44	5	telnet
user12	ttypb	2:43pm		2:08	2:07	nn
user6	ttypc	4:22pm		7	3	vi testmail
maint	ttypf	5:33pm		10	4	nn
hbrown	ttyq0	5:55pm		9	5	mail
jonesy	ttyq1	5:58pm		4	2	pico /usr/tmp/ nn.a27675
clinton	ttyq2	4:37pm		20	20	vi intellect

—More—

Getting Out Gracefully

This has been a lot for your first session. You have learned how to get in and how to do several interesting things. Now it's time to leave. As we mentioned before, there are three ways to leave:

1. The graceful exit;

2. The trouble exit; and

3. The "when all else fails" exit.

While you will rarely need the last two, you should know about them. We will begin with the graceful exit.

The Graceful Exit

When you are finished with any session, you will usually be at a prompt. At this prompt you can just type:

logout

NOTE: *While some systems use* **logoff** *or* **quit** *or* **bye**, **logout** *is the preferred form.*

The system will usually confirm your command and your session will have ended gracefully. The lack of a new prompt from the host is also an indication that the session has ended.

REMINDER: If you were using a dial-up connection, you will also need to tell your program to hang up and return to your PC operating system (DOS, Windows, etc).

The Trouble Exit

In the unlikely event that the system responds with some comment and a new prompt, don't panic. Just type **logout** again and the session will end.

You may have started a program running and the host was just reminding you that there were still processes or programs still running. You can find them and stop them or you can let the host do it for you by typing **logout** again.

The "When All Else Fails" Exit

The last method should only be used when nothing else works. When the host keeps responding with confusing messages and **logout** doesn't seem to work, just hang up.

Most communications programs will have a hang-up command that literally will hang up the telephone line. Nothing is hurt or damaged by doing this, but it should be reserved for the times when all else fails. We all have had to do this from time to time; don't feel bad when it happens to you.

End of Session One

Congratulations! You have completed your first session. You should now be more comfortable with connecting to the host, looking around, and getting out. This means you are ready for Session Two - Electronic Mail. We're ready as soon as you are.

■ ■ Session One Vocabulary and Command Summary

login .... signing onto a host computer

loginname .... the name that you use on that computer

password .... the special word that you use to identify yourself

pwd .... print working directory to tell where you are

cd .... the command used to change directories

ls .... list files in the directory

more .... the command that permits you to read one screen at a time

cat .... the command that lists things one after another, with no break

man .... the command used to provide you with the manual for a given command — for example, man pwd

who .... the command used to tell you who else is currently logged onto your host system

w | more .... the command that is used to tell you what everyone else is doing and that will permit you to view screens, one screen at a time

whatis .... permits you to get a brief amount of information — for example, whatis pwd

logout .... to leave your Internet host account

SESSION TWO

Electronic Mail

In our first session, we got into the Internet, looked around, and got out. We hope that during this new session you will be a little more comfortable with the process of "logging in." This time, we are going to explore a few of the many things we can actually do once we are "on the Internet." We will try out electronic mail, but we will do it without bothering anyone else. By the time we finish Session Two, you will be ready to send and receive electronic mail just like an old pro.

Just What is Electronic Mail?

We are all familiar with writing or typing letters, addressing envelopes, and "mailing" them at a post office or mail collection box. This is something we have been doing since someone told us that we had to write our first "thank you" note when we were small children. It may be something we like doing or it may be a chore, but we all know how to mail a letter.

There are, however, some annoying problems with paper mail. For starters, we send off a letter and sometimes have to wait weeks or months before we get a letter back. Or, worse, we get a letter from the person we wrote to, just a day or two after we mailed ours. The letters "crossed" in the mail.

Some people who use electronic mail (or **email**, as it is known) refer to such paper letters as "snail mail" because of these issues. Email can help solve these problems. In fact, the speed of email can be dazzling!

What is **email**, really? Simply put, it is just sending a file from your account across the Internet to someone else's account; that's all.

It is just that simple, once we understand what is happening. That is what we will do in this session. So let's get started!

Send Yourself a Message

What you will do now is send yourself an email message. We will walk through the steps to create a short message. You will then send it. Later in this session, we will show you how to do several things with this (and other) messages.

By the way, there are more elaborate message handling programs or mail systems available on your host. We will show you how to use them later. We think it's important that you first learn how to send and receive email with just the basic commands. After that, you can get fancy and use mail systems. However, you may always want to use the simple mail program for short messages.

1. login to your account as you learned to do in Session One.

NOTE: *Be sure to note your login name; we will use that as your email address in just a moment.*

2. After you are at the host prompt (% or $), type the word **mail** (all lower case) followed by a space and your login name. It should look like this:

   mail loginname

NOTE: *Remember that your login name must be typed exactly (lower case or upper and lower case) as it is when you login.*

3. The host should reply with a new line saying:

   Subject:

   We have begun an email message.

4. Type the following after the word Subject:

   Test Message Number One

Press the **ENTER** key. This will move the cursor to the line below **Subject**.

5. Press the **ENTER** key again to give us some space for the actual message.

6. We are about to type a message. Note that unlike most word processors, the mail program will not wrap your text at the end of the line. Use the **ENTER** key at the end of each line to keep all your text on the screen. If you make any typing mistakes, don't worry. We'll talk about correcting and editing your messages later.

Here is the message for you to type:

This is my first test message via electronic mail (email). As I type this I am learning the basics of composing and sending text messages. Soon I will be able to send email like this to anyone with an email address. The number of people with email ad-dresses is now estimated to be over 10 million people in over 90 countries.

This is the end of my first try at email.

Regards, me

7. Now press the **ENTER** key to move the cursor to the beginning of a new line.

8. Press the period (.) key and press **ENTER**.

9. The system should respond with **EOT** (which means End of Text) and a new host prompt.

NOTE: *If for some reason it does not do so, hold down your CONTROL key and press the D key.*

*Some systems may ask for **Cc:** ((carbon copy) here for copies to anyone else. Just press the Enter key and your message will be on its way. Don't worry if there were a few errors or extra lines in your message. You are the only one who will see it.*

Well done! You have just sent your first email message!

Receiving Your Message

Now you should have some email to receive and read. On most systems, the mail moves so fast, it will already be in your mailbox. We'll talk more about mailboxes later; for now, let's look and see what you have.

At the host prompt, type the command

> **mail**

with no name or address and press the **ENTER** key.

You should see a screen very much like the one below. (If you don't, wait another moment and then type **mail** again.)

```
host% mail
Mail version SMI 4.0 Thu Jan 1 12:00:00 EST  Type ? for help.
"/usr/spool/mail/loginname": 1 message 1 new
>N 1 loginname
Sun Jan 1 17:54  30/852 Test Message Number One
&
```

The first line shows the **host%** prompt and the **mail** command.

The second line is a notice by the **mail** command about its program. You can ignore this line.

The third line tells you that you have one message and that it is a new message.

The fourth line is what is called the **header** and tells you a lot about each message:

>   means that it is the "current" message

N   means that it is a new message

1   means that it is the first message in the message list

loginname tells you who it's from (this is your login name)

Following these four items are:

1. the date and time the message was sent;

2. the number of lines and the number of characters in the message; and

3. the subject of the message.

Finally, there is an **ampersand** (&).

The ampersand is the prompt for the mail program and it is waiting for you to tell it what to do with your current message. Why don't we take a look at the first message?

Type a **t1** or a **p1** for **type** or **print**.

NOTE: *The number 1 following the t or p tells the mail program which message to type out. If you don't use a number, it will type the "current" message.*

If you have not done so yet, type a **t1** and press **ENTER** now. You should see the following screen:

```
& t
Message 1:
From loginname Sun Jan  1 17:54:50
Return-Path: <loginname>
Received: by host.com (5.65c/here-2.0)
id AA19664; Sun, 1 Jan 17:54:49 -0400
Date: Sun, 1 Jan 17:54:49 -0400
From: Loginname (that's you)
Message-Id: <199305092154.AA19664@host.com>
To: loginname
Subject: Test Message Number One
Status: R

This is my first test message via electronic mail ( email ).
As I type this I am learning the basics of composing and
sending text messages. Soon I will be able to send email like
this to anyone with an email address. The number of people
with email addresses is now estimated to be over 10 million
people in over 90 countries.

This is the end of my first try at email.

Regards, me
&
```

Keeping Your Message

1. Type **new** at the **&** prompt.
   (This tells the mail program not to mark the message as "already read."

2. You will see a new **&** prompt. At this prompt, type **q** .
   This will end the mail program and return you to the system prompt.

Here is what it looks like:

```
& new
& q
Held 1 message in /usr/spool/mail/loginname
host%
```

Brief Explanation: The reason we had you type **new** was to hold the message as a new one. We'll use it again in a moment as a brand new message. Normally you would not use **new** here.

The **q** told the mail program to quit and to send you back to the **host%** prompt.

Another way to leave the mail program is to **exit** or **xit**. This leaves everything as it was when you entered the mail program. It's the same as using **new** and then **quit**.

At this point, we will continue to learn more about email, but it could be a good time for a break. If you would like to break here, just type **logout** at the host prompt. You can come back at your convenience and start up again right here.

Answering Yourself

1.   Type **mail** at the **host%** prompt.

NOTE: *If you have logged out, login again and type **mail**.*

Again, you will see the notice of a new message. It's really just your first message. Now we are going to answer this email. The answer will really be going to you; it's just for practice.

2.   At the **&** prompt, type:

reply

NOTE: *The screen looks very much like the first one we used to send mail. But notice that there is a **To:** line and that the subject line has been filled in for us. It should look like this:*

```
To: loginname
Subject: Re:  Test Message Number One
```

3.   Type in a reply, such as:

Here is an answer to our original message.

4.   Press the **ENTER** key and type a (.) period to send the message.

5.   Type a **q** to quit mail and you will be back at the **host**% prompt.

Saving Mail Messages

1.   Type **mail**. The reply you just sent is waiting for you. (Again, you may have to wait a moment.)

2.   Type the word **type** and look at it.

3.   To save this message in a file, do the following:

At the **&** prompt, type:

save 1

Brief Explanation: The mail program will usually save the message in a file called **mbox**. This is your "mailbox" for old messages.

You may also tell the command what file to use by just typing the filename. This would look like this:

save 1 myfile

If **myfile** doesn't exist, the program will create it for you. (The program may ask if you want such a file created.)

Remember from Session One that you could use the **more** command to look at a file. Go ahead now and save the message without a filename. Type:

save 1

Now type:

more mbox

and look at your message.

This file, **mbox**, will accumulate the mail you wish to have saved in one file. You can use the **save** command with different filenames if you wish to keep your messages separated.

Deleting Mail Messages

To delete your messages instead of saving them, just type:

delete 1

This will erase the message.

Let's review what we've done so far.

1. We have used the **mail** program and a **login name** (yours) to get to a screen where we could enter an **email** message.

2. We have typed a **subject** and some text for the message.

3. We have used **ENTER** and the **period key** to tell the mail program to send our message.

4. We have again used the mail program with **no name** to see if we had mail. We found our first message.

5. We have used the **type** or **t** or the **print** or **p** commands at the mail command's **&** prompt to enable us to read our message(s).

6. We have used the **reply** or **r** command to reply to the sender of the message. (The sender, of course, was you.)

7. We have saved or deleted our messages to the mailbox (**mbox**).

This completes the on-line part of the session on email. You may wish to continue trying various commands in the mail program or you may logout. If you choose to stay and play, we have included several of the commands you may use at the mail program's **&** prompt. Notice that although we have been using whole word commands, you may use just the first letter of some of the commands and get the same results.

You can continue to use your login name as an address to which you can send your email. This way, you may try many activities without having to bother other people.

If you choose to **logout**, type that now and jump ahead to the section entitled "What are Internet email Addresses?"

If you choose to stay, here is a more complete listing of the mail program's commands. The names shown in the brackets are the items you may type to tell the program which messages or users you want to indicate.

Mail Command	What it Does
?	lists this set of commands (and a few more)
d [message list]	**delete** messages
f [message list]	show the "**from**" lines of messages
h	show the **headers** of all the messages
inc	**incorporate** new messages that may have arrived
m [user list]	**mail** to specific users
p [message list]	**print** messages
q	**quit**, saving unresolved messages in mbox
r [message list]	**reply** to sender (only) of messages
R [message list]	**reply** to sender and **all recipients** of messages
t [message list]	**type** messages (same as print)
top [message list]	show **top lines** of messages
u [message list]	**undelete** messages

The [message list] consists of integers separated by spaces. If it is omitted, **mail** uses the current message.

When you are done, logout, and we will discuss sending email to others.

Some of the things we have NOT talked about yet include:

1. how to forward messages;

2. how to edit your outbound or forwarded messages; and

3. how to organize your mail.

These are somewhat more advanced topics.

For now, you know how to send email, how to receive email, and how to reply to email. That's most of what you will need to know, once you learn how to find email addresses.

What are Internet Email Addresses?

We took a simplified step during your second "online" session. When you typed the **mail** command and your **login name**, it worked because both you and the person you were addressing (you again) were on the same system. This will always work as long as both parties are on the same system.

Now we need to talk about the other cases, that is, when the parties are on different hosts. First, you need to be sure of your own complete email address. For the practice messages above we used just your login name.

Your REAL email address is a combination of both:

1. Your login name and

2. The name of the host.

It is almost always shown in the following form:

loginname@full_host_name

or

loginname@host_name.domain_name

NOTE: *There are no spaces between your login name, the @ symbol and the full_host_name. The full_host_name is really in two parts: the host name and the domain name. They are separated by periods and there may be several "pieces."*

When you obtained your account, you should have been provided with your full email address. It should look like one of the following:

loginname@world.std.com

loginname@epa.rtpnc.epa.gov

loginname@coombs.anu.edu.au

loginname@lawmail.law.columbia.edu

loginname@netcom.com

loginname@nri.reston.va.us

loginname@vnet.ibm.com

loginname@cerf.net

loginname@eff.org

NOTE: *On the left side is the login name (with no spaces).*
Next, there is an AT symbol (@), which is found above the number "2" on your keyboard.
This symbol is used to separate the loginname from the part on the right side.
This right side part completely defines the host system. It is only on a host system that a
specific login name can be found.

Understanding Host Names

There is a pattern to these host names. The key is to start from the right and work back towards the left. When the whole name is used, it is called the "fully qualified domain name."

Domains describe the parts of the name, and **fully qualified** means that all parts are shown.

When the Internet began many years ago, it was primarily an American network. The original naming scheme divided the country by organizational type. Thus, the endings were as follows:

.gov for **government**

.edu for **education**

.com for **commercial**

.net for **networks**

.org for other **organizations**.

When the international Internet community began to become sizeable, a different naming scheme began. This one uses **country codes** (a little like state abbreviations in the United States) as the final part of the domain name. For example:

loginname@nri.reston.va.us

Notice the following:

> **.us** (country) is preceded by
>
> **.va** (state), which is preceded by
>
> **.reston** (city), which is preceded by
>
> **.nri**, which is the actual host (or mail entry system) name.

Now it may be a little easier to understand the host name part of your email address. It will be made up of your:

1. login name;

2. an AT symbol (@);

3. a host identifier; and

4. a domain name.

Notice once more that the parts of the address are usually in lower case. Remember again that when you are on the Internet, case sensitivity (meaning the difference between upper and lower case letters) is very important.

If you are in doubt about your own email address, you may wish to take one or more of the following steps:

1. Contact your system help desk and ask;

2. Ask the person who helped you set up your account;

3. Call your commercial service help staff and ask;

4. Login and send mail to your full email address.

If the mail from you comes through to you with this full address, then you have found your address and tested it. This will be your email address until you change hosts. Note it down carefully with the correct lower case letters.

This email address becomes your gateway to the world. You can now tell people what your email address is. You can put it in your letters and on your business cards.

This is half of the battle. The other half is to find other people's addresses.

How Do I Find Addresses?

One of the oldest sayings in the Internet community is the answer to this question. The answer: **call them up and ask them**.

It is still the best advice. While there are a few experimental directories, it is still quite difficult to find the equivalent of telephone white pages or an information operator on the Internet.

Ask your correspondents to try to send you mail and try to send them some. Once mail comes in, pay very close attention to the many lines of text that form the top part or header of their message. Buried there is a reply address, which is their email address (or an email address that will reach them).

It may take a few tries to get it right, but the rewards will be immediate. Not only will you be able to reach your correspondents, but you will also have become a bit more confident about your growing skills on the Internet.

Addresses From Other Mail Systems.

There are also many other network and information systems connected to the Internet by what are known as **gateways**. This means that email to people on these other systems must pass through the gateway and be converted to the mail system that they are using.

We have chosen to list just three of these other systems and explain how to address them. **Appendix A** lists several more advanced books that will help you with all of the other systems.

Our example systems are **America Online, CompuServe,** and **MCI-Mail**. All of the subscribers on these systems may be reached by electronic mail and they can reach people on directly connected Internet hosts. But there are some complications of which you should be aware.

MCI-Mail and CompuServe, for instance, use only numeric login names for email from the Internet.

Electronic
Mail

America Online

For America Online, you would use the name and their **aol.com.** It would look like:

username@aol.com

MCI-Mail

On MCI-Mail, users have login names (for Internet email purposes) that look like:

1234567@mcimail.com

Notice that the host identifier (**mcimail**) and the domain name (**com**) are in lower case, although the correct name of the system is MCI-Mail, a mixed case name.

When you ask for the email address of an MCI-Mail subscriber, remember to get it in this numeric form. The subscriber may have to look it up, as they often use their initial and last name when they directly access MCI-Mail.

CompuServe

For CompuServe, there is an additional complication. CompuServe's users have login names that look like:

12345,6789

To use this address from the Internet, the comma must be converted to a period or dot. Thus it becomes:

12345.6789@compuserve.com

Composing (And Editing) Your Messages

There are many ways to compose and edit or change your text before sending it on the Internet. In fact, there are too many ways. Several text editors may be found on almost all systems. However, you should know that there is another way.

Composing On Your PC

Assuming that you are working from a PC, you are most likely familiar with creating notes and letters. You may have a simple editor like the DOS Editor (not EDLIN) or Window's Write. Whatever you use, you will need to be able to create a simple **ASCII** file.

By ASCII, we mean that there can be no word processing features in the file, just plain text characters and numbers. All popular word processors can produce files of just ASCII characters, but they need to be given special directions how to do so.

If you do not know what an ASCII file is, or how to create one, consult the manual of your word processing program.

NOTE: *If you choose to use a PC editor or word processor to create your notes, two things will happen:*
1. You will be working in a more familiar place, your PC;
2. You will not be on-line with the host. If you use dial-up to reach your host this may reduce your on-line and telephone costs a little.

Moving Notes Between The Host And Your PC

You will need to know how to move an ASCII message from your PC to the host so that it may be sent across the Internet. We will show you several ways how to do this.

1.   Create a short test message on your PC;

2.   When you are done, save your test message as an ASCII file, using a filename of **TEST1.MSG**;

3.   Now, login to your host account;

4.   Type **mail loginname** to send mail to yourself as you did before.

5.   After you have typed in a subject, the host mail program will wait for you to type in your message.

Instead, we will **upload** the message text. Upload means sending information from your (lower down) PC to the (larger, higher) host.

For illustration purposes, we will use examples from two programs: deltaComm'sTelix Lite and Microsoft Windows. Many other programs will work in similar ways.

Uploading With Telix Lite

Telix Lite uses a very simple method to upload.

1. Once you are connected to your host, pressing the **PAGE UP** key will pop up an upload menu on your screen.

2. Select **A** for ASCII and another pop up box will ask for the file name.

3. Tab to the **Path/Directory** box.

4. Type the name of the drive where your file may be found (for example, A: or C:) and press **ENTER**. You will be prompted to "**Insert diskette for drive A: and press any key when ready.**"

5. Tab to the filelist box. Highlight the file you wish to send (**TEST1.MSG**).

6. Then press **F10** to upload the file.

7. The upload boxes will disappear and you will see the text from your file appear on your screen as if you were typing it.

8. When the upload is complete, your keyboard will again be able to be used to enter text.

NOTE: *If all has worked well, your file from the PC is now in the body of your new email message. You may add additional text or just enter and press the period key to send it on its way. Give the system a moment and then use the mail command to look at your new message.*

Uploading With Windows

If you have been using the Windows Terminal accessory to communicate with your host account, then you will have noticed the word "Transfers" on the toolbar across the top of Terminal's window.

1. Before using "Transfers," begin a new message to yourself by typing:

    mail loginname

2. Type in a subject.

3. Next, move to the Transfers tool by clicking on the word Transfers on the toolbar or by typing **Alt**, then **T**.

4. The first line of the drop-down menu is "**Send Text Files...**" Click on that line. You will see a menu that requests a File Name.

5. Type the drive name, the directory name, and **TEST1.MSG** and click on "**OK**." Your file will be "typed" onto the host screen, as if you were typing it.

6. When the upload finishes, you may add to your message or just send it by pressing **ENTER** and the **period key**.

NOTE: *If the word "Stopped" appears when the upload completes, just type fg and you will be back in your mail program. The word "continue" may appear, which means that you can do just that.*

The reason the host may have "stopped" is that the DOS/Windows end-of-file character is a "stop" signal to your host. The **fg** command is an abbreviation for the word "foreground," which means "get the mail program going again."

Review these examples and then explore your own software (if it is different from these) to find the section on "Uploading." Follow the instructions from your particular program and try to upload your test message. Don't be discouraged if it doesn't work the first time. It didn't work the first time for us either.

Downloading Messages

As you might imagine, the opposite of uploading is **downloading**. That is, downloading is the moving of files or messages from the host "down" to your PC.

Downloading Using Telix Lite

In Telix Lite, there are two ways to bring information from the host to your PC:

1. The easiest method is to "capture" a screen image by pressing the **ALT** and the **I** keys. This captures just the screen that you are looking at.

NOTE: *The file will be called TELIX.IMG and may be found in your TELIX subdirectory.*

2. The other method, which is used by most communications programs, is to turn on a capture program.

In Telix Lite, pressing **ALT** and **L** opens a box that will prompt you to type in a capture file name.

While your file is being "captured," a **CAP** message will appear at the bottom of your screen. The biggest risk is forgetting to turn it off!

Downloading Using Windows

In Window's Terminal accessory, the last 100 lines may be saved by clicking on **File** on the toolbar. You will be prompted for a filename to use.

Wrapping Up

At this point, you have learned many of the basics of email on an Internet connected host. With what you have learned, you may actually be somewhat ahead of many "old hands." Now you are ready to let others know your email address and to enter the real world of electronic mail. We have been using a single command, **mail**, to do all of this.

If you would like to learn more about **mail**, type the following command:

man mail | more

This will send the manual pages for the **mail** command to your screen one at a time by the **more** filter.

If you want to "download" the manual pages, turn on your capture function and type:

man mail | cat

You can then read all the details of the **mail** command at your leisure and become even more proficient. As you become more comfortable with mail, you may find much more capable and friendly mail programs. Explore them as you wish; you can always come back to **mail**.

Letting People Know Your Address

When you are ready to join others in the fast and wonderful world of electronic mail, just note down or remember your full email address. It will look like:

loginname@full_host_name

Initially, you may wish to try this with one or two friends to make sure it's right. After that, you are on your way. Be careful! Email is a little bit addictive. Your authors are fully addicted. Once you are ready, you can broadcast your address to the world. Many of us have it printed on our business cards and stationery.

Sending Mail to Others

Now you are ready and well on your way. You can seem very assured as you ask people for their email addresses with a knowing look. A lot of people have signed up for email, including the occupants of the White House; more about that later. Good Luck and happy emailing.

Electronic Mail

■ ■ Session Two Vocabulary and Command Summary

mail .... the command used to begin the mail program

mail loginname@host .... the command used to send a particular individual an email message

t1 .... type (meaning display on the screen) the first message

p1 .... print (meaning display on the screen) the first message

q .... used to quit the mail session

new .... the word that is used to keep holding a message as a new one

reply .... the word that permits you to respond to an email message

save1 .... the command that is used to save the first message

mbox .... your "personal" mail box

more mbox .... the command that will permit you to view what is in your mail box, one screen at a time

delete 1 .... the command that is used to delete the first message

upload .... sending text or a file from your personal computer "up" to the mainframe host computer

download .... moving files or messages from the host "down" to your personal computer

man mail | more .... the command used to send the manual for the mail command to your screen, one screen at a time

man mail | cat .... the command used to send the entire mail manual to your screen, so that you might "capture" it onto a disk

SESSION THREE

The News

Introduction

It has been said that while email brings people to the Internet, it's the news that keeps them coming back. The news on the Internet is possibly the most misunderstood aspect of this worldwide collection of people and computers. Here in Session Three, we will make a tentative and gentle entry to "the news."

Perhaps one of the reasons for the misunderstanding has to do with the name "news." While news from several regular news sources may be found here, most of what you will find is not really what is commonly referred to as news. Instead, you will find questions and answers and opinions and fact and fancy and much discussion. Its real name is Usenet.

Here's the definition of Usenet from one of Usenet's own newsgroups:

news.announce.newusers

```
WHAT USENET IS
Usenet is the set of people who exchange articles tagged with
one or more universally-recognized labels, called "newsgroups"
(or "groups" for short).
(Note that the term "newsgroup" is correct, while "area,"
"base," "board," "bboard," "conference," "round table," "SIG,"
etc. are incorrect. If you want to be understood, be accurate.)
```

The history of Usenet is explained in greater detail in several of the books referenced in **Appendix A**, but our immediate concern is to get you started reading this "news." To begin, we will give you some idea of the scope of this truly huge resource.

There are well over 2,000 sections in this immense pool of information and they are called **groups** or **newsgroups**. Each group is devoted to a specific subject area and there may be many related groups. Each newsgroup contains any number of **articles**. The articles are just that; they detail information and discussion on (or hopefully close to) the group's subject.

With this many groups, you would think it would be hard to locate a subject. However, it's really not.

The organization of the groups follows a very simple structure, called a **hierarchy**. At the top of the hierarchy, there are headings called **categories**.

NOTE: *All hosts do NOT necessarily carry all categories. Therefore, when you are using your particular host system, you may not find some of the samples we list in the following pages. What is carried by a host is strictly up to the host's administrator.*

The Categories

There are a number of major categories for us to consider:

1. The main ones;

2. The alternative groups;

3. Local and campus groups.

The Main Groups Are:

comp ... Topics of interest to both computer professionals and hobbyists, including topics in computer science, software sources, and information on hardware and software systems.

misc .... Groups addressing themes not easily classified under any of the other headings or that incorporate themes from multiple categories.

news ... Groups concerned with the news network and software themselves.

sci .... Discussions marked by special and usually practical knowledge, relating to research in, or application of, the established sciences.

rec .... Groups oriented towards the arts, hobbies, and recreational activities.

soc .... Groups primarily addressing social issues and socializing.

talk ...... Groups that are primarily debate-oriented and that tend to feature long discussions without resolution and without appreciable amounts of generally useful information.

The above descriptions of the main groups are taken from an article in a specific group: **news.announce.newusers** .

If we look for a moment at the structure of the name of the group that is entitled **news.announce.newusers**, it will be possible to begin to understand the organization of all newsgroups.

Reading from left to right:

1. The first word before the **dot** is the major group name (**news**).

2. The next word (**announce**) tells us what the group is about.

3. Finally, the third word (**newusers**) completes the outline description.

As new users, **news.announce.newusers** is a group that we may wish to follow.

Rules For Naming Groups

1. There may be only two names or as many as four or five in the structure.

2. The names are always separated by periods or "dots."

3. The structure is always from highest level (left) to most specific level (right).

As an example: **rec.sport.baseball.college** tells us that it is about recreation, sports, and baseball and is focused on the college level.

Most of our examples will be self-explanatory if you use this structure. Occasionally, a word or abbreviation (or acronym) may be a bit obscure. We'll show you a way to look at groups individually so you can make a judgement about following that group.

Following Newsgroups

While you can look at newsgroups individually, most likely you will follow the custom that most of us do. Typically, that allows us to follow a few groups of particular interest. If we want to look into other groups occasionally, we'll usually use the individual method. Shortly we will show you both methods.

The Alternative Groups

In the alternative way of looking at things, there are groups and subgroups that represent many differing points of view. Some will not cause anyone any concern. An example is **alt.boomerang** , which is clearly about boomerangs. However, there are some groups in the **alt** category that will offend someone.

We could make an analogy here. In New York City, a stroll across 42nd Street will take you past the United Nations, Grand Central Terminal, The New York Public Library, Times Square, some off-Broadway theaters, and the Hudson River. Along this stroll, there will be places to either delight or offend almost anyone. So it is with the **alt** group (and perhaps some with others).

The solution to this is similar to the one you would come up with on your walk. No one will make you stop at any of the places or shops on 42nd Street that you might find offensive. Similarly, no one can make you read any of the groups that you do not wish to see. However, just as we would warn you about 42nd Street, so too do we warn you about the newsgroups, particularly the **alt** groups.

As mentioned earlier, not all groups are distributed to all hosts. The systems people at each host decide which groups they will carry. If you want groups that they don't carry or want them to stop carrying particular groups, you must speak to them. They may or may not choose to listen. After all, it's their system to manage.

Distributions

The main groups are usually distributed to most systems, but there are also national and local groups. These groups may be local to a particular host or campus or they may be local to a state or area. Most are easily identified by the leftmost word. There are several, however, that don't translate easily. These are groups from countries outside of North America. Some examples are:

> **fj. ... from Japan**
> **de. ... from Germany**
> **sf. ... from Finland**

and so on. There are also local groups that are particular to a given state or province within North America and groups that are specific to college campuses. We will show some examples later. The groups may be distributed widely or only within their particular area.

Two Notes of Caution

1. Before we begin some sample sessions to read the news, we are going to list some samples of various newsgroups, including the **alt** groups. If, after you select a group, you find that you are offended by its contents, just leave it. This is not *The New York Times*; some things here are not "fit to print."

2. Please, don't even think of trying to add your input to one of the newsgroups just yet. In the next session, we will walk you slowly through the contributing process. First, for your sake and peace of mind, you will need to understand the etiquette of the network and the risks of contributing too quickly. This is a well established community and you are still a beginner.

Reading the News

There are many ways to read the news, but we will start you off with just two. First, we will show you how to look at individual groups. Then, we will describe how to regularly "follow" a set of groups that may be of interest to you.

There are several programs that should be available on your host account. An older program **rn** or **read news** is available. However, we will recommend that you use **nn No News (is good news)**. That is actually its name and if you ask this program to show you news where there is none, it will say: No News (is good news). We are going to assume **nn** is available on your host. If it is not, check with your host administrator.

We will use **nn** in two ways:

1. First, to read just one group;

2. Second, to read a list of groups you have selected so that you can read them any time you choose.

Reading Individual Groups

Logon to your host computer as you have already done several times already. After you have taken care of your mail and are back at the host prompt, type the following:

```
rm  .newsrc
rm  .newsrc.bak
```

The News

These two commands remove (rm) two files that may interfere with our examples. Soon, we will create new ones with just your selections in them. You may be asked to confirm the removal.

If you get something like:

rm: .newsrc: No such file or directory
rm: .newsrc.bak: No such file or directory

don't worry. It's just the host complaining that these files can't be found (which is what we want right now).

Now, we will look at just one group.

Type the following just as we show it and press **ENTER**:

nn -x news.announce.newusers

The program **nn** is started with the **-x** option and the group **news.announce.newusers** is presented. The **-x** option keeps the **nn** program from making a new **.newsrc**.

The resulting screen should look something like this:

```
Newsgroup: news.announce.newusers      Articles: 29 NO UPDATE

  a  Gene Spafford        798  Answers to Frequently Asked Questions
                               about Usenet
  b  Gene Spafford        367  A Primer on How to Work With the
                               Usenet Community
  c  Gene Spafford        387  Emily Postnews Answers Your Questions
                               on Netiquette
  d  Gene Spafford        106  Hints on writing style for Usenet
  e  Gene Spafford        105  Introduction to news.announce
  f  Gene Spafford        628  List of Active Newsgroups, Part I
  g  Gene Spafford        316  Rules for posting to Usenet
  h  Gene Spafford        417  Usenet Software: History and Sources
  i  Gene Spafford        354  What is Usenet?
  j  taylor               246  A Guide to Social Newsgroups and
                               Mailing Lists
  k  David C Lawrence     157  How to Create a New Usenet
                               Newsgroup
  l  Gene Spafford        107  How to Get Information about Networks
  m  Gene Spafford        810  List of Moderators for Usenet
```

```
n  Gene Spafford     1149  Alternative Newsgroup Hierarchies,
                            Part I
o  Gene Spafford      687  >Alternative Newsgroup Hierarchies,
                            Part II
p  Gene Spafford      461  >List of Active Newsgroups, Part II
q  Jonathan Kamen    1462   List of Periodic Informational
                            Postings, Part 1/5
r  Jonathan Kamen    1454  >List of Periodic Informational
                            Postings, Part 2/5
s  Jonathan Kamen    1464  Changes to List of Periodic
                            Informational Postings

— 15:05 — SELECT — help:? ——Top 64%—
```

This screen shows some (about 64%) of the current articles you have not seen or read. This is the way **nn** usually shows you what is current.

A few words of explanation:

1. The word **current** means that you have not yet seen the articles and that they have not yet been tossed out by the system to conserve space.

2. The word **seen** means that you have been shown the index;

3. The word **read** means that you have selected the article to read.

Now, press the **SPACEBAR**.

This tells **nn** to move to the next page of the index for **news.announce.newusers**. Now you should see:

```
Newsgroup: news.announce.newusers    Articles: 29 NO UPDATE
a  Jonathan Kamen    1407  >List of Periodic Informational
                            Postings, Part 3/5
b  Jonathan Kamen    1449  >List of Periodic Informational
                            Postings, Part 4/5
c  Jonathan Kamen    1576  >List of Periodic Informational
                            Postings, Part 5/5
d  Jonathan Kamens    770  How to become a Usenet site
e  Jonathan Kamens    276  Introduction to the *.answers
                            newsgroups
f  Stephanie Silva    932  Publicly Accessible Mailing Lists,
                            Part 1/5
```

```
     g  Stephanie Silv    1247  >Publicly Accessible Mailing Lists,
                                 Part 2/5
     h  Stephanie Silv    1093  >Publicly Accessible Mailing Lists,
                                 Part 3/5
     i  Stephanie Silv    1219  >Publicly Accessible Mailing Lists,
                                 Part 4/5
     j  Stephanie Silv    1285  >Publicly Accessible Mailing Lists,
                                 Part 5/5
     — 15:05 — SELECT — help:? —Bot—
```

Directions

1. Pick out one of the articles.

2. Press the letter key of the letter you find at the far left of your article.

   WARNING: Do **NOT** press ENTER.

   The article index line will now change on your screen, most likely by becoming highlighted.

3. Press the **SPACEBAR** and the article you have selected will be displayed.

Example:

We will use article **e** from the screen above as an example:

1. Select article **e** by pressing the e key. We should see:

```
     Newsgroup: news.announce.newusers Articles: 29 NO UPDATE
     a Jonathan Kamen     1407  >List of Periodic Informational
                                 Postings, Part 3/5
     b Jonathan Kamen     1449  >List of Periodic Informational
                                 Postings, Part 4/5
     c Jonathan Kamen     1576  >List of Periodic Informational
                                 Postings, Part 5/5
     d Jonathan Kamens     770  How to become a Usenet site
     e Jonathan Kamens     276  Introduction to the *.answers
                                 newsgroups
     f Stephanie Silva     932  Publicly Accessible Mailing Lists,
                                 Part 1/5
     g Stephanie Silv     1247  >Publicly Accessible Mailing Lists,
                                 Part 2/5
     h Stephanie Silv     1093  >Publicly Accessible Mailing Lists,
```

```
                                Part 3/5
i Stephanie Silv     1219  >Publicly Accessible Mailing Lists,
                                Part 4/5
j Stephanie Silv     1285  >Publicly Accessible Mailing Lists,
                                Part 5/5

— 15:23 — SELECT — help:? ——Bot——
```

2. Press the **SPACEBAR** twice and the article will begin to display. It should look like this:

```
Jonathan Kamens: Introduction to the *.answers newsgroups
Archive-name: news-answers/introduction
          Introduction
This is the monthly introductory article for the moderated
newsgroups alt.answers, comp.answers, misc.answers,
news.answers, rec.answers, sci.answers, soc.answers, and
talk.answers (hereafter collectively referred to as
"*.answers"). It explains the purpose of the newsgroups, what
kinds of articles should be submitted to them, how to submit,
how to participate in the mailing list for periodic posting
maintainers, and where to find archives of *.answers postings.
Comments about, suggestions about or corrections to this
posting are welcomed. If you would like to ask me to change
this posting in some way, the method I appreciate most is for
you to actually make the desired modifications to a copy of
the posting, and then to send me the modified posting, or a
context diff between my posted version and your modified
version (if you do the latter, make sure to
— 15:23 —.announce.newusers— LAST —help:?—Top 8%—
```

The News

At this point, you may read each page of the article.

1. Press the **SPACEBAR** when you are ready to move to the next page.

2. If you want to back up a page, press the **BACKSPACE** key.

3. After you have finished with this article, you will come back to the host prompt.

At any point, you may press the **?** key and get a one page help screen of what various characters will do.

If you wish to quit early, type **Q** (that's a capital q). This will stop (Quit) the **nn** program and bring you back to the host prompt.

You may wish to look at other newsgroups this way. Find another one from the lists on the following pages and try it out. Just remember to use the command:

nn -x   (newsgroup full name)

Remember that the **-x** option before the newsgroup name tells the program to ignore the file called **.newsrc**. That was the one we removed just before you started. Later, we will create a new **.newsrc** for you that contains just your articles of interest.

Let's stop for a moment, however, to look again at the newsgroup index and see what the index lines mean.

What the Index Means

Each line of the index screens you have just seen contains a lot about the newsgroup.

1.   You have already used the letter at the left of the line to **select** an article to read.

2.   After the letter comes the name of the author of the article.

3.   Then there is a number to tell you how many characters are in the article.

4.   Finally, there is the subject or title of the article.

Look carefully at the titles for a moment. Some of them begin with the character **>** . This means that the program **nn** has found an original article and this is a second article referencing the first one.

The string of articles with the same subject is called a **thread** .

Threads

Many newsreader programs, like **nn** , arrange the articles in order for you. If the articles use the same subject line, the **nn** program will put them together in date order so that you can "follow the thread."

Moderated Groups

Some newsgroups have volunteers who **moderate** the group. This usually means that articles are submitted to the moderator before being put into the group. Other groups are unmoderated and anything that is sent in will go into the groups. Note that the group **news.announce.newusers** is moderated.

At this point, you may wish to **logout** while we prepare you to look at several newsgroups at the same time just by typing **nn**.

Reading Several Groups Regularly

To read several groups when you login, you will need a file called

.newsrc

This is a file (rc = run command) for the news reader programs such as **nn**. What you will need for this file are the exact names of groups you would like to follow. To help you out, we have listed just a sample of some of the groups from each major category. Scan the lists on the following pages and write down a few (not too many). Then we will begin another session in which you will have a chance to create your own personal **.newsrc** .

Some Alternative Groups

alt.3d	alt.folklore.computers
alt.archery	alt.folklore.science
alt.autos.antique	alt.fractals
alt.bbs.lists	alt.gopher
alt.books.reviews	alt.guitar
alt.books.technical	alt.history.living
alt.cad.autocad	alt.life.internet
alt.dcom.catv	alt.meditation
alt.dcom.telecom	alt.radio.internet
alt.desert.toppings	alt.rock-n-roll
alt.education.disabled	alt.sewing
alt.education.distance	alt.snowmobiles
alt.fan.douglas-adams	alt.sport.bowling
alt.fan.elvis-presley	alt.tennis
alt.fan.monty-python	alt.test
alt.fishing	alt.tv.simpsons

The News

The next set is a mix of local interest groups and specialty groups. Note the heading **atl** for Atlanta, the heading **ba** for San Francisco Bay Area, the heading **ca** for California, etc.

Two other categories here include **bionet** for biological research and **biz** for business (**comp** means computer).

atl.general	bit.listserv.scuba-l
atl.test	biz.comp.hardware
austin.general	biz.comp.software
austin.test	biz.comp.software.demos
ba.general	biz.test
ba.test	boulder.general
bionet.announce	ca.earthquakes
bionet.general	ca.general
bionet.journals.contents	ca.test
bit.general	can.general
bit.listserv.bitnews	capdist.general
bit.listserv.circplus	capdist.test
bit.listserv.ibmpc-l	cern.online
bit.listserv.literary	chi.general
bit.listserv.mednews	chi.test

The Clarinet (that's right, Clarinet) newsgroups collect real news from United Press International (UPI) and other sources. The **nb** series groups are from a news source called **"newsbytes."**

clari.biz	clari.nb.index
clari.biz.economy	clari.nb.review
clari.biz.economy.world	clari.nb.telecom
clari.biz.features	clari.nb.top
clari.biz.finance	clari.nb.trends
clari.biz.market	clari.nb.unix
clari.biz.market.amex	clari.net.announce
clari.biz.market.dow	clari.net.newusers
clari.biz.market.ny	clari.news.arts
clari.biz.market.otc	clari.news.aviation
clari.biz.market.report	clari.news.books
clari.biz.mergers	clari.news.briefs
clari.biz.misc	clari.news.bulletin
clari.biz.top	clari.news.canada
clari.biz.urgent	clari.news.consumer

clari.canada
clari.canada.biz
clari.canada.briefs
clari.canada.briefs.ont
clari.canada.briefs.west
clari.canada.features
clari.canada.general
clari.canada.newscast
clari.feature
clari.feature.dave_barry
clari.feature.miss_manners
clari.feature.movies
clari.local.arizona
clari.local.bc.briefs
clari.local.california
clari.local.chicago
clari.local.florida
clari.local.georgia
clari.local.headlines
clari.local.illinois
clari.local.indiana
clari.local.iowa
clari.local.los_angeles
clari.local.louisiana
clari.local.maryland
clari.local.massachusetts
clari.local.michigan
clari.local.minnesota
clari.local.missouri
clari.local.nebraska
clari.local.nevada
clari.local.new_england
clari.local.new_hampshire
clari.local.new_jersey
clari.local.new_york
clari.local.nyc
clari.local.ohio
clari.local.oregon
clari.local.pennsylvania
clari.local.sfbay
clari.local.texas

clari.news.economy
clari.news.election
clari.news.entertain
clari.news.europe
clari.news.features
clari.news.flash
clari.news.goodnews
clari.news.gov
clari.news.gov.state
clari.news.gov.taxes
clari.news.gov.usa
clari.news.headlines
clari.news.health
clari.news.interest
clari.news.movies
clari.news.music
clari.news.politics
clari.news.top
clari.news.top.world
clari.news.trends
clari.news.tv
clari.news.urgent
clari.news.weather
clari.sfbay.general
clari.sports
clari.sports.baseball
clari.sports.basketball
clari.sports.features
clari.sports.football
clari.sports.hockey
clari.sports.misc
clari.sports.motor
clari.sports.olympic
clari.sports.tennis
clari.sports.top
clari.tw
clari.tw.aerospace
clari.tw.computers
clari.tw.defense
clari.tw.education
clari.tw.electronics

clari.local.utah
clari.local.virginia+dc
clari.local.wisconsin
clari.nb
clari.nb.apple
clari.nb.business
clari.nb.general
clari.nb.govt
clari.nb.ibm

clari.tw.environment
clari.tw.health
clari.tw.health.aids
clari.tw.misc
clari.tw.nuclear
clari.tw.science
clari.tw.space
clari.tw.stocks
clari.tw.telecom

Most of the next groups are from the major **comp** (computer) category.

cmh.general
cmh.test
co.general
co.test
comp.ai
comp.ai.philosophy
comp.ai.shells
comp.ai.vision
comp.apps.spreadsheets
comp.compilers
comp.compression
comp.dcom.cell-relay
comp.dcom.fax
comp.dcom.isdn
comp.dcom.lans.ethernet
comp.dcom.lans.fddi
comp.dcom.lans.misc
comp.dcom.modems
comp.dcom.servers
comp.dcom.telecom
comp.editors
comp.groupware
comp.human-factors
comp.infosystems
comp.infosystems.gis
comp.infosystems.gopher
comp.infosystems.wais
comp.internet.library
comp.lang.ada

comp.lang.apl
comp.lang.c++
comp.lang.forth
comp.lang.fortran
comp.lang.lisp
comp.lang.logo
comp.lang.pascal
comp.lang.postscript
comp.lang.rexx
comp.lang.smalltalk
comp.lang.visual
comp.laser-printers
comp.multimedia
comp.music
comp.newprod
comp.object
comp.periphs.printers
comp.periphs.scsi
comp.programming
comp.protocols.appletalk
comp.protocols.ibm
comp.protocols.tcp-ip
comp.research.japan
comp.risks
comp.robotics
comp.society
comp.sys.ibm.pc.digest
comp.sys.ibm.pc.games
comp.sys.ibm.pc.hardware
comp.sys.laptops

These groups, from all over contain the **k12** groups that might be of interest to teachers and students in kindergarten through the 12th grade.

dc.general	k12.chat.senior
dc.test	k12.chat.teacher
dfw.general	k12.ed.art
dfw.news	k12.ed.business
dfw.test	k12.ed.comp.literacy
erg.general	k12.ed.health-pe
erg.test	k12.ed.life-skills
ga.general	k12.ed.math
ga.test	k12.ed.music
harvard.science-review	k12.ed.science
houston.general	k12.ed.soc-studies
houston.test	k12.ed.special
hsv.general	k12.ed.tag
ie.general	k12.ed.tech
ie.test	k12.lang.art
ieee.announce	k12.lang.deutsch-eng
ieee.general	k12.lang.esp-eng
in.general	k12.lang.francais
k12.chat.elementary	k12.lang.russian
k12.chat.junior	k12.library
	k12.sys.projects

Next, we have included some of the miscellaneous groups and the groups about Usenet (news).

kw.general	msen.reuters.general
la.general	msen.reuters.urgent
la.test	mtl.general
milw.general	mtl.test
misc.books.technical	nbg.general
misc.consumers	ne.general
misc.education	news.announce.conferences
misc.fitness	news.announce.important
misc.forsale.computers	news.announce.newgroups
misc.forsale.wanted	news.announce.newusers
misc.test	news.answers
misc.writing	news.future
mn.general	news.groups
mn.test	news.lists

mscs.general	news.newsites
mscs.test	news.newusers.questions
msen.reuters.biz	news.software.nn
msen.reuters.financial	news.software.readers
msen.reuters.food	news.test

This next set is mostly local, although it's from all over the globe.

nj.general	or.general
nj.housing	or.test
nj.test	ott.general
nlnet.general	pa.general
nlnet.test	pa.test
no.general	pdx.general
no.test	pdx.golf
ny.general	pdx.movies
ny.test	pdx.music
nyc.general	pdx.online
nyc.test	pdx.running
nz.general	pdx.sports
oc.general	pdx.telecom
oc.test	pdx.test
oh.general	pgh.general
oh.test	pgh.test
ok.general	phl.test
ont.general	phri.general
ont.test	pnw.general
opinions.supreme-court	pnw.test
	qtp.general

The recreational category contains a wealth of information from enthusiasts who are interested in many forms of recreation. Here is just a sample.

rec.antiques	rec.music.classical
rec.arts.animation	rec.music.compose
rec.arts.bonsai	rec.music.country.western
rec.arts.books	rec.music.dementia
rec.arts.cinema	rec.music.dylan
rec.arts.comics	rec.music.early
rec.arts.dance	rec.music.folk
rec.arts.disney	rec.music.funky
rec.arts.drwho	rec.music.gaffa

rec.arts.movies.reviews
rec.arts.poems
rec.arts.sf.movies
rec.arts.sf.reviews
rec.arts.sf.tv
rec.arts.startrek
rec.arts.theatre
rec.arts.tv
rec.arts.tv.soaps
rec.arts.wobegon
rec.audio
rec.audio.car
rec.autos
rec.aviation
rec.backcountry
rec.bicycles
rec.birds
rec.boats
rec.boats.paddle
rec.climbing
rec.collecting
rec.crafts.brewing
rec.crafts.misc
rec.crafts.textiles
rec.equestrian
rec.folk-dancing
rec.food.cooking
rec.food.drink
rec.food.historic
rec.food.recipes
rec.food.restaurants
rec.food.sourdough
rec.food.veg
rec.games.backgammon
rec.games.board
rec.games.bridge
rec.games.chess
rec.games.mud
rec.games.pinball
rec.games.trivia
rec.games.video

rec.music.gdead
rec.music.indian.misc
rec.music.industrial
rec.music.info
rec.music.makers
rec.music.marketplace
rec.music.misc
rec.music.newage
rec.music.phish
rec.music.reviews
rec.music.synth
rec.music.video
rec.org.mensa
rec.outdoors.fishing
rec.pets
rec.pets.birds
rec.pets.cats
rec.pets.dogs
rec.photo
rec.puzzles
rec.puzzles.crosswords
rec.pyrotechnics
rec.radio.amateur.misc
rec.radio.cb
rec.radio.shortwave
rec.radio.swap
rec.railroad
rec.roller-coaster
rec.running
rec.scouting
rec.scuba
rec.skate
rec.skiing
rec.skydiving
rec.sport
rec.sport.baseball
rec.sport.basketball
rec.sport.cricket
rec.sport.football.college
rec.sport.football.pro
rec.sport.golf

The News

rec.gardens
rec.golf
rec.guns
rec.humor.funny
rec.hunting
rec.juggling
rec.kites
rec.martial-arts
rec.models.railroad
rec.models.rockets
rec.motorcycles
rec.music.afro-latin
rec.music.beatles
rec.music.bluenote
rec.music.cd
rec.music.christian

rec.sport.hockey
rec.sport.hockey.field
rec.sport.olympics
rec.sport.pro-wrestling
rec.sport.rugby
rec.sport.soccer
rec.sport.swimming
rec.sport.tennis
rec.sport.triathlon
rec.sport.volleyball
rec.travel
rec.travel.air
rec.video
rec.video.cable-tv
rec.windsurfing
rec.woodworking

The sciences are represented by the next set of samples.

sci.aeronautics
sci.anthropology
sci.aquaria
sci.archaeology
sci.astro
sci.astro.hubble
sci.bio
sci.bio.technology
sci.chem
sci.classics
sci.cognitive
sci.comp-aided
sci.cryonics
sci.crypt
sci.econ
sci.edu
sci.electronics
sci.energy
sci.engr
sci.engr.biomed
sci.engr.chem
sci.engr.civil

sci.geo.meteorology
sci.image.processing
sci.lang
sci.lang.japan
sci.logic
sci.materials
sci.math
sci.math.num-analysis
sci.math.research
sci.math.stat
sci.math.symbolic
sci.med
sci.med.aids
sci.med.occupational
sci.med.physics
sci.nanotech
sci.optics
sci.physics
sci.physics.fusion
sci.psychology
sci.psychology.digest
sci.research

sci.engr.mech
sci.environment
sci.geo.fluids
sci.geo.geology
sci.space
sci.space.news
sci.space.shuttle
sci.systems
sci.virtual-worlds

The social sciences and other sociological discussions are next.

scruz.general
scruz.test
sdnet.general
sdnet.test
seattle.general
seattle.test
slo.general
soc.bi
soc.college
soc.college.grad
soc.college.gradinfo
soc.couples
soc.culture.afghanistan
soc.culture.african
soc.culture.arabic
soc.culture.asean
soc.culture.australian
soc.culture.bangladesh
soc.culture.brazil
soc.culture.british
soc.culture.bulgaria
soc.culture.canada
soc.culture.caribbean
soc.culture.celtic
soc.culture.china
soc.culture.czecho-slovak
soc.culture.esperanto
soc.culture.europe
soc.culture.filipino
soc.culture.french
soc.culture.german
soc.culture.greek

soc.culture.indian
soc.culture.indian.telugu
soc.culture.iranian
soc.culture.italian
soc.culture.japan
soc.culture.jewish
soc.culture.korean
soc.culture.lebanon
soc.culture.magyar
soc.culture.mexican
soc.culture.misc
soc.culture.nepal
soc.culture.netherlands
soc.culture.new-zealand
soc.culture.nordic
soc.culture.pakistan
soc.culture.polish
soc.culture.portuguese
soc.culture.romanian
soc.culture.soviet
soc.culture.spain
soc.culture.sri-lanka
soc.culture.taiwan
soc.culture.tamil
soc.culture.thai
soc.culture.turkish
soc.culture.usa
soc.culture.vietnamese
soc.culture.yugoslavia
soc.feminism
soc.history
soc.veterans
soc.culture.hongkong

Our last sample set includes the **talk** major category. It's probably very well named.

stgt.general	triangle.general
stl.general	tub.general
stl.test	tx.general
swnet.general	tx.test
swnet.test	uc.general
talk.abortion	uc.test
talk.bizarre	uch.general
talk.environment	uiuc.general
talk.origins	uiuc.test
talk.philosophy.misc	uk.general
talk.politics.animals	uk.test
talk.politics.china	ut.general
talk.politics.drugs	ut.test
talk.politics.guns	utcs.general
talk.politics.mideast	uw.general
talk.politics.misc	uw.test
talk.politics.soviet	uwisc.forum
talk.politics.space	uwisc.general
talk.politics.theory	uxa.general
talk.rape	uxa.test
talk.religion.misc	va.general
talk.religion.newage	va.test
talk.rumors	well.general
tamu.general	wi.general

Building a News File

To read the set you have selected, you will need to create a file called

.newsrc

As an example, we will pick half a dozen groups and show you how to create this file on your host account. Just substitute the groups you selected to replace our samples. We will use an editor on the host to create the file.

You won't need to know anything about the host editor; just follow the example we give. The final file on your host account will look exactly like this (with your group names instead of ours):

    clari.news.weather:
    clari.sports.basketball:
    news.announce.important:
    news.announce.newusers:
    news.newusers.questions:
    rec.food.cooking:
    rec.arts.movies.reviews:

The key to this file is the colon (:) at the end of each line. This colon tells the news program that you are "subscribed" to this group. Once you have this file in your host account, you can just type **nn** to read these groups. They will be presented to you in the order you listed. If there are no new articles, the group will be skipped. If there is nothing new, **nn** will respond with;

No News (is good news)

Now, let's create the file. We are going to use a host editor found on almost all UNIX hosts called **vi**. We are not really going to try to show you how to use **vi** here, since it is actually somewhat complicated. We just want you to follow the instructions below to create this file.

1. Login again to your account (if you logged out).

2. At the host prompt, type the following:

        vi .newsrc (this opens the .newsrc file)
         I (this sets up for entry)

3. Now very carefully type in the name of each newsgroup that you wish to have included.

    IMPORTANT: End each line with a colon (:) and press the **ENTER** key at the end of each line after the colon.

NOTE: *If something goes wrong, press the ESCAPE key and then type the following: :q!*
This stops the editor and throws away what you have done. You can start over until you are happy with what you have.

4. When you are done typing in the names of the groups you wish to have included, press the **ESCAPE** key and type:

        ZZ   (this closes and saves the file)

5. You can look at your file with the **more** command. Type:

   more .newsrc

Using nn and Your New File

Now when you type **nn**, you will be shown only the groups you entered in your **.newsrc** file. Each time you start **nn** it will check to see what you have already seen or read and it will show you only the "new" news. **nn** does this by adding article numbers after the colons in your file named:

   .newsrc

After you finish using **nn** the first time, you can type:

   more .newsrc

to see the numbers **nn** has added to your file.

New Newsgroups

New newsgroups are constantly being created. These will be automatically added to the end of your **.newsrc** file. As each new group is shown, you may decide either to keep it or to "unsubscribe" to it.

1. To keep a new newsgroup, just do nothing. The news from the new group will come up every time there is new news.

2. To "unsubscribe" to a new newsgroup, just type a U and it will go away. This method works while you are at the index or while you are reading an article.

Unsubscribed Newsgroups

Even after you have set up a **.newsrc** file, you can still use the earlier form of **nn** to look in on other groups. Just remember to use the **-x** option like this:

   nn -x the.group.name

The **-x** option will keep **nn** from changing your **.newsrc** file.

Finding What Exists

We have shown you how to read some of the newsgroups. You may wish to see a more complete and current list. Information on all widely distributed groups is carried monthly (or so) in the groups:

> **news.announce.newusers**
> **news.announce.newsgroups**

This completes our introduction to the "news." It is a huge and fascinating aspect of the Internet and one place where you can go on to learn a great deal more. Good Luck!

As you become more experienced in using **nn** (or other newsreader programs), you will want to look at many more groups and do many more things. One of those things may be to contribute to the newsgroups. That will be the subject of our next session.

■ ■ Session Three Vocabulary and Command Summary

Usenet .... The set of people who exchange articles tagged with one or more universally recognized labels, called "newsgroups"

news.announce.newusers ... a newsgroup particularly designed for new users

nn .... a "newsreader" program that is used to begin a newsgroup session

rm .... remove a file; that is, delete it

.newsrc .... the special file that contains the names of the newsgroups you would like to read when you login to nn (literally, the news run command program)

.newsrc.bak .... the backup file for the .newsrc file

Continues on next page

SPACEBAR .... used to move forward through the index of articles that are presented by nn
also used for displaying news articles once they have been selected

BACKSPACE key .... used to move back up a page through articles

? .... used to provide one page help screens

Q .... used to stop (Quit) the nn program and to take you back to the host prompt

thread .... a string of articles with the same subject

vi .... the editor you use to create your own .newsrc file

vi .newsrc .... the command used to begin the creation of a .newsrc file

I .... the command used to set up the file for entry

Esc key and :q! .... the sequence to type if you make a mistake while creating your .newsrc file

Esc key and ZZ .... the sequence to type when you are done creating your .newsrc file

nn -x the.group.name .... the sequence to type if you wish to read a particular newsgroup file, but do NOT wish to change the .newsrc file. For example, nn -x news.announce.newusers will permit you to read this file without changing your .newsrc file

U (Capital U) .... Unsubscribe to a particular group

SESSION FOUR

Contributing to Usenet

So far, we have shown you how to login to the Internet, how to send mail to yourself and to others, and how to read the news. All of these activities involve you and, at most, a few other people. We now enter an area where some may fear to tread - contributing to Usenet newsgroups. There is reason to hesitate here, as one will be quickly reminded that one is a beginner. However, everyone here was once a beginner and there is room for us all.

A Few Rules

These are not so much rules as they are suggestions for neophytes. By observing the suggestions, you will enter with understanding and be welcomed. Some of those who participate in Usenet Groups have little patience for those who have not done their homework to "understand the territory."

Before considering contributing to a real newsgroup, there is some information that you should review. We have included some of it below. Additional information may be found in the newsgroup **news.announce.newusers**.

This information includes:

1. Rules for posting to Usenet

2. Answers to frequently asked questions about Usenet

3. Hints on writing style for Usenet

4. Emily Postnews answers your questions on Netiquette

We strongly recommend that you read all of it before you venture into this territory. The natives are, for the most part, friendly, but have been known to take scalps from "tenderfeet."

Before you tread in the real water here, we will show you how to contribute to "test" newsgroups where you can learn without fear. However, before doing so, we would like you to read a wonderful file from **news.announce.newusers** called:

A Primer on How to Work With the Usenet Community
by Chuq Von Rospach

   *** You now have access to Usenet, a network of thousands of computers. Other documents or your system administrator will provide detailed technical documentation. This message describes the Usenet culture and customs that have developed over time. All new users should read this message to find out how Usenet works. ***

*** (Old users could read it, too, to refresh their memories.) ***

Usenet is a large collection of computers that share data with each other. It is the people on these computers that make Usenet worth the·effort to read and maintain, and for Usenet to function properly those people must be able to interact in productive ways. This document is intended as a guide to using the net in ways that will be pleasant and productive for everyone.

This document is not intended to teach you how to use Usenet. Instead, it is a guide to using it politely, effectively and efficiently. Communication by computer is new to almost everybody, and there are certain aspects that can make it a frustrating experience until you get used to them. This document should help you avoid the worst traps.

The easiest way to learn how to use Usenet is to watch how others use it. Start reading the news and try to figure out what people are doing and why. After a couple of weeks you will start understanding why certain things are done and what things shouldn't be done. There are documents available describing the technical details of how to use the software. These are different depending on which programs you use to access the news. You can get copies of these from your system administrator. If you do not know who that person is, they can be contacted on most systems by mailing to account "usenet".

Never Forget that the Person on the Other Side is Human

Because your interaction with the network is through a computer it is easy to forget that there are people "out there." Situations arise where emotions erupt into a verbal free-for-all that can lead to hurt feelings.

Please remember that people all over the world are reading your words. Do not attack people if you cannot persuade them with your presentation of the facts. Screaming, cursing, and abusing others only serves to make people think less of you and less willing to help you when you need it.

If you are upset at something or someone, wait until you have had a chance to calm down and think about it. A cup of (decaf!) coffee or a good night's sleep works wonders on your perspective. Hasty words create more problems than they solve. Try not to say anything to others you would not say to them in person in a room full of people.

Don't Blame System Admins for their Users' Behavior

Sometimes, you may find it necessary to write to a system administrator about something concerning his or her site. Maybe it is a case of the software not working, or a control message escaped, or maybe one of the users at that site has done something you feel requires comment. No matter how steamed you may be, be polite to the sysadmin — he or she may not have any idea of what you are going to say, and may not have any part in the incidents involved. By being civil and temperate, you are more likely to obtain courteous attention and assistance.

Be Careful What You Say About Others

Please remember — you read netnews; so do as many as 3,000,000 other people. This group quite possibly includes your boss, your friend's boss, your girl friend's brother's best friend and one of your father's beer buddies. Information posted on the net can come back to haunt you or the person you are talking about.

Think twice before you post personal information about yourself or others. This applies especially strongly to groups like soc.singles and alt.sex but even postings in groups like talk.politics.misc have included information about the personal life of third parties that could get them into serious trouble if it got into the wrong hands.

Be Brief

Never say in ten words what you can say in fewer. Say it succinctly and it will have a greater impact. Remember that the longer you make your article, the fewer people will bother to read it.

Your Postings Reflect Upon You — Be Proud of Them

Most people on Usenet will know you only by what you say and how well you say it. They may someday be your co-workers or friends. Take some time to make sure each posting is something that will not embarrass you later. Minimize your spelling errors and make sure that the article is easy to read and understand. Writing is an art and to do it well requires practice. Since much of how people judge you on the net is based on your writing, such time is well spent.

Use Descriptive Titles

The subject line of an article is there to enable a person with a limited amount of time to decide whether or not to read your article. Tell people what the article is about before they read it. A title like "Car for Sale" to rec.autos does not help as much as "66 MG Midget for sale: Beaverton OR." Don't expect people to read your article to find out what it is about because many of them won't bother. Some sites truncate the length of the subject line to 40 characters so keep your subjects short and to the point.

Think About Your Audience

When you post an article, think about the people you are trying to reach. Asking UNIX(*) questions on rec.autos will not reach as many of the people you want to reach as if you asked them on comp.unix.questions or comp.unix.internals. Try to get the most appropriate audience for your message, not the widest.
It is considered bad form to post both to misc.misc, soc.net-people, or misc.wanted and to some other newsgroup. If it belongs in that other newsgroup, it does not belong in misc.misc, soc.net-people, or misc.wanted.
If your message is of interest to a limited geographic area (apartments, car sales, meetings, concerts, etc...), restrict the distribution of the message to your local area. Some areas have special newsgroups with geographical limitations, and the recent versions of the news software allow you to limit the distribution of material sent to world-wide newsgroups. Check with your system administrator to see what newsgroups are available and how to use them.
If you want to try a test of something, do not use a world-wide newsgroup! Messages in misc.misc that say "This is a test" are likely to cause large numbers of caustic messages to

flow into your mailbox. There are newsgroups that are local to your computer or area that should be used. Your system administrator can tell you what they are.

Be familiar with the group you are posting to before you post! You shouldn't post to groups you do not read, or post to groups you've only read a few articles from — you may not be familiar with the on-going conventions and themes of the group. One normally does not join a conversation by just walking up and talking. Instead, you listen first and then join in if you have something pertinent to contribute.

Be Careful with Humor and Sarcasm

Without the voice inflections and body language of personal communications, it is easy for a remark meant to be funny to be misinterpreted. Subtle humor tends to get lost, so take steps to make sure that people realize you are trying to be funny. The net has developed a symbol called the smiley face. It looks like ":-)" and points out sections of articles with humorous intent. No matter how broad the humor or satire, it is safer to remind people that you are being funny.

But also be aware that quite frequently satire is posted without any explicit indications. If an article outrages you strongly, you should ask yourself if it just may have been unmarked satire. Several self-proclaimed connoisseurs refuse to use smiley faces, so take heed or you may make a temporary fool of yourself.

Only Post a Message Once

Avoid posting messages to more than one newsgroup unless you are sure it is appropriate. If you do post to multiple newsgroups, do not post to each group separately. Instead, specify all the groups on a single copy of the message. This reduces network overhead and lets people who subscribe to more than one of those groups see the message once instead of having to wade through each copy.

Please Rotate Messages With Questionable Content

Certain newsgroups (such as rec.humor) have messages in them that may be offensive to some people. To make sure that these messages are not read unless they are explicitly requested, these messages should be encrypted. The standard encryption method is to rotate each letter by thirteen characters so that an "a" becomes an "n". This is known on the network as "rot13" and when you rotate a message the word "rot13" should be in the "Subject:" line. Most of the software used to read usenet articles have some way of encrypting and decrypting messages. Your system administrator can tell you how the software on your system works, or you can use the Unix command "tr [a-z][A-Z] [n-z][a-m][N-Z][A-M]". (Note that some versions of Unix don't require the [] in the "tr" command. In fact, some systems will get upset if you use them in an unquoted manner. The following should work for everyone, but may be shortened on some systems:

    tr '[a-m][n-z][A-M][N-Z]' '[n-z][a-m][N-Z][A-M]'

Don't forget the single quotes!)

Summarize What You are Following Up

When you are following up someone's article, please summarize the parts of the article to which you are responding. This allows readers to appreciate your comments rather than trying to remember what the original article said. It is also possible for your response to get to some sites before the original article.

Summarization is best done by including appropriate quotes from the original article. Do not include the entire article since it will irritate the people who have already seen it. Even if you are responding to the entire article, summarize only the major points you are discussing.

When Summarizing, Summarize!

When you request information from the network, it is common courtesy to report your findings so that others can benefit as well. The best way of doing this is to take all the responses that you received and edit them into a single article that is posted to the places where you originally posted your question. Take the time to strip headers, combine duplicate information, and write a short summary. Try to credit the information to the people that sent it to you, where possible.

Use Mail, Don't Post a Follow-up

One of the biggest problems we have on the network is that when someone asks a question, many people send out identical answers. When this happens, dozens of identical answers pour through the net. Mail your answer to the person and suggest that they summarize to the network. This way the net will only see a single copy of the answers, no matter how many people answer the question.

If you post a question, please remind people to send you the answers by mail and at least offer to summarize them to the network.

Read All Follow-ups and Don't Repeat What Has Already Been Said

Before you submit a follow-up to a message, read the rest of the messages in the newsgroup to see whether someone has already said what you want to say. If someone has, don't repeat it.

Check the Headers When Following Up

The news software has provisions to specify that follow-ups to an article should go to a specific set of newsgroups — possibly different from the newsgroups to which the original article was posted. Sometimes the groups chosen for follow-ups are totally inappropriate, especially as a thread of discussion changes with repeated postings. You should carefully check the groups and distributions given in the header and edit them as appropriate. If you change the groups named in the header, or if you direct follow-ups to a particular group, say so in the body of the message — not everyone reads the headers of postings.

Be Careful About Copyrights and Licenses

Once something is posted onto the network, it is *probably* in the public domain unless you own the appropriate rights (most notably, if you wrote the thing yourself) and you post it with a valid copyright notice; a court would have to decide the specifics and there are arguments for both sides of the issue. Now that the US has ratified the Berne convention, the issue is even murkier (if you are a poster in the US). For all practical purposes, though, assume that you effectively give up the copyright if you don't put in a notice. Of course, the *information* becomes public, so you mustn't post trade secrets that way.

When posting material to the network, keep in mind that material that is UNIX-related may be restricted by the license you or your company signed with AT&T and be careful not to violate it. You should also be aware that posting movie reviews, song lyrics, or anything else published under a copyright could cause you, your company, or members of the net community to be held liable for damages, so we highly recommend caution in using this material.

Cite Appropriate References

If you are using facts to support a cause, state where they came from. Don't take someone else's ideas and use them as your own. You don't want someone pretending that your ideas are theirs; show them the same respect.

Mark or Rotate Answers and Spoilers

When you post something (like a movie review that discusses a detail of the plot) that might spoil a surprise for other people, please mark your message with a warning so that they can skip the message. Another alternative would be to use the "rot13" protocol to encrypt the message so it cannot be read accidentally. When you post a message with a spoiler in it make sure the word "spoiler" is part of the "Subject:" line.

Spelling Flames Considered Harmful

Every few months a plague descends on Usenet called the spelling flame. It starts out when someone posts an article correcting the spelling or grammar in some article. The immediate result seems to be for everyone on the net to turn into a 6th grade English teacher and pick apart each other's postings for a few weeks. This is not productive and tends to cause people who used to be friends to get angry with each other.
It is important to remember that we all make mistakes, and that there are many users on the net who use English as a second language. There are also a number of people who suffer from dyslexia and who have difficulty noticing their spelling mistakes. If you feel that you must make a comment on the quality of aposting, please do so by mail, not on the network.

Don't Overdo Signatures

Signatures are nice, and many people can have a signature added to their postings automatically by placing it in a file called "$HOME/.signature". Don't overdo it. Signatures can tell the world something about you, but keep them short. A signature that is longer than the message itself is considered to be in bad taste. The main purpose of a signature is to help people locate you, not to tell your life story. Every signature should include at least your return address relative to a major, known site on the network and a proper domain-format address. Your system administrator can give this to you. Some news posters attempt to enforce a 4 line limit on signature files — an amount that should be more than sufficient to provide a return address and attribution.

Limit Line Length and Avoid Control Characters

Try to keep your text in a generic format. Many (if not most) of the people reading Usenet do so from 80 column terminals or from workstations with 80 column terminal windows. Try to keep your lines of text to less than 80 characters for optimal readability. If people quote part of your article in a followup, short lines will probably show up better, too. Also realize that there are many, many different forms of terminals in use. If you enter special control characters in your message, it may result in your message being unreadable on some terminal types; a character sequence that causes reverse video on your screen may result in a keyboard lock and graphics mode on someone else's terminal. You should also try to avoid the use of tabs, too, since they may also be interpreted differently on terminals other than your own.

Summary of Things to Remember

Never forget that the person on the other side is human

Don't blame system admins for their users' behavior

Be careful what you say about others

Be brief

Your postings reflect upon you; be proud of them

Use descriptive titles

Think about your audience

Be careful with humor and sarcasm

Only post a message once

Please rotate material with questionable content

Contributing to Usenet

```
Summarize what you are following up

Use mail, don't post a follow-up

Read all follow-ups and don't repeat what has already been
said

Double-check follow-up newsgroups and distributions.

Be careful about copyrights and licenses

Cite appropriate references

When summarizing, summarize

Mark or rotate answers or spoilers

Spelling flames considered harmful

Don't overdo signatures

Limit line length and avoid control characters

Although this file is in the public domain, we would like to
thank all those who have contributed to and maintained it over
the years. It remains the best advice for newcomers.
```

Test Groups

We hope that by now you have read some of the other Usenet "how to" articles. Before contributing to "real" newsgroups, we will begin by contributing to test groups that have been created especially for beginners.

On almost every host, there are newsgroups just for that purpose. They are called **test** groups. We have listed a few of them below. After the list, we will begin several sessions that should allow you to test the process of submitting articles. The test groups are there to allow you to practice without bothering anyone. They were put there to be sure that you wouldn't add to the "noise" on the network. Please follow our lead and use these groups as often as you would like. Even after you are an experienced contributor, you may wish to try out ideas here to see how they look.

There are several other reasons to use test groups:

1. They are usually closer to you than are other computers on the whole Usenet. This means that you are not using up the resources of the network by posting to a very wide audience.

2. Your messages will be seen by very few people (just you and a few other self-conscious testers). You vastly reduce your risk of being "flamed." After our practice sessions, we will explain flames and why you should avoid them.

The Test Groups

Following is a partial list of some test groups. You should pick one from either your host system (check for that one first) or from one close to you. This is a worldwide listing of test groups; you will find test groups that speak English as well as many other languages.

NOTE: *There are test groups to test other than Usenet contributions. You should always read a group before contributing to be sure of its purpose. You can also see if the group is really close to you as the names are sometimes a little cryptic. As a reminder, you can use the command:*

> *nn -x (test.group.name)*

where you substitute the real name of the group for (test.group.name).

Test Group Names

atl.test	Testing in Atlanta, GA.
austin.test	Usenet testing in Austin, TX.
ca.test	Tests of 'ca' distribution articles.
capdist.test	For testing the capdist distribution.
chi.test	Usenet testing in Chicago.
cos.test	Test group for Colorado Springs regional hierarchy.
cth.test	Test messages.
dc.test	Testing in the Washington, DC area.
dfw.test	Testing in Dallas/Fort Worth.
dnet.test	Usenet testing in dnet.
fl.test	Testing workspace in Florida.
ga.test	Testing in Georgia.
houston.test	Testing in Houston, Texas.
ita.test	Test of ita distribution.
kc.test	Usenet testing in Kansas City.
la.test	Testing in Los Angeles, CA.

mhk.test	Test messages.
mit.test	For mit.all test Usenet news messages. Boring.
mn.test	Testing in Minnesota.
mtl.test	Usenet testing in Montreal.
nbg.test	Reflektorfutter (was: Fuer Jastel's wilde Testereien).
nj.test	Tests news and uucp software or news connections.
ny.test	Usenet news testing in New York.
nyc.test	Usenet testing in NYC.
oc.test	Usenet testing in Orange County, CA.
ont.test	Testing in Ontario, Canada.
or.test	Testing in Oregon.
pa.test	Usenet testing in Pennsylvania.
pdx.test	Testing in Portland, OR.
pgh.test	Testing in Pittsburgh.
phl.test	Usenet testing in Philadelphia.
pnw.test	Your vanilla test group.
princeton.test	Testing of the Princeton distribution.
rpi.test	For testing Usenet.
ruhr.test	Die obligatorische Testgruppe.
sac.test	Test Posting Group.
sat.test	Testing in San Antonio.
scruz.test	Usenet testing in Santa Cruz.
sdnet.test	Usenet testing in San Diego.
seattle.test	Usenet testing in Seattle, Washington.
slac.test	Netnews Testing Group.
stgt.test	Testing in Stuttgart.
stl.test	Testing in St. Louis.
sub.test	Fuer Superschachteln und andere wichtige Tests.
tn.test	Usenet Testing in Tennessee.
tor.test	Testing in Toronto, Canada.
tue.test	Test messages for tuenet (Eindhoven Univ. of Technology).
tx.test	Testing in Texas.
ucb.test	General UCB test group.
uchi.test	Test postings at the University of Chicago.
uiuc.test	Testing local news/notesfile network.
umiami.test	Test group for the University of Miami newsgroups.
ut.test	Test postings at UTexas.
uw.test	Testing.
va.test	Testing in Virginia.
resif.test	Pour vos tests de diffusion.
ie.test	For testing within Ireland.
nordunet.test	Just for testing.
sfnet.test	Testiryhm (Finland).
muc.test	Tests in and around Munich.
sta.test	Tests in and around Starnberg.
umn.cbs.test	Testing for the U of Minnesota College of BioSci.
umn.cis.test	Testing for the U of Minnesota Computer & Info. Svcs.

umn.cs.test	University of Minnesota CSci testing.
umn.csom.test	Testing for the U of MN Carlson School of Management.
umn.ee.test	Testing for the U of Minnesota EE dept.
umn.socsci.test	Testing for the University of Minnesota Social Sciences.
su.test	Testing news.
no.test	Testing the Norwegian News network.
uc.test	A place to post test messages.
nlnet.test	Voor testdoeleinden.
bit.listserv.test	Test Newsgroup.
biz.test	Biz newsgroup test messages.
bln.test	Testgruppe - Achtung: Reflektoren.
de.alt.test	Tests im de.alt-Teilnetz. Achtung Reflektoren!
de.test	Tests. Vorsicht Reflektoren!
eunet.test	EUnet-wide test group.
fj.test	Testing all over JUNET. (Japanese Universities, et al)
gnu.gnusenet.test	GNU's Not Usenet alternative sub-network testing.
hanse.test	Lokale Test-Gruppe.
schule.test	Fuer allgemeines Testen in den schule.-Gruppen.
trial.test	Testing of the Trial distribution.
vmsnet.test	Test messages.
fr.test	Testez la diffusion de vos articles dans fr.
uk.test	UK wide tests.
ba.test	Tests of 'ba' distribution. (Some sites autorespond.)

A Note about Editors

During the following session, you will most likely be presented with an "editor" screen to help you to compose your contribution. If you are not familiar with the editors on your host system, you should break here for a little while. You will need to become familiar with at least one text editor if you wish to contribute to Usenet groups.

If you are already comfortable with an editor, you can proceed. Ask your systems people or the staff at your host to help you a little here. If you are comfortable with **vi** and would like to use this editor for making contributions, ask your administrator how to make the **vi** editor the Usenet "default." They will also be able to help you select an editor and make it your "default."

Practice Posting

Contributing to a newsgroup is called **posting**. Posting means adding a new article to a newsgroup. After we try our first **post** we will show you how to reply to the **thread** that you have started. A thread is a series of articles on the same subject and is indicated (under the newsreader **nn**) by one or more > marks in the subject line.

1. Login to your host

2. Begin the **nn** newsreader as follows:

    nn -x (your.test.group)

    where (your.test.group) is replaced by the name of the test group you have selected.

3. When the selection screen appears, type **:post**

4. You will see something like the following screen. We have used a fake newsgroup called **host.test** here . You will be asked a series of questions about your posting. Key in answers similar to those we have shown and press **ENTER** after each one.

```
:post
POST to: host.test
Subject: A Test
Keywords: Test
Summary: A Test
MessageDistribution: (default 'world')
WAIT
```

5. Now you will be shown a partially filled in screen with your test posting, subject, etc. listed. The lines below the Keywords are blanks which are indicated by the ~ (tilde) characters.

6. If you are using the **vi** editor, **press A** to begin the append mode and begin typing your test message.

7. When you are done, remember to put your (real) name at the end of the message. Just type it in. You don't need to put your email address in, as the posting program will do that for you automatically.

```
Newsgroups: host.test
Subject: A Test
```

```
Summary: A Test Message
Keywords: Test

Here is a test message to try out the local test group. You
can put as much text in here as you would like, but you don't
need to put in any more than you want. The key is to get used
to the editor and to feel comfortable with what you are
saying.

Your Name
~
~
~
~
~
~
~
~
```

8. End your message (with Escape and ZZ if you are using vi) and you will be provided with a series of options:

```
a)bort e)dit h)old m)ail r)eedit s)end v)iew w)rite
Action: (post article)
```

At this point, you may make any of the selections indicated. If you would like to post the article, just press **ENTER**. The (post article) indicates the default action if you press **ENTER**.

9. Now you will have to be patient. The host will usually respond with:

```
Be patient! Your new article will not show up immediately.
```

NOTE: *Each system is different. You may have to wait somewhere between minutes and hours. In rare cases, it could even take a day. Most of the time, however, your test posting will appear within the hour. Your best bet would be to go and do something else while you wait.*

Replying to Postings

Under ordinary circumstances, when you see something in an article that you would like to discuss with the author of the posting, email is preferred over posting a response in the newsgroup.

For these test sessions, however, we will use both the reply-by-mail and the followup posting. After all, it's your first posting and anyone who reads a lot of test newsgroups deserves the boredom.

When you have let enough time elapse (it will depend on your system and how far away the test group is), again enter the test newsgroup with the command:

nn -x (your.test.group)

1. If your test posting now appears (you can tell; it's from you), select it by pressing the letter key that corresponds to your posting.

2. You will now see your posting as others see it. This is a good time to take a few notes for your next posting. You may wish to change a few things the next time you post.

Reply to Your Test

3. With your test posting on the screen, press a capital **R**
   This will put you into **reply** mode. This means that you will send an email note to the original poster of the article (you) and you can include the original posting.

4. After you are asked if you wish to include the original article (answer y), you will see something like this:

```
Newsgroups: host.test
Subject: A Test
Summary: A Test Message
Keywords: Test
Here is a test message to try out the local test group. You
can put as much text in here as you would like, but you don't
need to put in any more than you want to. The key is to get
used to the editor and to feel comfortable with what you are
saying.

Your Name
~
```

```
~
~
~
~
~
~
~
```

5. Move the cursor down to the last line of the original test (your signature line) and press **A** **(if you are using vi)**

6. Press ENTER to get to the next line and begin your reply message. Notice that the original posting is included above and that the system has been smart enough to know that it is from you.

7. Compose your reply message and press ESCAPE when you are done.

8. Then type **ZZ** to leave the **vi** editor.

9. You will then have a series of options:

    a)bort e)dit h)old m)ail r)eedit s)end v)iew w)rite

    Action: (send letter)

10. By pressing ENTER, you will send the message, including your original posting, to yourself.

    You can use the mail program demonstrated in Session Two to see what your reply looks like. It might appear to be something like this:

Contributing
to Usenet

```
Mail version SMI 4.0    date & time    Type ? for help.
 "/usr/spool/mail/user": 1 message 1 new
>N  1 user                      Re: Another Test
& t1
Message 1:
From user
Return-Path: <user>
Received: by host.com
id AA23506; day, date & time
Date: date & time
From: user (Your Real Name)
Message-Id: <199307012022.AA23506@host.com>
To: user@host.com
```

```
Subject: Re: A Test
Newsgroups: host.test
References: <C8xsnr.DH9host.com>
Status: R

In host.test you write:

>Here is a test message to try out the local test group.
>You can put as much text in here as you would like, but
>you don't need to put in any more than you want to.
>The key is to get used to the editor and to feel
>comfortable with what you are saying.

>Your Name

Here is the reply-by-mail that you just typed in a few moments
ago.
Regards, You
—
Your Real Name                          user@host.com
```

This is what your reply-by-mail will look like to the person who posted the original article. Again, you can see what your mail reply will look like.

Followup Postings

When you feel that you have something substantive to add to the newsgroup as a followup to someone else's posting, you can **followup**. This will be similar to reply-by-mail, but will appear in the newsgroup as another posting. If people read the group with a reader like **nn** , the subject line may appear as one or more > to indicate that the articles are followups.

Let's practice doing a followup to your original test posting.

1. Login to your host, and type:

    nn -x (your.test.group)

2. Select your original posting by pressing the correct letter key.

3. This time you will press the followup key, a capital F. Type **F** now.

4. As before, you will be asked a few questions and then will be presented with the original posting on an editor screen.

```
Newsgroups: host.test
Subject: A Test
Summary: A Test Message
Keywords: Test

Here is a test message to try out the local test group. You
can put as much text in here as you would like, but you don't
need to put in any more than you want to. The key is to get
used to the editor and to feel comfortable with what you are
saying.

Your Name
~
~
~
~
~
~
~
~
```

5. Move the cursor down to the last line of the original message and press an **A** to append to the message.

6. Type your followup posting.

7. When you have finished, press **ESCAPE** and **ZZ**. You will see:

```
a)bort e)dit h)old m)ail r)eedit s)end v)iew w)rite
Action: (post article)
```

8. Pressing the ENTER key will send your followup article off to be posted. As with your original article, you will have to wait for your article to appear. You may wish to logout and come back later.

Another Option

There is another option to discuss here, but we won't use a screen session to show it. You may wish to login and try this for yourself. We are talking about the

Contributing
to Usenet

mail option. This is not the same as reply-by-mail to the originator. This is a simple emailing of the article to someone else.

1. Use the same approach to bring the article up on your screen and then type a capital **M**.

2. You will be asked for a recipient. If you just press ENTER, most systems will send the article to you.

You can practice doing this and sending test or real articles to yourself and then reading them with the mail program. There are a number of opportunities here to practice and build your proficiency.

Getting Ready for Real Submissions

There are always a number of people who read but don't often contribute to the newsgroups. Sometimes this is called "lurking," but there is certainly nothing wrong with it. Many clashes on the Internet are caused by people submitting articles before they are really ready to do so, or while they are really angry about a topic.

The best advice continues to be to read the groups that interest you for some months before you contribute. This will give you a feel for the "culture" of the group and what subjects are really appropriate. Usually the worst mistakes are made by people submitting the wrong content to a group. After reading for a while, you will know what is really discussed in a group. The group titles are not always the best descriptions. Often a group may have shifted its focus over a number of months or years and the title may be a little off. Be prepared for the occasional "flame" and stand back from "flame wars."

Flames and Flame Wars

People will be people when they try to communicate (perhaps more so electronically). This means that disagreement and misunderstandings will occur and sometimes the language becomes abusive. When this happens, it's called "flaming" or a "flame." While our Rules section at the front of this session talks about spelling flames, many other subjects will trigger a flame.

If you post, you will probably be flamed at some point. Even if you don't intend it, you may get someone's temper up. Please don't start a "flame war" in a newsgroup. If you think you can calm someone down from a misunderstanding, try email directly to that person. If that doesn't work, back off. There is probably no worse use of host and network resources than a flame war.

Automatic Signatures

You can create a file on your host account called **signature**. When the posting part of the news reader finds that file, it will add the contents of the file to the end of your posting. You can use the **vi** editor to create a small **.signature** file for yourself. It can be serious or it can be (hopefully) humorous, but custom calls for it to be short!

A signature of more than four lines is considered very bad manners and a shorter signature is probably in very good taste. If you have a saying you think is funny, it may grow old quickly after the newsgroup has seen it many times. Using the automatic signature is fine, but you don't see it as often as everyone else. Keep it short and to the point. Remember that your email address already appears in the posting.

You may want to use the **.signature** file to show things like a phone number or a FAX number or other ways of reaching you. It can show your educational or business affiliations and indicate that these opinions may not be those of your employer. Try out a few different **.signature** files by posting to test groups and seeing how they look.

Go For It!

Now it's up to you to contribute. When you feel you have something to add, jump in. Just review the rules at the front of this session and you will be welcomed into the group. Have fun and share your views and knowledge!

Contributing
to Usenet

■ ■ Session Four Vocabulary and Command Summary

nn -x test.group.name ....the command used to "test" out your usenet abilities - be sure to substitute the name of the test group located nearest to you

vi...the text editor that may be used to write messages

A (capital a) ....the key to be pressed so that you might append your message

Esc key and ZZ....................the sequence used to end your vi session

R (capital r) ....the key to be pressed so that you might reply to your test message

F (capital f) ....the key to be pressed so that you might follow up to a message

.signature ....the file that you can create that will automatically be added to the end of each message you post

SESSION FIVE

Mailing Lists

Mailing lists differ from newsgroups in that they are distributed electronically only to those who request them. You may subscribe to a list and you may unsubscribe. Each list has an "owner" or a "coordinator," although that individual may or may not look at each item distributed to the list. Some lists are very active and send out many messages; others have very little "traffic."

In this session, we will show you how to subscribe to a list and how to unsubscribe if you no longer want the electronic mailings. We also will help you to figure out how to contact the owner or coordinator if you have questions. This information is particularly useful, since most of the subscriptions (and unsubscriptions) are handled by computer software.

After these simple instructions, we list a small but hopefully representative sample of the mailing lists. The entire "list of lists" may be found monthly in **news.announce.newusers** or it may be found in a hardcopy, indexed version available from Prentice Hall. It is titled *Internet: Mailing Lists* and has an ISBN number of 0-13-327941-3. It is available in many book stores, and may be ordered directly from Prentice Hall by calling 515-284-6751.

Subscribing to a List

Subscribing follows a convention that allows the subscription software to sign you up automatically. If you follow the convention, it all works reasonably well. Here's how to subscribe to a list:

1. Find the exact name of the mailing list from the samples below, from the Prentice Hall book or from the "list of lists" in **news.announce.newusers**

2. Send email to a contact address as in the following example.

3. Include specific subscription information in the body or text part of the email.

Constructing Contact Addresses

1. Take the exact list name and add

    -request

    to the part before the @ symbol.

2. Complete the address with the exact host part of the email address.

Constructing Contact Addresses — Practice

1. We will pick as our example:

    bicycles@BBN.COM

    which is a discussion of all matters related to bicycles and bicycling.

2. Send email to: **bicycles-request@BBN.COM**

3. IMPORTANT: Leave the Subject line blank.

4. In the body of the message, type the following:

    subscribe bicycles (your_firstname your_lastname)

Remember that the receiving host computer can interpret your email address from the message. It would like to know your real first and last names.

In the lists that are included below, you will note that the "subscribe convention" varies a bit from list to list, but for the most part, it follows the general pattern we have described.

Unsubscribing from a List

If you later decide that you no longer wish to receive the mailings of a list, you just send another message to reverse the process. Here is how you would unsubscribe to bicycles:

1. Send email to: **bicycles-request@BBN.COM**

2. IMPORTANT: Leave the Subject line blank.

3. In the body of the message, type the following:

unsubscribe bicycles (your_firstname your_lastname)

NOTE: *Be careful not to send email to the mailing list name (bicycles@BBN.COM); it might end up going out to the whole mailing list. You would not appreciate receiving subscribe and unsubscribe requests; neither do others.*

Contacting the Coordinator/Owner

Many of the lists show the email address of the coordinator separately from the list-request address. If the list description shows that person, then you may contact him or her through regular email. Otherwise you can send specific inquiries to the **list-request** address.

A Brief Sample of Mailing Lists

These few lists have been selected by the authors so that you might have an indication of the many lists out there. For more detailed information, please refer to the complete lists in either the referenced book or in the newsgroup **news.announce.newusers**.

In this newsgroup, you will find the lists (in multiple parts) under the name:

Publicly Accessible Mailing Lists

NOTE: *Some lists, while publicly accessible, are restricted to people who are involved with specific types of research or inquiry. For these very few lists, you may have to establish your bona fides to join. Most lists, however, are open to any interested person.*

Sample Lists

ADV-ELO on LISTSERV@UTFSM.BITNET   [Last Update 11/92]

ADV-ELO is a list to discuss the latest advances in electronics.

Archives of ADV-ELO can be listed by sending the command INDEX to LISTSERV@UTFSM.

To subscribe, send the following command to LISTSERV@UTFSM via mail or interactive message: **SUB ADV-ELO your full name** where "your full name" is your name. For example: SUB ADV-ELO Francisco Fernandez

Mailing Lists

Owner: Francisco Javier Fernandez (FFERNAND@UTFSM.BITNET)

ALBION-L on LISTSERV@UCSBVM.BITNET

ALBION-L is an electronic discussion list for British and Irish history. All time-periods and fields are welcome.

To subscribe, send e-mail to LISTSERV@UCSBVM.BITNET with the BODY of the mail (NOT the subject) containing the command: **SUBSCRIBE ALBION-L yourfirstname yourlastname**

Owner: Questions about ALBION may be addressed to Joe Coohill at: 2120jtc@ucsbuxa.bitnet or gd03jtc@ucsbvm.bitnet

ANCIEN-L on LISTSERV@ULKYVM or LISTSERV@ULKYVM.LOUISVILLE.EDU

ANCIEN-L is a forum for debate, discussion, and the exchange of information by students and scholars of the history of the Ancient Mediterranean. ANCIEN-L is ready to distribute newsletters from study groups, and to post announcements of meetings and calls for papers, short scholarly pieces, queries, and other items of interest.

The list currently does not maintain a FTP directory nor is archiving available. Hopefully, this will change in the near future.

ANCIEN-L is associated with the general discussion list HISTORY, and co-operates fully with other lists similarly associated.

To subscribe, send a message to LISTSERV@ULKYVM on BITNET or LISTSERV@ULKYVM.LOUISVILLE.EDU. In BODY of the message state: **SUB ANCIEN-L yourfirstname yourlastname**

Adding your full name, LISTSERV will accept both BITNET and Internet addresses. Postings should be made to ANCIEN-L@ULKYVM.

If you have any questions please contact the owner:

James A. Cocks   BITNET:JACOCK01@ULKYVM
                  Internet: JACOCK01@ULKYVM.LOUISVILLE.EDU

AUDIO-L on LISTSERV@VMTECMEX

A **listserv** list providing a forum to discuss all topics related to audio, this includes theories, commercial equipment, applications, etc. The list runs unmoderated and it's located in AUDIO-L@VMTECMEX.BITNET

As in any listserv list, send the following command to LISTSERV@VMTECMEX to subscribe: **SUB AUDIO-L yourfirstname yourlastname** in the text of a message or mail.

Coordinator: Alejandro Kurczyn S.

BGRASS-L on L   ISTSERV@UKCC.BITNET   Last Updated 6/92] or LISTSERV@UKCC.UKY.EDU

The purpose of BGRASS-L is to be a forum for discussion of:

1.   Issues related to the International Bluegrass Music Association (IBMA)

2.   Bluegrass music in general, including but not limited to recordings, bands, individual performers, live performances, publications, business aspects, venues, history, you-name-it. Old-time music and early commercial country music are also acceptable topics.

Archives of traffic since 1 Feb. 1992 are available from the LISTSERVer; earlier by special arrangement.

To subscribe, send e-mail to: LISTSERV@UKCC or LISTSERV@UKCC.UKY.EDU with the following command in the BODY of the mail (NO subject:): **SUB BGRASS-L your full name**

To communicate, send e-mail to: BGRASS-L@UKCC or BGRASS-L@UKCC.UKY.EDU

For information, send e-mail to: UKA016@UKCC or UKA016@UKCC.UKY.EDU

Owner: Frank Godbey, University of Kentucky, Lexington, KY
              BITNET:UKA016@UKCC.BITNET
              Internet: UKA016@UKCC.UKY.EDU

bicycles@BBN.COM

Mailing list for topics relating to bicycles including:

1.   Racing: How do I get started? What do I need for equiment?Why do they shave their legs anyway? Are there any big races coming to this area?

2.   Touring: Where are some great places to ride? Stories of some of your bike trips. What are some of the things I should take for an overnight trip?

3.   Commuting: What is the best way to get by major traffic roads?

4.   Plus: Equipment, Repairs, Good places to buy a bike, Cars vs Bicycles, Human

Powered Vehicles, Fitness, Bike path construction, or anything else you might want to ask or talk about.

To be added to the list: **bicycles-request@BBN.COM**

Coordinator: Craig MacFarlane <cmacfarl@SOCRATES.BBN.COM>

Bread@cykick.infores.com   [Last Update 6/93]

A list to discuss all aspects of bread making.

Send digest submissions to: Bread@cykick.infores.com

Send add/unsubscribe requests to: **bread-digest-request@cykick.infores.com** (send HELP for more information)

Send problems about the list to: Bread-Mgr@cykick.infores.com

Archives for the Bread list are only available by mail-server. Send a message containing HELP in the body of the message to: bread-archive@cykick.infores.com

camelot@castle.ed.ac.uk   [Last Updated Feb 92]

A mailing list on the subject of Arthurian legend and Grail Lore. The 'Matter of Britain', as it is known, in all its guises and all related subjects, discussed in an unmoderated mailing list.

Technical Details: There are two mailing addresses you will need to know:

1.   camelot-request@castle.ed.ac.uk – If you wish to be added to or removed from the mailing list or if you want to report a bug or if you want info on the mailing list or any other such technical stuff, this is the address to use.

2.   camelot@castle.ed.ac.uk – This is for your articles and chat. It is unmoderated and unfiltered, so anything goes. This is the address you will post to mainly.

In addition, there is an FTP address with up-to-date archives and some GIF pictures and interesting articles. The address is: 129.215.56.11 (sapphire.epcc.ed.ac.uk) The login name is anonymous with your mail address as the password. Then type **cd pub/camelot** and get the README to find the contents.

Owner: Chris Thornborrow <ct@castle.edinburgh.ac.uk>

CANINE-L on LISTSERV@PCCVM or LISTSERV@PSUVM.BITNET

The CANINE-L list has been created to discuss matters of interest to dog owners. A full statement of purpose, plus any applicable restrictions, will be automatically mailed to new subscribers.

Monthly notebooks will be kept at PCCVM.

To subscribe, send an interactive message or e-mail to LISTSERV@PCCVM.BITNET or LISTSERV@PSUVM.BITNET with the following text in the body: **SUB CANINE-L your-full-name**

List Owner: W. K. (Bill) Gorman <34AEJ7D@CMUVM>

CLASSICS@uwavm.u.washington.edu or CLASSICS@UWAVM.BITNET

An unmoderated list for discussing ancient Greek and Latin subjects. This list is open to everyone interested in Classics, and prospective members are warmly welcomed. The discussions assume a background in ancient Greek and/or Latin. The CLASSICS list is neither run by nor directly affiliated with the University of Washington Classics Department.

All requests to be added to this list should be sent to listserv@uwavm.bitnet or listserv@uwavm.u.washington.edu with the one-line message: **SUBSCRIBE CLASSICS your-full-name**

To unsubscribe, send: UNSUBSCRIBE CLASSICS

Coordinator: Linda Wright <lwright@u.washington.edu>

CLASSM-L@BROWNVM.BROWN.EDU   [Last Updated 12-October-1991]
CLASSM-L@BROWNVM.BITNET

The Classical Music List was created to discuss classical music of all kinds. All topics and periods are welcome, from Gregorian Chants to George Crumb.

To subscribe to CLASSM-L, send a mail message to:
Internet: LISTSERV@brownvm.brown.edu BITNET: LISTSERV@BROWNVM
with the text: **SUB CLASSM-L <First Name> <Last Name>**

Owner: Catherine "Pumpkin" Yang
Internet: cyang@brownvm.brown.edu
BITNET:CYANG@BROWNVM

Coins@rocky.er.usgs.gov   [Last Update 4/93]

This list is for the discussion of Numismatics, the study of coins, American and International. Paper currency is also a welcome topic.

This list is for discussion and not for trading (use of the internet for commercial profit is illegal).

THIS WILL NOT BE A LISTSERVed LIST, at least not initially. All administrative issues will be handled by me. To get subscribed or unsubscribed, send me a message at: robert@whiplash.er.usgs.gov

ANYONE INTERESTED IN COINS IS WELCOME TO JOIN!

List Owner: robert holder   robert@whiplash.er.usgs.gov
                unix troll   us geological survey
                st petersburg florida usa

CTI-L on LISTSERV@IRLEARN.UCD.IE

CTI-L is an unmoderated list to facilitate the discussion of issues in the use of computers in teaching. The list is intended to promote discussion on how computers can be used in learning and teaching via the following:

CTI Computers in Teaching Initiative CAT Computer Aided Teaching CBT Computer Based Training CAL Computer Aided Learning CBL Computer Based Learning TBT Technology Based Training

To subscribe, send a message to LISTSERV@IRLEARN.UCD.IE with the following line of text in the BODY: **SUB CTI-L Your_full_name** where Your_full_name is your firstname lastname .

List co-ordinator: Claron O'Reilly <CLARON@IRLEARN.UCD.IE>

DANCE-L%HEARN.BITNET@CUNYVM.CUNY.EDU
DANCE-L on LISTSERV@HEARN

The purpose of DANCE-L is to create a global electronic forum and medium for information exchange between all who are interested in folkdance and traditional dance.

This list hopes to contribute to a better contact between dancers, dancing masters, choreographers, dance documentalists, choreologists, organizers of folkloristic festivals and performances, dance and folklore organizations, publishers of dance books, records, videotapes.

The information in this list should concentrate on: addresses of the above-mentioned groups, terminology, bibliographies, discographies, facts on historic and social backgrounds of folkdance, dance and choreography descriptions, costumes, announcements and reports of performances and festivals.

The list participants will be stimulated to actively engage and share responsibility in a number of projects:

- to establish an INTERNATIONAL FOLKDANCE DATABASE, by using a standard exchange record format, with the dance name as the main entry.

- to establish a FOLKDANCE DOCUMENTATION DATABASE, also by using a standard exchange record format, with book or article title as the main entry.

- to establish a MULTILINGUAL FOLKDANCE TERMINOLOGY DATABASE, also by using a standard exchange record format, with the English term as the main entry.

To subscribe to DANCE-L send a message or MAIL to one of the addresses above: **SUB DANCE-L your full name eg. SUB DANCE-L Ginger Rogers**

Description of List

DINOSAUR@donald.WichitaKS.NCR.COM [Last Update 4/93]

DINOSAUR is an open, unmoderated discussion list about dinosaurs and other archosaurs of the Mesozoic Era. Subjects range from popular press and news items to detailed paleontological theories.

To subscribe, send a regular email request to: dinosaur-request@donald.WichitaKS.NCR.COM

Note that the list is currently maintained by hand. In addition, the list does not change "From" on submitted items. That means replies will go to the originator, not the list.

Owner: John Matrow <John.Matrow@WichitaKS.NCR.COM>EMEDCH-L on LISTSERV@USCVM.BITNET

EMEDCH-L on LISTSERV@USCVM.BITNET

EMEDCH-L is devoted to promoting discussion centered around the studies of the period of Chinese history between the Han and the Tang dynasties (3rd through 6th centuries A.D.). Membership is unrestricted.

To subscribe, send a mail message to LISTSERV@USCVM.BITNET with the body of the mail containing the line: **SUB EMEDCH-L yourfirstnameyourlastname**

EV on LISTSERV@sjsuvm1.sjsu.edu

The EV Electric Vehicle Discussion Mailing List is intended to provide a forum to discuss the current state of the art and future direction of electric vehicles. It is not intended to discuss either EV appropriateness or comparisons with other transportation primary drive modes such as the venerable internal combustion engine. Those "discussions" are best relegated to the appropriate usenet newsgroup.

An electric vehicle is any vehicle which uses an electric motor as the primary or sole motive force. The energy storage device used to drive said motor can use any technology including, but not limited to, solar electric, electric battery, internal combustion engine coupled with a electric generator, or any combination of these. Production electric vehicles are currently available. Internal combustion engine vehicles can be converted to electric. There exist a number of companies who perform this conversion. There is also a number of manufacturers of equipment allowing you to do-it-yourself.

To subscribe, send the following command to LISTSERV@SJSUVM1 (bitnet) or LISTSERV@SJSUVM1.SJSU.EDU (in the BODY of e-mail): **SUBSCRIBE EV firstname lastname**

After subscribing, messages may be sent to the list by sending to: EV@SJSUVM1 (bitnet) or ev@sjsuvm1.sjsu.edu.

Owner: Clyde R. Visser, KD6GWN <cvisser@ucrmath.ucr.edu>

FIT-L on LISTSERV@ETSUADMN.BITNET

FIT-L is a discussion list for exchanging ideas, tips — any type of information about wellness, exercise, and diet.

To subscribe, send the following command to LISTSERV@ETSUADMN.BITNET in the BODY of mail or interactive message : **SUB FIT-L your full name** where "your full name" is your name. For example: SUB FIT-L Jon Doe

Owner: Chris Jones <JONES@ETSUADMN.BITNET>

FLEXWORK on LISTSERV@PSUHMC.BITNET

FLEXWORK (Flexible Work Environment List) is a list to discuss how people are handling flexible work situations. Telecommuting, work-sharing and flex-time are some examples.

Archives of FLEXWORK back issues can be listed by sending the command **INDEX FLEXWORK** to LISTSERV@PSUHMC.BITNET

To subscribe, send the following command to LISTSERV@PSUHMC.BITNET in the BODY of the mail or message: **SUB FLEXWORK your full name** where "your full name" is your name. For example: SUB FLEXWORK Joan Doe

Owner: MHOLCOMB@PSUHMC.BITNET Maria Holcomb

Folk_Music@nysernet.org

New American Folk Music discussion List

Folk_Music is a moderated discussion list dealing with the music of the recent wave of American singer/songwriters. List traffic consists of tour schedules, reviews, album release info and other information on artists like Shawn Colvin, Mary-Chapin Carpenter, David Wilcox, Nanci Griffith, Darden Smith, Maura O'Connell, Don Henry, and others.

Membership to this discussion list is open free of charge to all interested individuals or organizations.

There are no archives as of yet.

To subscribe, send mail to <listserv@nysernet.org> with this request: **SUBSCRIBE FOLK_MUSIC Your Fullname**

To unsubscribe, send: UNSUBSCRIBE FOLK_MUSIC

To post a message, send it to: folk_music@nysernet.org

We also will maintain files for FTP at nysernet.org. To access these files via anonymous FTP logon as GUEST giving your user-id@your.local.host as a password. Files and subdirectories are contained within the directory /FOLK_MUSIC. These may not be available until July, 1993.

All questions, requests for information, etc., should be sent to the moderator.
List Moderator: Alan Rowoth <alanr@nysernet.org>

Golf-L on LISTSERV@ubvm.bitnet   [Last Update 9/92]
or LISTSERV@ubvm.cc.buffalo.edu

The Golf-L discussion list was formed to give golfers and those interested in golf a place to discuss all forms of golf and all topics related to golf. Some topics may be current tournaments, etc.

To subscribe to Golf-L, send the following command to LISTSERV@UBVM via mail text or interactive messaging: **SUBSCRIBE GOLF-L your name**. For example: SUBSCRIBE GOLF-L John Doe

Owner: Chris Tanski captanski33@snycorva.bitnet
              cttx@vax5.cit.cornell.edu

Mailing Lists

HOCKEY-L@MAINE.MAINE.EDU

College_Hockey discussion list.

This list is for the discussion of collegiate ice hockey, including scores, team info, schedules, etc. allowing fans to become more involved and knowledgeable about the game.

Owner: WTS@MAINE (Wayne T. Smith)

homebrew%hpfcmr@HPLABS.HP.COM
hplabs!hpfcmr!homebrew (UUCP)

The Homebrew Mailing List is primarily for the discussion of the making and tasting of beer, ale, and mead. Related issues, such as breweries, books, judging, commercial beers, beer festivals, etc, are also discussed. Wine-making talk is also welcome, but non-homemade-wine talk is not.

Archives are now available from Mthvax.CS.Miami.EDU via the netlib program and anonymous ftp; please use anonymous ftp if you can, if not send mail to netlib@Mthvax.CS.Miami.EDU with subject index for a top level index and help file.

All requests to be added to or deleted from this list, problems, questions, etc., should be sent to homebrew-request%hpfcmr@HPLABS.HP.COM (or UUCP hplabs!hpfcmr!homebrew-request).

Coordinator: Rob Gardner <rdg%hpfcmr@HPLABS.HP.COM>

home-ed@think.com   [Last Update 11/92]

Purpose: This mailing list is for the discussion of all aspects and methods of home education. These include the "unschooling" approach, curricula-based home-schooling, and others. The list is currently unmoderated and welcomes everyone interested in educating their children at home, whatever the reasons.

Contact: home-ed-request@think.com (David Mankins)

Coordinator: David Mankins (dm@think.com)

ibmpc-kids@minerva.sws.uiuc.edu   [Last Update 3/93]

Mailing list for the discussion of children's software on IBM-pc and compatible computers. This is an unmoderated list. To subscribe, send a message to: ibmpc-kids-request@minerva.sws.uiuc.edu with the subject "subscribe ibmpc-kids"

List owner: Bob Larson blarson@uiuc.edu

INFO-HAMS@WSMR-SIMTEL20.ARMY.MIL

A mailing list for Amateur Radio (not CB) operators. INFO-HAMS is gatewayed to/ from Usenet's rec.ham-radio so Usenet people will get it there.

Mail archives are kept on host WSMR-SIMTEL20.ARMY.MIL as TOPS20 mail files named yymm.n-TXT, where n starts with one and increments by one into another file as each file reached 150 disk pages. To conserve disk space, all the mail files in the archive, except for the current year, are individually compressed. The compressed files have the suffix -Z as part of the filetype field; they should be renamed to have the suffix .Z (uppercase Z) when transfered to a Unix system so the uncompress program will find them. The current month's mail is still kept in HAMS-ARCHIV.TXT. The archives are stored in directory: PD2:<ARCHIVES.HAMS> Archive files are available via ANONYMOUS FTP for those with TCP/IP access to the Internet.

Phil Howard KA9WGN <PHIL%UIUCVMD.BITNET@CUNYVM.CUNY.EDU> also archives the INFO-HAMS mailing list on BITNET node UIUCVMD using the LISTSERV mailing list server (subscriptions disabled for this). Users on BITNET may request files to be sent to them by sending commands, either by interactive message or in the message body by mail, to the address LISTSERV@UIUCVMD.

The command to see the current online list of files is: **INDEX INFOHAMS** (Note there is no dash "-"). To obtain volume 88 issue 73, send the command: **GET INFOHAMS 88-00073** INFO-HAMS is a digested mailing list, and each digest is available separately from LISTSERV@UIUCVMD.

All Internet requests to be added to or deleted from this list, problems, questions, etc., should be sent to INFO-HAMS-REQUEST@WSMR-SIMTEL20.ARMY.MIL.

Coordinator: Keith Petersen <W8SDZ@WSMR-SIMTEL20.ARMY.MIL>

Info-IBMPC@WSMR-SIMTEL20.ARMY.MIL

Info-IBMPC is a forum for technical discussion of the IBM Personal Computer and compatible micro-computers, providing a way for interested members of the Internet community to compare notes, ask questions, and share insights of a technical nature about these machines. While it is not primarily a consumer's guide to the IBM PC, the digest may also be useful for that purpose.

Messages are collected, edited into digests and distributed as the volume of mail dictates (generally twice a week). All messages regarding hardware for IBM PCs, PC and compatibles and software are welcomed; messages on other topics will not be run. In addition, two topics are taboo and are routinely edited out: (1) self promotion of products for sale, and (2) anything about copy protection.

Mailing Lists

An archive of back issues and a program library are available to those with FTP access (essentially anyone on the Internet). Digests are archived at WSMR-SIMTEL20.ARMY.MIL in PD2:<ARCHIVES.IBMPC> in <YYMM.1-TXT> format. Digests from September 1982 through the current issue are available by ANONY-MOUS FTP login.

A library of free software in binary and source code form is maintained at SIMTEL20 in directory PD1:<MSDOS> and PD2:<MSDOS2>. A list of all MS-DOS programs available from WSMR-SIMTEL20.ARMY.MIL is contained in PD1:<MSDOS>FILES.IDX. Donations of source code are welcomed. Donated programs must be truly free and public domain, with no fee or contribution required or requested, and no license agreement. To donate a program to the library, send a description of the program along with a copy of the source code to: INFO-IBMPC-REQUEST@WSMR-SIMTEL20.ARMY.MIL.

Files may be FTP'ed by logging in to the SIMTEL20 FTP server with username ANONYMOUS, password GUEST. (Although GUEST is a perfectly good pass-word, a password of <YOUR-NAME@YOUR-HOST> is preferred.) For those subscribers without Internet FTP access, a file transfer mechanism has been set up with RPIECS.bitnet. For more details, send a message to <LISTSERV@RPIECS.bitnet> with the first line of 'HELP' or ask the editor for the Simtel-Bitnet FTP help file. Requested files are mailed to those users with a VALID Internet return address. WSMR-SIMTEL20.ARMY.MIL can be accessed using LISTSERV commands from BITNET and those users without Internet FTP access via LISTSERV@NDSUVM1, LISTSERV@RPIECS, LISTSERV@FINTUVM and in Europe from EARN TRICKLE servers. Send commands to LISTSERV or TRICKLE@<host-name> (example: TRICKLE@TREARN). The following TRICKLE servers are presently available: AWIWUW11 (Austria), BANUFS11 (Belgium), DKTC11 (Denmark), DB0FUB11 (Germany), IMIPOLI (Italy), EB0UB011 (Spain) TAUNIVM (Israel) and TREARN (Turkey).

All requests to be added to or deleted from this list, problems, questions, etc., should be sent to INFO-IBMPC-REQUEST@WSMR-SIMTEL20.ARMY.MIL.

BITNET users must join the INFO-IBMPC distribution list through the BITNET LISTSERV mechanism. There are IBMPC-L BITNET sub-distribution lists at the following BITNET hosts: BNANDP11, UTORONTO, CEARN, DEARN, EB0UB011, FINHUTC, HEARN, VTVM1, POLYGRAF, $$INFOPC@RICEVM1, TAMVM1, TAUNIVM, UBVM, UGA, and VTVM2. BitNet subscribers can join by sending a SUB command to the nearest LISTSERV node or to <LISTSERV@POLYGRAF.bitnet>. For example: SEND LISTSERV@CEARN SUB IBMPC-L Jon Doe
To be removed from the list substitute the keyword "SIGNOFF" for "SUB". To make contributions to the list, BITNET subscribers should send mail to <INFO-IBMPC@WSMR-SIMTEL20.ARMY.MIL> and NOT to the BITNET list name.

For those users on USENET, the Digest is available from newsfeed comp.sys.ibm.pc.digest. Since the current editor does not have a USENET feed, please include <INFO-IBMPC@WSMR-SIMTEL20.ARMY.MIL> as a CC: address on all messages sent to USENET.

On BITNET, the archives can be obtained from DATABASE@BITNIC.BITNET and the program library can be obtained from CCUC@UMCVMB.BITNET. The WSMR-SIMTEL20.ARMY.MIL FTP server may also be reached via <LISTSERV%RPICICGE.BITNET@CUNYVM.CUNY.EDU>. For more details, send a message to the above addresses with the first line of 'HELP'.

Editor: Gregory Hicks <GHICKS@WSMR-SIMTEL20.ARMY.MIL>

Former Editors: Billy Brackenridge <BRACKENRIDGE@C.ISI.EDU>
                       Richard Gillmann <GILLMANN@C.ISI.EDU>
                       Eliot Moore <Elmo@C.ISI.EDU>
                       Phyllis O'Neil

INFO-MAC@SUMEX-AIM.STANFORD.EDU

Network interest group for the Apple Macintosh computer. This list is SUMEX's contribution to the community of research and instructional developers and users of the Macintosh; all submissions of messages and programs in this spirit are welcome.

For those sites with FTP access to SUMEX-AIM, archives for INFO-MAC are kept under {SUMEX-AIM}/info-mac/digest/infomacvM-NNN, where M is the volume number and NNN is the digest number. These numbers have little to no bearing on reality.

Programs submitted to the bulletin board, along with documentation files and other references are also stored in the info-mac directory. With FTP access as user "anonymous" and any password, you can bring these files over to your host and download them to your Macintosh. "Usenet" and some of the other networks that copy info-mac will see sources redistributed at the time they are mentioned in the digest distributions.

Messages to INFO-MAC@SUMEX-AIM.STANFORD.EDU are scanned to filter out any list requests, questions previously answered, pure speculation or opinion, or message obviously not in line with the stated purpose of the list.

All requests to be added to or deleted from this list, problems, questions, etc., should be sent to INFO-MAC-REQUEST@SUMEX-AIM.STANFORD.EDU. Due to the size of this list, INFO-MAC only sends to relays, i.e. addresses such as INFOMAC@yoursite.whatever which then distribute it locally. Please check with your local gurus to gain access your local relay.

Mailing Lists

Moderators: Bill Lipa <Info-Mac-Request@SUMEX-AIM.STANFORD.EDU>
Jon Pugh <Info-Mac-Request@SUMEX-AIM.STANFORD.EDU>

INFO-MODEMS@WSMR-SIMTEL20.ARMY.MIL

Info-Modems is a discussion group of special interest to modem users. The list is gatewayed to/from Usenet newsgroup comp.dcom.modems.

Mail archives are kept on host WSMR-SIMTEL20.ARMY.MIL as TOPS20 mail files named yymm.n-TXT, where n starts with one and increments by one into another file as each file reached 150 disk pages. To conserve disk space, all the mail files in the archive, except for the current year, are individually compressed. The compressed files have the suffix -Z as part of the filetype field; they should be renamed to have the suffix .Z (uppercase Z) when transfered to a Unix system so the uncompress program will find them. The current month's mail is still kept in MODEMS-ARCHIV.TXT. The archives are stored in directory: PD2:<ARCHIVES.MODEMS> Archive files are available via ANONYMOUS FTP for those with TCP/IP access to the Internet.

All requests to be added to or deleted from this list, problems, questions, etc., should be sent to Info-Modems-Request@WSMR-SIMTEL20.ARMY.MIL.

Coordinator: Keith Petersen <W8SDZ@WSMR-SIMTEL20.ARMY.MIL>

J-FOOD-L%JPNKNU10.BITNET@CUNYVM.CUNY.EDU
J-FOOD-L on LISTSERV@JPNKNU10

This list, created at Kinki university in Japan, is for people interested in the Japanese food and culture.

If you wish to subscribe to the list, issue the following (FOR BITNET):
TELL LISTSERV AT JPNKNU10 SUB J-FOOD-L <your full name>

or send mail to LISTSERV%JPNKNU10.BITNET@CUNYVM.CUNY.EDU with the following in the text/body: **SUB J-FOOD-L <your full name>**

KIDSNET@VMS.CIS.PITT.EDU
KIDSNET@PITTVMS.BITNET (BitNet)
pitt!vms.cis.pitt.edu!kidsnet UUCP)

Mailing list formed to provide a global network for the use of children and teachers in grades K-12. It is intended to provide a focus for technological development and for resolving the problems of language, standards, etc. that inevitably arise in international communications.

All requests to be added to or deleted from this list, problems, questions, etc., should be sent to KIDSNET-REQUEST@VMS.CIS.PITT.EDU or to JOINKIDS@PITTVMS.BITNET (BitNet).

Coordinator: Bob Carlitz <carlitz@VMS.CIS.PITT.EDU>

LATIN-L on LISTSERV@PSUVM.BITNET   [Last Update 4/93]
or LISTSERV@PSUVM.PSU.EDU

Announcing a new electronic discussion group: LATIN-L, a forum for people interested in classical Latin, medieval Latin, Neo-Latin — the languages of choice are Latin (of course) and whatever vulgar languages you feel comfortable using. Please be prepared to translate on request. The field is open— name your topic!

To subscribe, BITNET users may send an interactive message such as:
TELL LISTSERV@PSUVM SUB LATIN-L <your name>

INTERNET and other domain users, send a mail message (without a subject line) to LISTSERV@PSUVM.PSU.EDU — the BODY should read: **SUB LATIN-L your full name**
For example: SUB LATIN-L Marcus Antonius

Send messages to LATIN-L@PSUVM or LATIN-L@PSUVM.PSU.EDU

Ave atque vale

Kevin Berland for LATIN-L

Owner: BCJ@PSUVM or BCJ@PSUVM.PSU.EDU

Library on ListServ@IndyCMS or ListServ@IndyCMS.IUPUI.Edu

Library (Libraries & Librarians) is dedicated to *general* news and information of interest to libraries, their employees and users.

Library seeks to complement and supplement preexisting specialized library-related lists.

Library is owned and coordinated by a retired professional archivist and librarian (Donna B Harlan) and an interested layperson and former library paraprofessional (John B Harlan). It is a mother and son project :-)

To subscribe to "Library" send e-mail to LISTSERV@INDYCMS on BITNET or ListServ@IndyCMS.IUPUI.EDU on the Internet with the following command in the BODY of the mail: **sub library yourfirstname yourlastname**

List owner/coordinators: Editorial: Donna B Harlan
    Harlan@IUBACS (CREN)
    Harlan@UCS.Indiana.Edu (Internet)

    Administrative: John B Harlan
    IJBH200@IndyVAX (CREN)
    IJBH200@IndyVAX.IUPUI.Edu (Internet)

LN on LISTSERV@FRMOP11.Bitnet

Bulletin Electronique LN

Le bulletin electronique LN a pour but de favoriser la circulation d'informations a travers la communaute "Informatique Linguistique": appels a communication, annonces de conferences ou seminaires, requetes specifiques concernant logiciels, corpus et donnees diverses, descriptions d'activites et de projets, discussions sur des sujets techniques, etc. Le bulletin est principalement francophone, mais de nombreuses informations sont retransmises sous leur forme originale en anglais. Il constitue un forum pour les chercheurs travaillant sur le Francais mais n'est en aucun cas restreint a ce seul champ d'etude.

Le bulletin est parraine par l'Association for Computational Linguistics (ACL) et l'Association for Computers and the Humanities (ACH). Ce double parrainage reflete l'interet croissant des linguistes informaticiens pour, a cote de domaines plus traditionnels, des domaines tels que la lexicographie informatique, l'etude et l'utilisation de corpus, les modeles statistiques, etc., qui sont depuis longtemps centraux dans l'ACH.

Le bulletin comporte a l'heure actuelle pres de 400 abonnes dans 25 pays. Il est edite par Jean Veronis (GRTC-CNRS, France) et Pierre Zweigenbaum (DIAM-INSERM, France).

Vous pouvez vous abonner au bulletin en envoyant un message compose de la seule ligne suivante a LISTSERV@FRMOP11.BITNET: **SUBSCRIBE LN Prenom Nom**

Vous pouvez transmettre des informations pour diffusion dans le bulletin en envoyant un message a LN@FRMOP11.BITNET.

En cas de probleme, adressez-vous directement aux editeurs:
    Jean Veronis VERONIS@VASSAR.BITNET
    Pierre Zweigenbaum ZWEIG@FRSIM51.BITNET

LN Electronic List

LN is an international electronic distribution list for computational linguists. Its goal is to disseminate calls for papers, conference and seminar announcements, requests for software, corpora, and various data, project descriptions, discussions on technical topics, etc. The list is primarily French-speaking, but many items are circulated in English. It provides a forum for scholars working on French, but it is by no means restricted to this field.

The list is sponsored by the Association for Computational Linguistics (ACL) and the Association for Computers and the Humanities (ACH). This joint sponsorship reflects the fact that in addition to more traditional concerns, computational linguists have a growing interest in areas such as computational lexicography, study and use of corpora, statistical models, etc., which have been traditionally central to ACH.

Currently the list consists of about 400 members in 25 countries. It is moderated by Jean Veronis (GRTC-CNRS, France) and Pierre Zweigenbaum (DIAM-INSERM, France).

To join LN, send a message to LISTSERV@FRMOP11.BITNET, containing only the following line: **SUBSCRIBE LN your name**

Send messages to be transmitted on the list to LN@FRMOP11.BITNET. In case of problems, send a message to one of the editors:

Jean Veronis
Pierre Zweigenbaum
VERONIS@VASSAR.BITNET
ZWEIG@FRSIM51.BITNET

LymeNet-L@Lehigh.EDU   [Last Update 3/93]

Lyme Disease is now the fastest growing infectious disease in the United States. In 10 short years, this little known bacterial infection has claimed half a million victims and the number of new patients continues to spiral upward with no relief in sight. It is estimated that in 1991, 100,000 Americans contracted this dangerous disease. If left untreated, LD can cause permanent nerve, musculoskeletal and cardiac damage.

Unfortunately, many in the medical and political arenas have not given this epidemic much thought. Self appointed experts in the academic community have declared that LD can always be cured with short courses of simple antibiotics. However, as the number of cases rise, doctors on the front lines are discovering that LD is more serious that previously suspected, requiring longer treatment therapies and more complex combinations of medicines. The battle lines have been drawn.

Mailing Lists

And the battles continue at LD conferences, and in the various State legislatures where insurance companies, terrified at the high cost of LD, are attempting to short change patients. Estimates show that the average cost of treatment for chronic LD patients ranges from $60,000 to $100,000 per patient.

MAILING LIST: To keep up with the latest developments, including new treatment protocols, research news and political events, we introduce the Lyme Disease Electronic Mail Network. LymeNet, in association with the Lyme Disease Network of New Jersey, Inc., with provide you with a periodic newsletter with the latest information. All you need is an Internet-accessible e-mail address.

INTERESTED INDIVIDUALS INCLUDE:

*   LD patients
*   Friends or family of LD patients, who may wish to forward the newsletter to an LD patient
*   Interested members of the medical community
*   Interested members of the press

To subscribe, send a memo to Internet address listserv@Lehigh.EDU In body type: **subscribe LymeNet-L <Your Real Name>**

Owner: Marc Gabriel <mcg2@lehigh.edu>

MEDSTU-L on LISTSERV@UNMVM

The University of New Mexico is pleased to announce that effective immediately, we are hosting a new Listserv discussion list for medical students worldwide. The name of the new list is MEDSTU-L and initially, the list will be unmoderated with subscriptions open. Due to a present limitation on disk storage, notebooks will be kept for a period of 30 days.

The impetus for this list was mail I sent out several weeks ago soliciting medical students with e-mail accounts to exchange mail with medical students here. As a result of that solicitation, I found that while there are many medical students with e-mail accounts, most of them are unaware of others with e-mail accounts. Thus, this list. While it is an open list and therefore there is no way of verifying the subscription request, the two list owners respectfully request that the list be limited to students in medical schools.

To subscribe to the list send e-mail to LISTSERV@UNMVM and in the body of the message say: **SUB MEDSTU-L your_first_name your_last_name**

If you have any questions, please let us know.

Owners:
Art St. George STGEORGE@UNMB or STGEORGE@BOOTES.UNM.EDU

David Goldstein DGOLDST@UNMB or DGOLDST@BOOTES.UNM.EDU

Art St. George, Ph.D.
Executive Network Services Officer
University of New Mexico

High-Tech Access:	Soft Touch Access
stgeorge@unmb (BITNET)	(505) 277-8046 VOICE
stgeorge@bootes.unm.edu (Internet)	(505) 277-8101 FAX

military@ATT.ATT.COM

Mailing list for discussions of military technology and related matters. The list is gatewayed bi-directionally with the Usenet newsgroup "sci.military," which is moderated; it is distributed in the form of a daily digest.

All requests to be added to or deleted from this list, problems, questions, etc., should be sent to military-request@ATT.ATT.COM.

Moderator: Bill Thacker <military@ATT.ATT.COM>
<military@CBNEWS.ATT.COM>

MUSEUM-L on LISTSERV@UNMVM.BITNE [Last Updated 12-October-1991]

Museum-L is a general interest dicussion list for museum professionals and others interested in museum related issues.

It is hoped that an open discussion by those who work in exhibits, education, collection, or curatorial positions can foster an understanding among those who work in museums. It is also hoped that the discussion can share ideas and information regarding new methods of interpreting information for visitors, both high tech and low tech.

To subscribe, send a one line message to LISTSERV@UNMVM.BITNET:
subscribe MUSEUM-L Your_Full_Name

If I can be of further assistance, please feel free to contact me.

Owner: john chadwick chadwick@unmb (bitnet)
chadwick@bootes.unm.edu (internet)

Nerdnosh@scruz.ucsc.EDU   [Last Update 4/93]

The origins of Nerdnosh were in the lowlands of the Red River years ago, with the water moccasins along the brakes and the mosquitoes swarming and the River rising and the wolves in the distance edging closer as the sun dropped, and a group of us were swapping stories and the rains began and one of us said, wouldn't this be a great idea without the water moccasins and the mosquitoes and the high water and the wolves and the rain?

Here it is. A virtual campfire gathering of storytellers. Bring us your tired yarns and your family fables and your yesterday's journals and your imprints on tomorrow. Send the command:

> SUBSCRIBE NERDNOSH
> END

to: majordomo@scruz.ucsc.edu

Owner: tcbowden@clovis.felton.ca.us (Timothy Bowden)
uunet!scruz.ucsc.edu!clovis.felton.ca.us!tcbowden
Clovis in Felton, CA

NORWAVES@nki.no   [Last Update 5/93]

This listserver list NORWAVES will distribute weekly news from Norway. The information is provided by NORINFORM. The NORINFORM press office was established by The Norwegian Information Council and provides overseas news services in several languages, daily (in English only) and weekly. NORINFORM also produces the monthly magazine "Norway Now" and a fulltext database containing bulletins and articles about Norway.

If you are interested you should subscribe to the list NORWAVES at listserv@nki.no by issuing the line: **subscribe NORWAVES <your full name>**

We would be grateful for any comments concerning the list. You may also send an "info" request for more information. If you have any questions, you may send a message to the list editors.

Editors: nwnews@nki.no
Andre Kristiansen
Per Staale Straumsheim

origami-l@nstn.ns.ca   [Last Update 12/92]

This unmoderated mailing list is for discussion of all facets of origami, the Japanese art of paper folding. Topics include bibliographies, folding techniques, display ideas, descriptions of new folds, creativity, materials, organizations, computer representations of folds, etc.

Archives available by anonymous ftp from rugcis.rug.nl:

Start FTP:	FTP rugcis.rug.nl
Login:	anonymous
Password:	'your IP-address'

Change dir: cd origami

All requests to be added to or deleted from this list, problems, questions, etc., should be sent to origami-l-request@nstn.ns.ca

Owner: Anne R. LaVin, lavin@mit.edu

PACIFIC on LISTSERV@BRUFPB.BITNET

The Forum for and about the Pacific Ocean and Islands

A forum for and about the Pacific Ocean and islands (Pacific Basin), the Pacific coastlines and hinterlands of those nations who border the edge of the Pacific (Pacific Rim), ie. Asia, Australia, North & South America - For those living within these areas, and by others who are interested in the Pacific Basin and Rim.

Ways to increase (electronic) communications with, and interaction between Pacific peoples will be of special interest, as will news, exchanges of informal interests and ideas, cultural and educational sharing, economic, and other material concerns, and activities, both lighthearted and serious.

To subscribe, send the following message to listserv@BRUFPB (Bitnet):
subscribe pacific Your Name Your Interests set pacific repro (so you will receive a copy of your own postings) eg. subscribe pacific John Doe oceanography set pacific repro

To get a list of current subscribers, and their interests, if provided, send the message "review pacific" to listserv@BRUFPB.BITNET.

List owner: CTEDTC09@BRUFPB.BITNET (Carlos Fernando Nogueira)

PCBUILD on LISTSERV@LIST.DSU.EDU   [Last Update 3/93]

PCBUILD is an open, unmoderated discussion list featuring PC hardware. We discuss such things as: upgrading your PC, building your own PC, hardware problems, questions, cheap businesses from which to buy hardware, etc. Hardware in general. This list is for owners of DOS, Windows, or OS/2 based machines, as we discuss hardware problems as they relate to the various operating systems as well.

TO SUBSCRIBE: Send a message to: LISTSERV@LIST.DSU.EDU
The first line of the message must be: **SUB PCBUILD Your Name**
For Example: SUB PCBUILD John Doe

Administrators of the PCBuild list: Mike Bitz

(BITZM@COLUMBIA.DSU.EDU), and Anthony Anderberg
(ANDERBEA@COLUMBIA.DSU.EDU)

PHOTO-L%BUACCA.BITNET@CUNYVM.CUNY.EDU

This list is a forum for discussion of all aspects of photography, including esthetics, equipment, technique, etc.

To subscribe to this list issue the command: **TELL LISTSERV AT BUACCA SUB PHOTO-L your_full_name**
or on VMS systems: **SEND LISTSERV@BUACCA SUB PHOTO-L your_full_name**

Non-BitNet users can subscribe by sending the text: **SUB PHOTO-L your_full_name** in the body of a message to: LISTSERV%BUACCA.BITNET@CUNYVM.CUNY.EDU.

Coordinator: Mark Hayes <MARK@BUIT32.BU.EDU>
<CCMLH%BUACCA.BITNET@CUNYVM.CUNY.EDU>

PUBLIB@nysernet.org   [Last Update 5/93]

PUBLIB, initiated on December 1, 1992, is a new discussion list concerned with use of the Internet in public libraries. Issues to be examined include connectivity, public access to the Internet, user and staff training, resources of interest to public librarians (online, print, video, other), electronic freedoms and responsibilities, new technologies for public library Internet access, National, International, and regional public telecommunications policy and public libraries, and more.

To join the list and receive the mailings from PUBLIB: Send a message to LISTSERV@nysernet.org (no subject necessary) saying: **subscribe PUBLIB "your full name here"**

For example: To: LISTSERV@nysernet.org
            Subject:
            Message:
            subscribe PUBLIB Melvil Dewey

Please introduce yourself to the list after you receive the welcome message back from the listserv.

Co-moderators: John Iliff   jiliff@nysernet.org
            Pinellas Park Public Library
            7770 52nd St.   Pinellas Park, FL 34665
            (813) 541-0719   Fax (813) 541-0818

            Jean Armour Polly   jpolly@nysernet.org
            NYSERNet, Inc.
            111 College Place   Syracuse, NY 13244-4100
            (315) 443-4120   Fax (315) 425-7518

RAILROAD on LISTSERV@CUNYVM or
LISTSERV@CUNYVM.CUNY.EDU [Last Update 11/92]

The RAILROAD list - for the discussion of anything about railroads, real and model.

To subscribe, you may send an interactive message (from BITNET sites which provide such a facility), or mail (with the command as the body of the mail - *NOT* in the subject field -) to: LISTSERV@CUNYVM or LISTSERV@CUNYVM.CUNY.EDU

The command should be in the form: **SUB RAILROAD full name**
... where "full name" is your full (and correct) name.

To contribute to the list, send your mail messages to:
RAILROAD@CUNYVM or RAILROAD@CUNYVM.CUNY.EDU

For further information, please contact the list owner:

Geert K. Marien - GKMQC@CUNYVM.CUNY.EDU (BITNET node CUNYVM)

SCUBA-L@BROWVM.BITNET [Last Updated 28-Janaury-1992]

Mailing list for discussion of all aspects of SCUBA diving. Any articles, views, ideas, and opinions relating to SCUBA diving are welcome. Areas discussed will include, but are not limited to:

Safety/First Aid	Places to Dive
Decompression computation	Best Places to Dive
Decompression Tables	History
New Equipment	Dive Shops
New Technologies	Mail/order Shopping
Diving Science & Technology	Travel
Dive Computers	Tropical Diving
Underwater Photography	Underwater Animal Life
Underwater Vehicles	Questions/Quizzes
PADI certifications	
NAUI certifications	
YMCA certifications	

BitNet users can subscribe by sending the following interactive command to LISTSERV@BROWNVM: **TELL LISTSERV AT BROWNVM SUB SCUBA-L your_full_name** (where "your_full_name" is your real name, not your loginid) or by sending mail to LISTSERV@BROWNVM.BITNET with the first text line in the BODY of the mail being: **SUB SCUBA-L your_full_name**

Non-BitNet users can subscribe by sending the above SUB command in the body of a message to LISTSERV%BROWNVM.BITNET@CUNYVM.CUNY.EDU

Coordinator: Catherine Yang (CYANG@BROWNVM.BITNET)

SPACE@ANDREW.CMU.EDU

Discussions (daily digest) on space-related topics.

Archives are not available by ANONYMOUS FTP. Requests for back issues should be directed to SPACE-REQUEST@ANDREW.CMU.EDU.

All requests to be added to or deleted from this list, problems, questions, etc., should be sent to SPACE-REQUEST@ANDREW.CMU.EDU.

There is a BitNet sub-distribution list, SPACE@UGA; BitNet subscribers can join by sending the SUB command with your name. For example, **SEND LISTSERV@UGA SUB SPACE Jon Doe**

To be removed from the list, SEND LISTSERV@UGA SIGNOFF. To make contributions to the list, BitNet subscribers should send mail to the Internet list name, NOT to the BITNET list name.

Coordinator: Owen T. (Ted) Anderson <OTA@ANDREW.CMU.EDU>

Stagecraft@Jaguar.cs.utah.edu   [Last Updated 12-October-1991]

Mailing list is for the discussion of all aspects of stage work, including (but not limited to) special effects, sound effects, sound reinforcement, stage management, set design and building, lighting design, company management, hall management, hall design, and show production. This is not a forum for the discussion of various stage productions (unless the discussion pertains to the stagecraft of a production), acting or directing methods (unless you know of ways to get actors to stand in the right spots), film or video production (unless the techniques can be used on the stage). The list will not be moderated unless problems crop up.

Archives will be kept of the discussion (send mail to stagecraft-request for copies).

Requests to be added, problems, questions, etc., should be sent to: stagecraft-request@Jaguar.utah.edu

Coordinator: Brad Davis <b-davis%CAI@CS.UTAH.EDU>

STAMPS on LISTSERV@CUNYVM or LISTSERV@CUNYVM.CUNY.EDU

The STAMPS list - for those who collect, or just have a passing interest in, stamps and related items.

To subscribe, you may send an interactive message (from BITNET sites which provide such a facility), or mail (with the command as the body of the mail - *NOT* in the subject field -) to: LISTSERV@CUNYVM or LISTSERV@CUNYVM.CUNY.EDU

The command should be in the form: **SUB STAMPS full name**
... where "full name" is your full (and correct) name.

To contribute to the list, send your mail messages to:

STAMPS@CUNYVM or STAMPS@CUNYVM.CUNY.EDU

For further information, please contact the list owner:
Geert K. Marien - GKMQC@CUNYVM.CUNY.EDU (BITNET node CUNYVM)

SWIM-L on LISTSERV@UAFSYSB.BITNET (BITNET)
[Last Updated 28-January-1992]
or LISTSERV@UAFSYSB.UARK.EDU (Internet)

SWIM-L is a list which is dedicated to the discussion of all phases of swimming. To subscribe, send your request to the LISTSERV at UAFSYSB.Bitnet with the following message in the body: **SUB SWIM-L firstname lastname**

This should prove to be a fun list for all those who are interested in swimming!

Contact: "L. C. Jones" <LJ27524@UAFSYSB.BITNET>

TOLKIE@JHUVM.BITNET   [Last Updated 12-October-1991]
or LISTSERV@PUCING.BITNET (Chile)

The purpose of this list is to discuss and to exchange information on subjects related to J.R.R. Tolkien's mythological books. Now, TOLKIEN has two peered nodes, which allows me (the current owner of the list) to invite EVERYONE who wishes to chat about TOLKIEN my -thos to enter this List.

For 'Tolkien Lore' reasons, you're expected to have already read the major books, such as the Silmarillion and The Lord of the Rings. If you want to enter the list, just send your request to the owner OR to LISTSERV@JHUVM.BITNET with the body containing:
SUB TOLKIEN yourfirstname yourlastname

A "peer" list is hosted on LISTSERV@PUCING.

Owner: Escuela de Ingenieria <GANDALF@PUCING>

Mailing Lists

travel-advisories@stolaf.edu

This list distributes US State Department Travel Advisories.

Please send requests for subscription/removal to travel-advisories-request@stolaf.edu

This list is also archived - the form of the archive is yet to be determined, but you can start by looking (via anonymous FTP) in ftp.stolaf.edu:/pub/travel-advisories/archive and ftp.stolaf.edu:/pub/travel-advisories/advisories

The latter contains the most recent advisory for a particular country.

The most recent Travel Advisories for each country are also available from St. Olaf's "gopher" server: gopher.stolaf.edu:/gopher/Databases/US-State-Department-Travel-Advisor

Owner: Craig D. Rice <cdr@stolaf.edu>

YACHT-L%GREARN.BITNET@VM1.NODAK.EDU

Yachting, Sailing, Design and amateur BoatBuilding mailing list. The list offers to the people that are interested in these subjects a way to communicate. Discussions about new yachts, designs, construction techniques, races, etc., are welcome.

To subscribe to the list, send the following command to LISTSERV@GREARN:

VM/CMS:
>   **TELL LISTSERV at GREARN SUB YACHT-L Your_Full_Name**
VMS:
>   **SEND LISTSERV@GREARN SUB YACHT-L Your_Full_Name**

Non-BitNet users can subscribe by sending a message to LISTSERV%GREARN.BITNET@VM1.NODAK.EDU with the message text/body:
SUB   YACHT-L Your_Full_Name

Coordinator: Kostas Antonopoulos
<NETMAINT%GREARN.BITNET@VM1.NODAK.EDU>
<Gandal%GGRCRVAX1.BITNET@VM1.NODAK.EDU>

■ ■ Session Five Vocabulary and Command Summary

-request ....the word that is added to the part before an @ symbol when you wish to subscribe or unsubscribe to a list — for example, bicycles-request@BBN.COM

subscribe ....the word that is used in the body of an email message when you wish to subscribe to the mailing list

unsubscribe ....the word that is used in the body of an email message when you wish to unsubscribe to the mailing list

SESSION SIX

Other Hosts - Telnet

Session Overview

This session will introduce you to some of the many resources that exist on computers other than your own. You will have a chance to get a feel for where these computers are located, how to sign on to them legally, and what happens once you have done so. The primary new vocabulary word for this session is **telnet**, which is the word that you will use whenever you want to login to another computer that is far from your own.

For each of the seven practice Telnet exercises in this session, we have provided a page or so of actual screens. With these you will have a better idea of what should be happening on your computer. There are many choices available once you have established a Telnet connection and your actual computer screen may look somewhat different from the examples shown.

Now let's get started.

Telnet Overview

Stated simply, the **telnet** command provides you with the ability to login remotely to another computer. This means that once the initial connection has been established, you will find that your computer acts as if it were directly connected to the computer where you have set up your Telnet connection. Many of the computers that provide these facilities have well-developed menu systems that will permit you to follow their directions once your connection has been established. Hopefully, you will be able to find and get what you want.

It is probably fair to say that the Telnet resources are limitless. In the following exercises, we have tried to provide you with a reasonably representative sample of the many resources that Telnet has to offer.

Before we start, we must tell you a little about proper behavior.

Telnet Netiquette

In these sessions, you will be using computer resources belonging to many other people and organizations. Remember that you are a guest. These computers are run and paid for by people with real work to do. Please don't abuse the guest privileges they offer. If too many of us overload these systems, they may close the guest doors.

Here are just a few suggestions of proper "guest" behavior.

1. Try to limit your sessions to "after hours."

2. Keep your sessions short, just enough to learn "how to."

3. If requested to do so, use your email address as a password.

4. Read any "guest" instructions carefully and follow them.

5. If asked to come back later, wait a while before trying again.

Telnet Basics

When you give the command **telnet** , you are telling your host account to connect you to another host. This means that you will need to complete the command with the full name of the destination host. In each of the following practice sessions, we will show you the full name of the destination.

This will usually look like:

telnet hostname.placename.typename

In addition, we will sometimes add a number after the host name. This number is called a "port" and tells the **telnet** command to ask for a specific connection (like a telephone extension at a campus or company). In a moment, our first practice will use the following command:

telnet madlab.sprl.umich.edu 3000

You can understand this command as follows:

madlab	is the destination host
sprl.umich	is the place
edu	tells us that it is an education organization
3000	is the port number

In Case Of Trouble

When you are first connected, you may see a message like the following:

> Trying 141.212.196.79...
> Connected to madlab.sprl.umich.edu
> Escape character is '^]'.

Here's what it means:

1. The "Trying" is just that, with the real numeric Internet address.

2. The next line tells us that the connection to our destination worked.

3. It's the next line, "Escape," that we should look at in detail.
   This "Escape" means that we can use a combination of keys to break the connection if something really goes wrong. This combination, which works on many systems, can be read as:

> Hold the Control Key (^) and press the] (right square bracket) key.

This will usually break the connection (similar to hanging up the phone) if no other action will let us out. This is worth noting, as sometimes sessions do not go as planned. Remember that you must hold down the "Control" or "CTRL" key while you press the] key.

Practice Sessions

What follows is a series of practice sessions to illustrate the uses of remote logins – the **telnet** command. In Appendix A, we will list a number of books that will tell you about other computers to which you may Telnet.

For each session, we will list where we are going, and what actual **telnet** command you should use, and then show you the sample screens which result. Not all of these sessions may be available from your host account or open to you at the time that you try them.

Now let's begin our practice sessions!

For each of these practice sessions, you should login to your host account and be at a host prompt. As before, this should look something like:

> **host%**

At this host prompt, you can then type the **telnet** commands we illustrate below.

TELNET PRACTICE #1:   **WEATHER UNDERGROUND**

Where we're going:

> Weather Underground
> University of Michigan
> College of Engineering

Directions

1. At your host prompt, type:

telnet madlab.sprl.umich.edu 3000

What Happens?

You will be presented with the following response:

(Note that we have selected option "H," which provides us with help for new users. Once you have read through the help, feel free to explore the many options that are presented by the Weather Underground.)

When you have finished exploring the Weather Underground, type "X" to Exit Program.

Session Printout

```
telnet madlab.sprl.umich.edu 3000
Trying 141.212.196.79...
Connected to madlab.sprl.umich.edu.
Escape character is '^]'.
-----------------------------------------------------------------
*                 University of Michigan                     *
*                 WEATHER UNDERGROUND                        *
-----------------------------------------------------------------


*     College of Engineering, University of Michigan         *
* Department of Atmospheric, Oceanic, and Space Sciences     *
*           Ann Arbor, Michigan  48109-2143                  *
*          comments: sdm@madlab.sprl.umich.edu               *
*                                                            *
*                                                            *
*   With Help from: The UNIDATA Project,                     *
```

```
*                     University Corporation for Atmospheric *
                      Research
*                     Boulder, Colorado  80307-3000          *
* NOTE:—> New users, please select option "H" on the main    *
          menu:
*   H) Help and information for new users                    *
*                                                            *
-------------------------------------------------------------
Press Return for menu, or enter 3 letter forecast city code:


    WEATHER UNDERGROUND MAIN MENU
    *****************************
      1) U.S. forecasts and climate data
      2) Canadian forecasts
      3) Current weather observations
      4) Ski conditions
      5) Long-range forecasts
      6) Latest earthquake reports
      7) Severe weather
      8) Hurricane advisories
      9) National Weather Summary
     10) International data
     11) Marine forecasts and observations
      X) Exit program
      C) Change scrolling to screeN
      H) Help and information for new users
      ?) Answers to all your questions
         Selection:h
```

INFORMATION FOR NEW USERS OF THE WEATHER UNDERGROUND

Welcome to the Weather Underground! Through our host
computer in Ann Arbor, Michigan, we provide a variety of
weather information through this menu-driven, interactive
program. Use of this service is free, as long as the
information is for personal or educational use. Feel free to
access the service as much as you like, but be aware that
during major weather events usage gets quite heavy, and you
may receive the following message:

The Weather Underground is fully loaded. Try again later.

The Weather Underground is limited to 100 simultaneous
users, so you will have to wait until someone else signs off
before you can get on. Once you do get on, please limit the

duration of your session so that others may sign on.

BYPASSING THE MAIN MENU

When first entering the Weather Underground, you will get
the following prompt:

Press Return for menu, or enter 3 letter forecast city code:

At this point, you can either hit <Return> to get the main
menu, or enter a special code that will immediately give you a
forecast or observation. The special codes are explained under
the various options available on the main menu. You may enter
any of the following codes at the initial prompt:

1) A 3-letter code for a U.S. city forecast. For example,
entering DTW will give the forecast, plus any warnings or
special weather statements for Detroit.

2) A 2-letter state or province code, to get current
observations for the U.S. or Canada. For example, entering MI
will give the current observations for Michigan.

3) A number between 1 and 20, to get the current forecast for
a Canadian Province. For example, entering 18 will give the
forecast for the Yukon.

Note that as a special feature for users who access the
Weather Underground non-interactively through special "script"
programs, an extra character can be entered after any of the 3
options described above to set unlimited scrolling. For
example, entering "DTWF" will give the Detroit forecast only
(no special weather statements or 3-5 day forecast included)
with unlimited scrolling. For more information on these
options, plus much more information on the Weather
Underground, select "?" from the main menu.

BYPASSING SUBMENUS

One can save keystrokes in the U.S. city forecast submenu
and current weather observation submenu by entering the
desired code immediately upon entering the submenu. For
example, upon selecting "1" from the main menu to enter the
U.S. city submenu, one can then immediately enter "MIA" to get
the forecast for Miami, instead of typing a "1", carriage

return, then "MIA". Similarly, one can enter the 2-letter
state or province code immediately upon entering the current
observations submenu.

```
WEATHER UNDERGROUND MAIN MENU
*****************************
                1) U.S. forecasts and climate data
                2) Canadian forecasts
                3) Current weather observations
                4) Ski conditions
                5) Long-range forecasts
                6) Latest earthquake reports
                7) Severe weather
                8) Hurricane advisories
                9) National Weather Summary
                10) International data
                11) Marine forecasts and observations
                X) Exit program
                C) Change scrolling to screen
                H) Help and information for new users
                ?) Answers to all your questions
                    Selection:
-------------------------------------------------------------
```

TELNET PRACTICE #2:   CLEVELAND FREENET

Where we're going:

> Cleveland Freenet
> Case Western Reserve University
> Community Telecomputing Laboratory

Directions

There are three sets of commands that will enable you to log on to the Cleveland
Freenet. Once you are there, follow the directions for new users. Should you
wish to continue to use the Cleveland Freenet, you may obtain an account to do
so.

When you are done exploring the Cleveland Freenet, type "x" to exit.

Let's get started:

Type one of the following commands:

telnet freenet-in-a.cwru.edu

telnet freenet-in-b.cwru.edu

telnet freenet-in-c.cwru.edu

Here is what should happen:

```
telnet freenet-in-a.cwru.edu
Trying 129.22.8.38...
Connected to hela.INS.CWRU.Edu.
Escape character is '^]'.

4.3 BSD UNIX (hela) (ttyrf)


                                    /\
WELCOME TO THE...              _|  |_
                            _|__  __|_
             __               |        |
          _|  |_              |  |  |   |
         |      |   /\        |  |  |   |
         |      | |  |  |     |  |  |   |___
         |      | |  |  |     |  |  |   |   |
         |      | |_|_  |     |  |  |   |   |
         |      |  | | |  |   |  |  |   |   |
        _|      |  |_|_  |    |     |   |_
                                    
         |        |    |_|            |     |
         |                           |
         |      CLEVELAND FREE-NET        |
         |    COMMUNITY COMPUTER SYSTEM   |
         |_____ |


              brought to you by
        Case Western Reserve University
        Community Telecomputing Laboratory

     Are you:
             1. A registered user
             2. A visitor

     Please enter 1 or 2: 2
```

Would you like to:
            1. Apply for an account
            2. Explore the system
            3. Exit the system

Please enter 1, 2 or 3: **2**
Last login: Fri Apr 9 16:00:57 from wugate.wustl.edu
SunOS Release 4.1.2 (SUN690) #6: Wed May 20 08:15:30 EDT 1992

WELCOME:

  As a visitor to the Cleveland Free-Net you are allowed to
go anywhere and read anything on the system. However, to
post messages, and send or receive electronic mail, use the
Cafe (chat area) and other features, you must be a REGISTERED
USER. To register, simply use the "Apply for an account"
option from the visitors menu and follow the directions.
  The registration process and all system usage is FREE.
You are limited to one hour per visit but there is no limit
to the number of visits you can have per day.
  Before you enter the system however, there are two things
we need to tell you.
  First we need to tell you that: By entering this system,
in consideration for the privilege of using the Cleveland
Free-Net and in consideration for having access to the free
information contained on it, that you hereby release Case
Western Reserve University, the National Public Telecomputing
Network, the Cleveland Free-Net Project, its operators, and
any institutions with which they are affiliated for any and
all claims of any nature arising from your use of this system.

(See, aren't you glad we told you that?)

  Second, once you are in the system you may want to try
some of these commands from any arrow ==> prompt:
            who - who is online with you. The Cleveland Free-
                   Net handles as many as 12,000 logins a day.
                   You might want to see who else is online at
                   the same time you are.
           time - tells you the date and time ('case ya don't
                   know), how long you have been online, and how
                   much time you have remaining in your session.
        go <name> - takes you to the place on the system you name
                   (like a building or an area). See the Index
                   in the Administration Building for a (more or
                   less) complete list of the features
                   available.

```
         x -  logs you off the system from any arrow prompt
```

Thank you for visiting the Free-Net. We hope you will
become a registered user and that we'll see you online often.

    Enjoy and Learn!

End of File, Press RETURN to quit

Press RETURN to continue:

FreePort Software copyright 1991 Case Western Reserve
University

        <<< FROM THE ADMINISTRATOR >>>

The "What's New in the Electronic City" BBS will now be used
to announce all new SIG's and features on Free-Net. Type
"go new" at any "==>" prompt to get to the BBS. [emr - 2/11]

There is a 60 minute time limit on this connection.

Last login: Fri Jan 10 11:18:51 1992

<<< CLEVELAND FREE-NET DIRECTORY >>>

```
 1 The Administration Building
 2 The Post Office
 3 Public Square
 4 The Courthouse & Government Center
 5 The Arts Building
 6 Science and Technology Center
 7 The Medical Arts Building
 8 The Schoolhouse (Academy One)
 9 The Community Center & Recreation Area
10 The Business and Industrial Park
11 The Library
12 University Circle
13 The Teleport
14 The Communications Center
15 NPTN/USA TODAY HEADLINE NEWS
```

```
h=Help, x=Exit Free-Net, "go help"=extended help

Your Choice ==>
```

TELNET PRACTICE #3:   NYSERNET

Where we're going:

> NYSERNet (New York State Education & Research Network)
> 111 College Place
> Syracuse, NY 13244

NYSERNet has published a wonderful guide about the Internet entitled "New User's Guide to Useful and Unique Resources on the Internet" which is available in a bound, paper version as well as via FTP.

In this practice session, we will learn how to browse interactively through the guide using the NYSERView system.

Directions

> **telnet nysernet.org**
> **login: nysrview** (NOTE: do NOT type nyserview with two e's)
> **password: nysrview** (NOTE: do NOT type nyserview with
> two e's)

As you will notice in the following, NYSERView provides a great deal of information about the Internet. As well, it enables the user to quickly, and easily, access many of the Internet Resources which you explored in earlier chapters.

Here is what happens when you follow the directions provided above:

```
telnet nysernet.org
Trying 192.77.173.2...
Connected to nysernet.org.
Escape character is '^]'.

SunOS UNIX (nysernet.org)

login: nysrview
Password:
```

** Try our new-and-improved gopherized NYSERView interface by
** logging into nysernet.org as "nysernet" instead of
   "nysrview" !!!!!

Welcome to NYSERView!

An interface to useful network information.

   1) General Information About NYSERView
   2) Connect to Internet Resources
   3) Read About Internet Resources
   99) Quit

Please enter your choice and hit return: 1

Welcome to NYSERView: NYSERNet's Internet Portal

This NYSERNet service provides:

   1. A one-step transport to the Internet's useful and
unique resources
   2. Online information about the Internet's resources

NYSERView is currently running as a beta or test version.
Please address comments or notice of problems to
consult@nysernet.org

Copyright(c) 1991, NYSERNet, Inc.
This work was developed by The Computing Support Team,
Syracuse, New York

Press return to continue:

** Try our new-and-improved gopherized NYSERView interface by
** logging into nysernet.org as "nysernet" instead of
**   "nysrview" !!!!!

Welcome to NYSERView!

An interface to useful network information

   1) General Information About NYSERView
   2) Connect to Internet Resources
   3) Read About Internet Resources
   99) Quit

```
Please enter your choice and hit return: 3

You have chosen to access information about resources found on
the internet. Please select a category you would like to see
information on:

0)  Library Catalogs & Campus Information Systems
1)  Databases
2)  Electronic Discussion Groups/Forums
3)  Directories
4)  Information Resources
5)  FTP Archives
6)  Fee-Based Information Services
7)  Software/Freeware
8)  Bulletin Board Services
9)  Miscellaneous
99)  Quit

Please enter your selection and hit enter: 99

99Connection closed by foreign host.
```

TELNET PRACTICE #4:   UNIVERSITY OF MARYLAND INFO

The following practice session introduces you to the many resources available
from the University of Maryland's INFO program. With directories of information available about Computers, Literature, NewsLetters, USGovt, UofMaryland,
Weather, etc. it is obvious that it includes more than we can cover here.

However, we will demonstrate what happens when we log onto this computer
and follow several menu driven screens in our pursuit of information!

Directions:

Before signing onto this system, it is useful to know that once you have signed
on, you will use the arrow keys to move your cursor. Then you will make
selections according to the following choices:

View Return Select X-fer Go-To Protocol Quit INFO

Pressing the first letter of one of these menu choices (i.e. V for View) will enable
you to make your selection.

To begin, type the following:

telnet info.umd.edu

login id: info

terminal: vt100

Our decision was to follow the series of menus which led us to Government (Selection 5), then to US (Selection 6), and finally, to the poem (Selection 16) that was read at President Clinton's inauguration. Here is what happened:

```
telnet info.umd.edu
Trying 128.8.10.29…
Connected to info.umd.edu.
Escape character is '^]'.

At the login: prompt below, enter:

    info    for access to the Information On-line files and
            programs.
    gopher  for access to the Gopher interface and Internet
            Resources

login: info
Last login: Mon Apr 12 14:31:15 from phybuscomp.umd.e
ULTRIX V4.2A (Rev. 47) System #1: Mon Mar 29 12:53:33 EST 1993

Please enter your terminal type (? for a list, RETURN for
'vt52'):
INFO 2.0k── VIEW Return Select X-fer Go-To Protocol Quit
──Welcome to INFO

Menus will be available after you press a key to clear this
screen.

To select a menu item, press the arrow keys to highlight the
item (such as VIEW or SELECT), and then press Return or Enter.

You can also select a menu item by typing the first letter of
that item. For example, pressing V selects the VIEW option.

Help is available everywhere. If you get stuck you can press
the ? key, and information about the highlighted menu item
will appear on the screen. Press any key to continue…
```

Creating File List   INFO 2.0k

14 FILES IN /NameDescriptionprotocol = None

--1

2	CampusServices	Directory	06 Apr,	1993	13.28	
3	Computers	Directory	29 Mar,	1993	14.54	
4	EconData	Directory	28 May,	1992	10.04	
5	**Government**	**Directory**	**08 Jan,**	**1993**	**11.12**	
6	ReadingRoom	Directory	23 Feb,	1993	10:01	
7	StudentOrg	Directory	27 Jan,	1993	16:04	
8	Teaching	Directory	08 Feb,	1993	09:03	
9	USAToday	Directory	05 Aug,	1992	15:22	
10	UofMd-System	Directory	09 Mar,	1993	15:17	
11	UofMd-UMCP	Directory	05 Feb,	1993	16:12	
12	INDEX	File11	Apr,	1993	19:00	138814 bytes
13	UPDATE	File12	Apr,	1993	07:00	21405 bytes
14	WELCOME	File	05 Feb,	1993	09:05	2023 bytesMOF

Use the up/down arrow keys to select a directory or file,
press the first letter of a menu item to act on the selection.
Press ? for help.

Creating File List   INFO 2.0k

6 FILES IN /Government

1	...(Previous)	04 Ma13:38
2	Factbook91	17 Jan2 14:01
3	Factbook92	08 Jan1:12
4	Maryland	02 Feb3 14.23
5	UN	21 Jul2 16:54
6	**US**	**30 Mar3:48**

Creating File List   INFO 2.0k

16 FILES IN /Government/US8   Jan1:1

2	ADARegulation		23 Feb3		15:28
3	Census-90 110:29				
4	Congress30		Mar3:42		
5	Constitution07		Jan0:13		
6	Election9202		Feb09		
7	GAO	Directory	02 Feb,	1993	15:50
8	Legislation	Directory	15 Jan,	1992	17:06
9	NATO	Directory	30 Mar,	1993	09:49
10	NutrientData	Directory	10 Jul,	1992	17:05

```
11  SupremeCt       Directory   24 Jul,  1992  08.23
12  Travel          Directory   16 Sep,  1992  09:11
13  WhiteHouse      Directory   09 Apr,  1993  09:20
14  education-goals File        04 Jun,  1991  12:00  11927 bytes
15  inaug-address   File        26 Jan,  1993  09:15  9225 bytes
16  inaug-poem      File        26 Jan,  1993  09:16  3701 bytes

[Retrieving File...]
INFO 2.0k TOP Bottom Up Down   Left    Right   Number
/Government/US/inaug-poem lines 1-17 of 126
```

Maya Angelou's Inaugural Poem   January 20, 1993

"ON THE PULSE OF MORNING"
A Rock, A River, A Tree
Hosts to species long since departed,
Marked the mastodon.
The dinosaur, who left dry tokens
Of their sojourn here
On our planet floor,
Any broad alarm of their hastening doom
Is lost in the gloom of dust and ages.
But today, the Rock cries out to us, clearly, forcefully,
Come, you may stand upon my

NOTE: *In this particular instance, should you wish to transfer the entire file, you must use FTP, which is discussed in Session 7.*

TELNET PRACTICE #5:   NSSDC

Where we're going:

> NSSDC — The National Space Science Data Center
> Goddard Space Flight Center
> Greenbelt, MD

This official clearing house for NASA data, contains a directory of publicly available data. Data includes Geophysical Models, Voyager and other planetary images, Earth observation data; and Star catalogs.

Directions

telnet: nssdca.gsfc.nasa.gov

Login: nodis

Here is what a typical session looks like:

```
telnet nssdca.gsfc.nasa.gov
Trying 128.183.36.23...
Connected to nssdca.gsfc.nasa.gov.
Escape character is '^]'.
   <<   NSSDCA   VAX 9410   >>    Monday, April 12, 1993
    ANY UNAUTHORIZED ATTEMPT TO ACCESS THIS SYSTEM IS A
                     FEDERAL OFFENSE
    ONLY ACCESS TO THE USERNAME=NODIS(=NSSDC) ACCOUNT IS
                    AUTHORIZED TO ALL

Username: NODIS
One moment ...

    Is your terminal:

          1] VT Compatible
          2] TEKTRONIX-4025 Compatible
          3] OTHER

Enter Selection # : 1

                  W E L C O M E   T O

    N     N   OOOOOO    DDDDDDD   IIIIIII   SSSSS
    N N   N   O     O   D     D      I      S
    N  N  N   O     O   D     D      I      SSSS
    N   N N   O     O   D     D      I          S
    N    NN   O     O   D     D      I      S   S
    N     N   OOOOOO    DDDDDDD   IIIIIII   SSSSS

    NSSDC'S   ONLINE   DATA  &  INFORMATION  SERVICE

To ABORT session, type <Ctrl-Z>

Enter Your Name (e.g. Johnson, Robert): Sachs, David

One moment please... Searching User database...?21
Your name could not be found in our user database. You may
choose to re-enter your name (option-0) specifying last name
only, or if youintend to use NODIS regularly, you may input
information below for the NODIS user database. If you're just
```

'browsing', choose option-2.

```
Title,Full Name: DAVID SACHS
Affiliation:
Address1:
Address2:
Address3:
Address4:
Address5:
Zip Code:                              Country:
Fax:                                   Telephone:
Electronic Address1:

Valid Options:

0 - Abort,Return to Name Prompt   1 - Save,Proceed to NODIS Menu
2 - Abort,Proceed as "Browser"    3 - Refresh Input Screen
(-) - Previous Field,             <Return> - Next Field
Enter Title (or option#): 2
```

```
    NODIS Main Menu   (Choose one option)
            <<Enter '?' for help information>>

        0  -  Logoff NODIS account
        1  -  Master Directory - NASA & Global Change
        2  -  Personnel Information Management System
        3  -  Nimbus-7 GRID TOMS Data
        4  -  Interplanetary Medium Data (OMNI)
        5  -  Request data and/or information from NSSDC
        6  -  Geophysical Models
        7  -  CANOPUS Newsletter
        8  -  International Ultraviolet Explorer Data Request
        9  -  CZCS Browse and Order Utility
       10  -  Astronomical Data Center (ADC)
       11  -  STEP Bulletin Board Service
       12  -  Standards and Technology Information System
       13  -  Planetary Science & Magellan Project Information
       14  -  Other Online Data Services at NSSDC
       15  -  CD-ROMS Available at NSSDC

    Enter Selection #: 13

        Planetary Science & Magellan Project
             Introductory Screen
```

The text files contained in this option describing planetary

science and Magellan project information were written by Dr.
David Okerson, SAIC, Magellan project engineer.

If you wish to place an order for any of the products
described here, please return to the NODIS menu and choose
option 5 to reach the NSSDC request coordination office. For
more information on CD-ROM's, NODIS option 15 will be
available in the near future .

To exit from any text file, press <Ctrl> Z and return to the
menu.

Press Return...

```
            PLANETARY SCIENCE & MAGELLAN PROJECT INFORMATION

                    1. Magellan Fact Sheet
                    2. Magellan Products Guide
                    3. Using Magellan CD-ROM's
                    4. NASA Teacher Resource Center Network
                    5. Regional Planetary Image Facilities
                    6. Planetary Data System Nodes

    * Enter your selection or 0 to exit menu:   4

                    NASA TEACHER RESOURCE CENTER NETWORK

    NASA Education Division

    NASA's Education Division provides educational programs and
    materials for teachers and students from the elementary to the
    university level.  The NASA Teacher Resource Center Network, a
    dissemination mechanism to provide educators with NASA
    educational materials, is one of the programs that has helped
    science and mathematics teachers over the years.

    Continued...
```

TELNET PRACTICE #6:   SPACELINK

The following session introduces you to a wonderful resource for teachers that is
very powerful, but also very easy to use.

Directions

Telnet: spacelink.msfc.nasa.gov

user-id: newuser

password: newuser

Here is what the session looks like:

```
world% telnet 192.149.89.61
Trying 192.149.89.61...
Connected to 192.149.89.61.
Escape character is '^]'.
                        WELCOME
                          to
                     NASA SPACELINK

            A Space-Related Informational Database
         Provided by the NASA Educational Affairs Division
          Operated by the Marshall Space Flight Center
          On a Data General ECLIPSE MV7800 Minicomputer


                   ******IMPORTANT!******
          Do not press RETURN until you have read the following
                         information.
          You are about to be asked to provide a Username and a
                          Password.
             If this is your first call to NASA Spacelink,
          Enter NEWUSER as your Username and enter NEWUSER as your
                          Password.
       If you have called before, enter your assigned Username and
                          Password.
         You may send Carriage Returns or Line Feeds but NOT BOTH.

                 You may now press RETURN, or
            To redisplay this message press CONTROL-D.


      AOS/VS II 2.20.00.66 / EXEC-32 2.20.00.07      12-Apr-93
      14:37:38      @TCON27

      Username: NEWUSER
      Password:
```

Last message change   8-Apr-93   0:51:46

***** IMPORTANT MESSAGES *****

Internet callers may try our new FTP capability (in
development). Username is anonymous and Password is guest.
Address is 192.149.89.61 READ README!

To transfer files on Internet, PLEASE use Kermit instead of
XMODEM or YMODEM.

For info on the current Shuttle flight, enter STS-56 at the GO
TO prompt. Don't forget the hyphen!

Spacelink's phone number is 205-895-0028.

Most recent logon   12-Apr-93   14:36:56
NASA/SPACELINK   REGISTRATION   Revision:1.10.00.00

======
NOTICE: We're delighted you called NASA Spacelink. This
service is free. But, you need to understand that you will be
charged by your phone service if you're calling long distance
to our computer in Huntsville, Alabama. So use it all you
like, but remember, it's your nickel.

This system is designed for 80 column text display. On
computers that display fewer than 80 columns, some text may be
distorted.

To allow time for reading, NASA Spacelink will pause
periodically, waiting for you to press RETURN. You must now
choose the number of lines NASA Spacelink will display on your
screen between pauses. Most home and school computers can
display 24 lines at a time. Please enter a number and press
return, or just press return to accept the default of 24
lines.

======
Enter the number of lines to scroll before
pausing:[default=24]

Text will pause after 24 lines.

Is this correct: [Y/N] Y

======
When the screen pauses, press return to continue.

This introduction is provided automatically only for callers who log on as NEWUSER. You may review it under main menu option 2 (NASA Spacelink Overview). After the introduction, you will be asked to assign yourself a personal Username and Password. When you use them to log on, you won't receive the introduction.

NASA SPACELINK BACKGROUND

NASA Spacelink runs on a Data General ECLIPSE MV-7800 minicomputer at the NASA George C. Marshall Space Flight Center in Huntsville, Alabama. NASA Spacelink software was developed and donated to NASA by the Data General Corporation. The system has a main memory of 14 megabytes (14 million characters), and disk storage space for 2 gigabytes. It runs at 300, 1200, 2400 or 9600 baud. Data word format is 8 data bits, no parity, and 1 stop bit. The system was made public in February, 1988.

Initial support for NASA Spacelink was provided by the Educational Affairs Division at NASA Headquarters. The NASA Spacelink data base is maintained by the Public Services and Education Branch of the Marshall Space Flight Center Public Affairs Office. Operational support is provided by the Information Systems Office at the Marshall Center. Information on NASA scientific projects and educational programs is provided to NASA Spacelink by education specialists at NASA Headquarters and the NASA field centers.

While NASA understands that people from a wide variety of backgrounds will use NASA Spacelink, the system is specifically designed for teachers. Unlike bulletin board systems, NASA Spacelink does not provide for interaction between callers. However, it allows teachers and other callers to leave questions and comments for NASA.

Continued...

TELNET PRACTICE # 7:　　GEOGRAPHIC NAME SERVER

Overview

As you might expect, this server provides geographic information for those who need it. The information includes zip codes, latitude and longitude, elevation, population, telephone area codes, and time zones.

Directions

telnet:　　martini.eecs.umich.edu 3000

As you will see below, there are no additional sign-on commands necessary for this program. It is useful to take a minute to read the help which is provided.

However, after doing that once, it is up to the individual user to determine what cities are of interest, and how that information will be used. Here is a sample session, in which we looked up several cities, just for the fun of it:

```
telnet martini.eecs.umich.edu 3000
Trying 141.212.99.9...
Connected to martini.eecs.umich.edu.
Escape character is '^]'.
# Geographic Name Server, Copyright 1992 Regents of the
University of Michigan.
# Version 8/19/92. Use "help" or "?" for assistance, "info"
for hints.
 .
help
Change summary:
1) ZIP codes now printed ten per line.
2) "info" command provided.
3) Handles urgent (out-of-band) data.

NOTE: This server is intended for use with clients which
interpret the raw protocol. However, you may also use the
server directly if you don't have the clients. There are
currently four clients:

1) A user agent which pretty-prints the raw protocol and
optionally computes distance and azimuth between any two
cities,

2) A filter for producing input files for Brian Reid's netmap
program,
```

3) A US map browser which uses the X Window System,

4) A prototype X-based network browsing tool.

Data came primarily from the US Geological Survey and the US
Postal Service. Coverage includes all US cities, counties, and
states, as well as some US mountains, rivers, lakes, national
parks, etc. A few international cities have also been
included. Unfortunately, some minor inaccuracies remain. Send
mail to info@comsol.com for information regarding the data.

Queries should generally look like the last line of a postal
address, as in "Ann Arbor, MI 48103".

All these queries will also work:
1) ed(1)-style regular expression, like "[Bb]os.*n$"
2) A city name alone, like "Ann Arbor"
3) A ZIP or ZIP+4 code alone, like this: "46556", "48103-2112"
   NOTE: only the first 5 digits in a ZIP+4 code are used.
4) As in 1) or 2) but with a state name or abbreviation, like
   this: "Ann Arbor, MI", "Los Angeles, California"
5) As above but with optional nation name or abbreviation,
   like "Toronto, , Canada". NOTE: there are currently very
   few foreign cities.

Punctuation, white space, and upper/lower case are ignored.
Any reasonable state/nation abbreviations are recognized.

Here are more example queries:

"Ann Arbor, Mich" "48103" "annarbor,mi" "Paris,,France"
"Mammoth Cave National Park" "mount mckinley" "lake michigan"

If a query fails, try expanding abbreviations (e.g. change
"Mt." to "Mount", etc.

Interpret server replies as follows:

0 <city name>
1 <county FIPS code> <county name>
2 <state/province abbreviation> <state/province name>
3 <nation abbreviation> <nation name>
A <telephone area code>
E <elevation in feet above mean sea level>
F <feature code> <feature name>
L <latitude DD MM SS X> <longitude DDD MM SS X>

```
P <1980 census population>
R <remark>
T <time zone>
Z <postal ("ZIP") code>
```

To exit the server, enter "stop", "end", "quit", "bye",
"exit", "logout", or "logoff".

Direct questions or comments to Tom Libert,
libert@citi.umich.edu,
or phone (313) 936-0827. Please let me know if you write new
clients.

.
```
south salem, ny
0 South Salem
1 36119 Westchester
2 NY New York
3 US United States
F 45 Populated place
L 41 16 20 N  73 33 12 W
Z 10590
```


.
```
new canaan, ct
0 New Canaan
1 09001 Fairfield
2 CT Connecticut
3 US United States
A 203
F 45 Populated place
L 41 08 48 N  73 29 43 W
E 340
Z 06840 06842
```


.
```
white plains, ny
0 White Plains
1 36119 Westchester
2 NY New York
3 US United States
R county seat
F 45 Populated place
L 41 02 02 N  73 45 48 W
P 46999
E 201
Z 10600 10601 10602 10603 10604 10605 10606 10607 10625 10629
```

```
Z 10650

.
quit
Connection closed by foreign host.
world%
```

Conclusion

As you can see from the examples we have included, there is an almost limitless amount of information available when one uses Telnet. For the most part the Telnet system works quite smoothly, with few or no complicated commands to learn or remember. As you read through the sources listed in the Appendix of this book you will find many other Telnet addresses. Feel free to try them, knowing that usually your success rate will be high and your enjoyment enormous. The screens you see may be different from those we show. All systems constantly undergo changes and improvements.

Remember that you are a guest. Be a caring and careful guest and we will all be welcome at these many fascinating places on the Internet.

■ ■ Session Six Vocabulary and Command Summary

telnet ....the command that enables you to logon to other mainframe computers

SESSION SEVEN

Getting Things: File Transfer Protocol

In this session, we will show you how to move files and programs from one host computer to another. The procedures we will follow here will work between any two host computers on which you have accounts. As a beginner, you most likely do not have two or more accounts, so we will talk primarily about something that is known as "guest" or "anonymous" file transfer.

Here, the transfers will be from another host on the Internet where you do not have an account, to the host computer where you do have one. As you saw in Session Six with Telnet, there are many places on the Internet that offer information, documents, and programs to anyone. You just have to know how to get to the computers that offer them, and how to move the files to your host account.

In this session, we will help you through several file transfers and provide you with a list of some sample places to look. Then we will show you how to move the files to and from your PC.

Good Manners – A Reminder

As we noted earlier in the session on Telnet, you must remember that you are using guest privileges. File transfer uses resources on computers owned and run by others. They have made some of those resources available to the Internet community as a public service. Please observe any conditions requested by those who manage the other computers. It is also polite to limit your use of the other computers during their prime working hours. As the Internet spans the entire globe, be sensitive to the fact that evenings for you in North and South America may be early in the working day in Asia.

Getting Files from Other Hosts

The file transfer process is actually very simple. There are really only a few new commands here and some are very much like ones you have seen when using

DOS commands on an IBM PC. The whole process is called **File Transfer Protocol** and is abbreviated as **FTP**.

You do not need to understand all of the complexities involved in the complete FTP process. You just need to know how to use the commands so that you may transfer files from a host computer to your own host computer account, and then, from there, to your own PC. This is what we will show you.

The FTP process goes like this:

1. You will use the command FTP and the full name of another host.

2. You may be asked for a login and a password (we'll show you what to use).

3. You will select a directory and look at its list of files (or some of them).

4. You will pick a file you wish to "get."

5. You will decide whether it is an ASCII or a BINARY file (we'll help you to decide).

6. You will use the "get" command with the file name.

7. You will "close" the connection and "quit" the FTP command.

That's all there is to it, but before we begin, we need to explain "anonymous" FTP. This is what you will be using during our practice sessions.

"Anonymous" FTP

There is a **convention** used in the Internet community for FTP. A convention is not really a standard in the formal sense; it's just a general agreement to do things in one common way. Anonymous FTP is such a convention. Here's how it works.

Many hosts offering publicly accessible files need to keep their usual login processes in place. They want, however, to allow public access to some parts of their system. The "anonymous FTP" convention allows them to do this.

Public users who wish to access their systems use the login name **anonymous**. This login name allows access to a restricted portion of the host system. Restricted access means access only to certain directories. The convention also may ask that you use your email address as the password to this anonymous login.

It's considered bad manners not to give your email address when asked.

You don't need to worry about being contacted; few systems administrators look at individual addresses. They often want them just to show that many people from many places are using their system. This can sometimes help them to get their funding. Not only should you provide your email address when asked, but you should type it very carefully. This is because, like any password, it will not show on your screen when you type it.

FTP PRACTICE #1

1. Begin by logging in as usual, and get to your host prompt.

2. At the host prompt, type:

   host%   ftp   nri.reston.va.us

   You will see something like the following screen. Notice that after the login, the prompt changes to:

   ftp>

   Ignore the numbers in front of the responses. They are there for programs to read, not people.

```
Connected to cnri.reston.va.us.
220 CNRI FTP server (SunOS 4.1) ready.
Name (nri.reston.va.us:user):
```

3. When you are prompted for a name, type (in lower case) the word

   anonymous

4. Press **ENTER**.

5. You will then be asked for a password.

```
331 Guest login ok, send ident as password.
```

6. Carefully type your complete email address (you won't see it on your screen) and press **ENTER**.

    Remember that your email address looks like:

    login_name@your.host.edu

    where you use your own actual full address.

    You should now see the following screen:

```
230 Guest login ok, access restrictions apply.
```

Commentary

You are still issuing commands to your usual host account. However, your host account has set up a communications "channel" with another host (the remote host). It may appear as if you are talking directly to the remote host; you are really still giving commands to the **ftp>** prompt on your host computer, and it is sending them on to the remote host.

Finding your Way Around

We will now practice moving around the directories at the remote host.

1. To start, let's see where we are. Remember the "print working directory" command? Type:

    pwd

2. Your host should respond with:

```
ftp> pwd
257 "/" is current directory.
```

---

3. Now we will change to another directory on the remote host. At the ftp> prompt, type:

cd isoc

4. The response should be:

```
250 CWD command successful.
```

5. Again, type the **pwd** command to verify that you have moved to the new directory. (This is more than just practice as the host only told us that some directory change was successful.)

6. The remote host will respond with:

```
ftp> pwd
257 "/isoc" is current directory.
```

7. Now we will use the **directory** command to list the files; we do this with the **dir** command (just like **dir** in PC-DOS). Type the following:

dir

```
ftp> dir
200 PORT command successful.
150 ASCII data connection for /bin/ls (131.215.48.62,2746) (0
bytes).
total 1623
-rw-rw-r-  1 1031  1000     830 Mar  1 22:14  0README
-rw-rw-r-  1 1031  1000     253 May19  23:16  Internet-Service-
                                             POC.txt
-rw-r-r-   1 1055  1000 11725 Apr 13 14:44  Internet.host.growth
-rw-rw-r-  1 1031  1000 16179 May 19 23:16  abstract.txt
-rw-rw-r-  1 1031  1000  3939 Jun  6 21:44  advisory-council.txt
-rw-rw-r-  1 1031  1000  2370 May 19 23:16  announcement.txt
-rw-rw-r-  1 1031  1000 19397 May 19 23:16  bylaws.txt
drwxr-xr-x 2 1045  1     1024 Jun 30 16:33  charts
-rw-rw-r-  1 1031  1000 37646 May 19 23:16  corp-isoc-pkg.txt
drwxrwxr-x 2 1055  1000   512 Mar 23 21:15  elections
-rw-rw-r-  1 1031  1000  2104 May 19 23:16  founding.txt
-rw-rw-r-  1 103   1000444808 Jan  5 22:27  future.inet.ps
-rw-rw-r-  1 1     1000  6816 May 19 23:16  incorp.txt
```

```
-rw-rw-r—  1 1031  1000  31004 May 19 23:16 indiv-isoc pkg.txt
-rw-rw-r—  1 1031  1000   9925 May 19 23:16 inet-connect.txt
-rwxrwxr-x 1 1031  1000  28845 May 19 23:16 inet93 adv.prog.txt
drwxrwxr-x 2 1031  1000   1024 May 21 14:50 info
-rw-r—r—   1 1055  1000  27090 Mar  4 13:13 internet.bibliography
-rw-rw-r—  1 1002  1000   8098 Mar  8 20:16 internet.biblio-
                                            graphy-2
-rw-r—r—   1 1055  1000   7337 Mar  3 14:14 internet.survey
-rw-rw-r—  1 1031  1000  60232 May 19 23:16 isoc-pkg.txt
-rw-rw-r—  1 1036 1000236683 Jan  8 19:47 isoc.application.ps
-rw-rw-r—  1 1036  1000  32864 Jan  6 15:39 isoc.logo1.ps
-rw-rw-r—  1 1036  1000  50083 Jan  6 15:39 isoc.logo2.ps
drwxrwxr-x 7 1031  1000    512 Mar 16 22:12 isoc_news
drwxrwxrwx 2 1045  1000    512 Apr  6 21:00 itu
drwxrwxrwx 2 1045  1000    512 Apr 19 03:02 k-12
-rw-rw-r—  1 1031  1000   4922 Jun  6 21:53 membership.txt
-rw-rw-r—  1 1031  1000   1408 Feb 19 20:38 org-paymentmethod.txt
-rw-rw-r—  1 1031  1000   1265 May 19 23:16 org-pymt method.txt
-rw-rw-r—  1 1031  1000   2416 May 19 23:16 payment method.txt
-rw-rw-r—  1 1031  1000   1159 May 19 23:16 secretariat.txt
-rw-rw-r—  1 1031  1000   1701 May 19 23:16 trustees.txt
-rw-rw-r—  1 1031  1000  54075 Jan  5 21:01 viewgraphs.ps
-r—r—r—    1 1002 1000492268 Apr  6 1992   worldmap.ps
226 ASCII Transfer complete.
2547 bytes received in 1.6 seconds (1.5 Kbytes/s)
```

Commentary

1. The letters on the left of the screen indicate whether the item is a directory (d) or a file (-) and whether or not you can read it (r).

2. The remaining letters will have to wait until you are more familiar with the host's operating system.

3. The numbers just before the file's or directory's date tell you the size of the file in bytes.

NOTE: *Be careful at this stage not to try to "get" very large files. Remember that you are just beginning.*

Getting a File

1. Let's pick a file to transfer to your host system account. For practice, we'll pick a small file to conserve host and network resources. We will use the file named:

   0README

2. Before we "get" the file, we must be sure that we have set our host computer for the correct type of transfer.

   There are two transfer types in FTP: ASCII and BINARY (or IMAGE, which is the same as BINARY).

   Most README files are created as text or ASCII files, although it does not necessarily tell you that. Therefore, for our transfer mode, we will use ASCII.

3. At the prompt, type:

   ascii

4. Press **ENTER**.

   Your host will respond with:

```
ftp> ascii
200 Type set to A.
```

5. Now we can begin the transfer. Type:

   get 0README

   Note that we have used capital letters in README, because that is exactly how the file was named when we listed it in the directory.

   Watch your screen. You should see something like the following.

```
ftp> get 0README
200 PORT command successful.
150 ASCII data connection for 0README (131.215.48.62,2748)
(830 bytes).
226 ASCII Transfer complete.
```

```
local: 0README remote: 0README
849 bytes received in 0.28 seconds (2.9 Kbytes/s)
```

This means that the file has been successfully transferred from the "other" computer to your host account and that the same filename (0README) has been used on your host.

6. We will now close this first practice connection to the remote host. To do this, type:

    close

7. After the host responds:

    221 Goodbye.

Type: **quit**

These two commands have told FTP to close or to end the connection to the remote host and then to quit the FTP program.

Looking at the File

Let's look at the file we have just transferred. You do that, remember, with the **more** command. Do that now by keying:

more 0README

You will see something like:

```
host% more 0README
FILENAME                  CONTENTS
0README                   This file
abstract.txt              Introduction to the Internet Society
advisory-council.txt      Members of the Internet Society
                          Advisory Council
announcement.txt          Announcement of the Internet Society
bylaws.txt                By-Laws of the Internet Society
payment-method.txt        Individual Member Dues Payment
org-payment-method.txt    Organizational Member Dues Payment
founding.txt              List of Charter, Founding, and
                          Organizational members of the Internet
                          Society
```

incorp.txt	Internet Society Articles of Incorporation
membership.txt	Description of membership types
secretariat.txt	The Internet Society Secretariat
trustees.txt	Board of Trustees for the Internet Society
isoc-pkg.txt	All the above (without 0README)

... and so on

Congratulations! You have just completed your first file transfer. A copy of the file is now on your host account.

FTP PRACTICE #2

There are many places on the Internet that make "anonymous" FTP publicly available. We have selected one more for you to try. Remember that you are a guest and behave accordingly. This session is from the Project Gutenberg at Illinois Benedictine College.

We will show the entire session this time as a series of screens. See if you can follow along with the FTP that we illustrate, and then do it on your own.

```
host% ftp mrcnext.cso.uiuc.edu
Connected to mrcnext.cso.uiuc.edu.
220 mrcnext.cso.uiuc.edu FTP server (Version 5.1 (NeXT 1.0))
ready.
Name (mrcnext.cso.uiuc.edu:user): anonymous
331 Guest login ok, send ident as password.
Password:
230 Guest login ok, access restrictions apply.
Remote system type is UNIX.
Using binary mode to transfer files.
```

Note that the default transfer type is BINARY. Let's change that to ASCII.

```
ftp> ascii
200 Type set to A.
ftp> dir
200 PORT command successful.
```

```
150 Opening ASCII mode data connection for /bin/ls.
total 137
```

-rw-r—r—	**1**	**187**	**micro**	**157**	**Jun 4**	**2000**	**README**
-rw-r—r—	1	109	micro	1798	Jan4	2000	README.bak
drwxrwxr-x	2	root	micro	1024	Oct 4	1999	amiga
dr-xr-xr-x	2	root	micro	1024	Jul 14	2000	bin
lrwxrwxrwx	1	root	micro	9	Aug 30	2000	cache -> pub/cache
drwxr-xr-x	2	187	wheel	1024	Mar 8	2000	compucom
drwxr-xr-x	2	root	micro	1024	Sep 6	1999	etc
lrwxrwxrwx	1	root	micro	9	Aug 30	2000	etext -> pub/etext
drwxr-xr-x	2	24	micro	3072	Jul 22	12:26	etext92
lrwxrwxrwx	1	root	micro	5	Jun 4	2000	gutenberg -> etext
-rw-r—r—	1	24	micro	4853	Jan 10	2001	gutnberg. doc
drwxr-xr-x	2	187	micro	1024	May 9	2000	kites
drwxrwxr-x	2	root	micro	1024	Dec 23	18:23	lists
drwxr-xr-x	3	root	micro	1024	Dec 30	12:51	mac
drwxr-xr-x	11	187	micro	2048	Jun 28	2001	nethack
-rw-r—r—	1	109	micro	52064	May 23	2000	odipkt .zip
drwxrwxr-x	9	root	micro	1024	Jul 3	2000	pc
drwxr-xr-x	2	root	micro	1024	Mar 7	2001	pcsig10
drwxr-xr-x	2	187	wheel	50176	Oct 24	17:37	pcsig2
drwxrwxr-x	2	root	micro	1024	Dec 19	1999	pspice
drwxrwxr-t	8	root	wheel	1024	Jul 16	15:03	pub
drwxrwxr-x	2	root	micro	6144	Jun 12	2000	simtel20
drwxrwxr-x	2	root	micro	1024	Aug 12	2000	uiuc
drwxrwxr-x	2	root	staff	1024	May 21	2000	unix
drwxr-xr-x	3	root	micro	1024	Jun 20	2000	usr
drwxrwxr-x	2	root	micro	1024	Dec 22	00:57	video
drwxr-x—	4	300	wp	1024	Jul 31	14:09	wp
drwxr-xr-x	2	24	micro	1024	Jun 19	2001	zip93

```
226 Transfer complete.
ftp> get README
200 PORT command successful.
150 Opening ASCII mode data connection for README (1579
bytes).
226 Transfer complete.
1632 bytes received in 0.21 seconds (7.6 Kbytes/s)
ftp> close
221 Goodbye.
ftp> quit
```

As before, we will look at the file we have just FTP'ed.

```
host% more README
This is an '040 NeXT cube with a 660 Meg hard drive.  In this
public directory is an NFS mount of the ftp directory on
ftp.cso.uiuc.edu, 128.174.5.59, labelled "ux1". It contains a
lot more than 660 Meg.
Files/directories of interest:
amiga              A few files for Amigans. Look in ux1/amiga
                   for more.
apple2             For necromechanomaniacs.
Bible              A copy of the KJB can be found on
                   uxc.cso.uiuc.edu
drivers.zip        A bunch of packet drivers for PC versions of
                   Telnet.
cwp.zip            Chinese Word Processor. This is NOT a product
                   of the University of Illinois, and we're NOT
                   doing support for it. It is nonetheless
                   useful, and it's here.
etext              Michael Hart's Project Gutenberg electronic
                   text collection.
lists              A bunch of lists:
... and so on
```

From this list, you should be able to determine that you could go back here and change the directory to **etext** and begin to look at the Project Gutenberg text files. Be careful if you do; some of the files are very large.

FTP PRACTICE #3

Our third practice session is with the Electronic Frontiers Foundation.

```
host%  ftp   ftp.eff.org
Connected to kragar.eff.org.
220 kragar.eff.org FTP server (Version 2.1WU(1)) ready.
Name (ftp.eff.org:stair): anonymous
331 Guest login ok, send your complete e-mail address as
password.
Password:
230 Guest login ok, access restrictions apply.
230-If your ftp client chokes on this message, log in with a
'-' as the
```

```
230-first character of your password to disable it.
230-
230-If you have problems with or questions about this service,
send mail to
230-ftphelp@eff.org; we'll try to fix the problem or answer
the question.
230-
230-Electronic Frontier Foundation newsletters and other
information     are in
230-pub/EFF and subdirectories thereof.  If you're interested
in     official
230-EFF positions and philosophies, look here.
230-
230-For general information on the EFF, get pub/EFF/about-eff.
230-
230-**** NOTICE ****
230-The files ending in ".z" are gzip'ed files.  Either get
gzip from a 230-GNU archive site (ftp.uu.net:/packages/gnu,
say) or use "get     filename"
230-(without the .z) to have it ungzip'ed on the fly.  (If you
have UNIX
230-compress compatible software, "get filename.Z" will
convert gzip     files
230-to compress files on the fly.)
230-
230-Remember to use binary mode with compressed or gzip'ed
files.
230-****************
230-
230-Please read the file README
230-  it was last modified on Sat May  2 18:10:09 1992 - 424
days ago
```

The README file tells us to go look in the **pub** directory, so we will skip some text and move there now.

```
ftp> cd pub
250 CWD command successful.
ftp> pwd
257 "/pub" is current directory.
ftp> dir
200 PORT command successful.
150 Opening ASCII mode data connection for /bin/ls.
total 28
```

```
rw-r–r—      1   root       12       0   Oct  18   1991   .notar
drwxrwxr-x 11   199        12     512   Apr  27  19:43   EFF
drwxrwsr-x  5   199        12     512   Apr   5  21:13   SJG
drwxrwsr-x 17   kadie      21    1024   May  15  04:21   academic
drwxr-sr-x  4   199        12     512   Jan   4  23:39   agitprop
drwxr-sr-x  2   hrose      12     512   Feb  17  18:27   airliners
drwxr-xr-x  2   ezf       146    1024   May  27   1992   cpsr
drwxrwsr-x  4   gnu       134     512   Jan   6  17:09   crypto
drwxr-xr-x 37   brendan    12    1024   Jun   2  05:02   cud
drwxr-sr-x  3   composer   15     512   Jul  20   1992   ftp.dreams
                                                         .org
drwxrwxr-x  4   199        12    1024   Feb  20  17:24   internet
info
drwxrwsr-x  5   hrose      14     512   May  13  01:57   irc
drwxr-xr-x 13   rita      148     512   May  14  13:55   journals
drwxrwsr-x  3   ckd        15     512   Nov  17  20:38   net-tools
drwxr-sr-x  2   1      daemon     512   May   8   1992   pub-infra
226 Transfer complete.
956 bytes received in 0.23 seconds (4 Kbytes/s)
ftp> cd EFF
250-Look at about-eff for general information on the
250-Electronic Frontier Foundation.
250-
250-Look at Index for a guide to the different subdirectories.
250-
250-Questions about items in this directory and subdirectories
thereof
250-should go to eff@eff.org
250-
250 CWD command successful.
ftp> dir
200 PORT command successful.
150 Opening ASCII mode data connection for /bin/ls.
total 50
-rw-rw-r—    1   199    12      234   Apr 27  19:52   message
-rw-r–r—     1   199   199     1137   Apr 27  19:56   Index
-rw-rw-r—    1   199   199    11688   Apr 23  18:50   about-eff
drwxrwsr-x   2   199    12      512   Oct 20  15:30   eff-issues
drwxr-xr-x   2   199   199      512   Apr 27  19:44   eff-misc
drwxrwsr-x   2   199    12      512   Feb 16  20:02   historical
drwxrwsr-x   2   199    12     1024   May 25  16:25   legal
                                                      issues
drwxrwsr-x   2   199    12     1024   May 13  19:51   legislation
drwxrwxr-x   4   199   199      512   Apr 23  14:53   local_
                                                      action
drwxrwsr-x   3   199    12     1536   Jun 11  22:09   newsletters
```

```
drwxrwsr-x   2  199   12    512    Jan 13 17:44   newsnotes
drwxrwsr-x   3  199   12   1024    Mar  9 00:31   papers
226 Transfer complete.
793 bytes received in 0.26 seconds (3 Kbytes/s)
ftp> get Index
200 PORT command successful.
150 Opening ASCII mode data connection for Index (1137 bytes).
226 Transfer complete.
local: Index remote: Index
1167 bytes received in 0.11 seconds (11 Kbytes/s)
ftp> close
221 Goodbye.
ftp> quit
host% more   Index
```

Index to ftp.eff.org pub/EFF – last changed 27 Apr 93

Note that most files are located in subdirectories. Archive-server users can access these files (and directories) by using commands like:

```
ls eff/newsletters
get eff/newsletters effector2.08
```

about-eff

A file of basic information about EFF. It includes our goals, mission, achievements, and current projects. This is current as of February 17, 1993. Includes a membership form.

mission-statement

The EFF's mission statement.

Subdirectories

eff-misc	- EFF bumper sticker GIFs, staff directory and membership form
historical	- documents on the EFF of historical interest
legal-issues	- papers and documents about various legal issues
legislation	- texts of various bills and proposals
local-action	- information on regional telecomm activist groups
newsletters	- back issues of EFFector Online and its predecessor EFFnews
newsnotes	- the EFF's "FYI" news bulletins
papers	- papers and testimony by EFF board members on various topics

... and so on

Getting the Files to Your PC

Although there are many ways to copy the file from your host account to your PC, we will outline just the basics. As you become more expert, you will uncover your own best method. The methods differ depending on what software you have been running on your PC while communicating with the host.

Copying the file to your PC will depend largely on the software you are using on your PC. If you are running a Windows or Works type of program, the information from the host will usually be captured. That is, at least a portion of it will be, and you can then save it in a file. If you are using a communications program, you will have some sort of "capture" or download capability. At this point you should consult the manuals for your specific setup.

Once you have found out how to capture information coming down to you from the host, all you have to do is to be sure that it is turned on. Then you can tell the host to "print" a continuous stream of data to your PC. This is unlike the **more** command in that it does not stop at the end of each page. It keeps on going until it reaches the end of the file. The command, already introduced in the Session on email, is:

> **cat**

The word **cat** is from "Concatenate and Print" files. You are not concatenating, but you are printing.

When you type the command **cat** followed by the filename, it will just stream down your screen without stopping. You may not be able to read it, depending on how fast your modem is, but if you are "capturing" it, that's OK.

1. Login to your host.

2. Select a filename to send down to your personal computer.

3. Turn on the "capture" command on your software. In Telix Lite you should press the **ALT** and **L** keys simultaneously. This will prompt you for a file name in which to save the download.

4. Type the command:

> **cat (filename)**

where you substitute the real filename for (filename).

5. When you are finished, turn off the capture command. To do this in Telix Lite, press the **ALT** and **L** keys simultaneously.

FTP PRACTICE #4

Our fourth practice session connects us to a remote computer at the University of Wisconsin. It is here that Scott Yanoff maintains a file called **inet.services.txt**, which provides a wonderful array of resources for Internet users.

We will login to this computer as we have done before. We will change to the **pub** directory, since this is often where files available to the public are kept. After using the **dir** (directory) command to see if the file is actually there, we will use the **get** command to bring a copy of the file to our host computer.

This time, we will use a different way to download the file to our personal computer. We will quit File Transfer Protocol mode, and return to our primary host prompt. At the host prompt, we will issue a command which will cause the file to be sent to our personal computer.

Put simply, we will use something called the **XMODEM** protocol which will enable us to send this file from the host computer to our own computer. As you will see, at one point you will be prompted to "turn on" your communications software so that it can receive the file.

NOTE: *A protocol is just a standard set of procedures which are used. There are several protocols available for transferring files. Among the best known are Kermit, XMODEM, YMODEM, and ZMODEM. Most good software packages such as Windows and Works will permit you to use one or several of these protocols.*

Here are the steps to follow. Read through them carefully, then review the printout of the actual session which follows, so that you may see how it worked for us.

1. At the host prompt, type:

   ftp

2. At the ftp prompt, type:

   open csd4.csd.uwm.edu

   (you could also do this by typing: ftp csd4.csd.uwm.edu)

3. When you are prompted for Name, type:

anonymous.

4. When you are prompted for Password, type your full internet id — for example, dsachs@world.std.com

5. Change to the pub directory by typing:

   cd pub

6. Check to see where you are by typing:

   pwd (print working directory)

7. Now, to get a listing of the files in this particular directory, type:

   dir

8. Since you will be transferring a text (ascii) file, at the ftp prompt, type:

   ascii

9. At the ftp prompt, type:

   get inet.services.txt

   You will note that 35,163 bytes of data were transferred to your host computer in 1.2 seconds (!)

10. Now, we will quit using ftp. At the ftp prompt, type:

    quit

11. You should be back at your host prompt. At the host prompt, type:

    sx -a inet.services.txt

    This tells your host computer to:

    a. send the file using the XMODEM protocol **(sx)**

    b. send an ascii file **(-a)**

    c. send the file named (inet.services.txt)

12. When you press ENTER, you will be prompted to give your local XMODEM receive command.

If you are using Microsoft Works, you will type:

alt   transfer   Receive File

and you will be prompted for the name which you wish to give to the file which is being transferred (for example, a:inetserv.927)

For other communications programs, follow a similar process.

At that point, a Transfer Status box should appear on your screen, and you will be able to watch the file being transferred to your own disk. The file will, of course, be named inetserv.927 or whatever you chose to name it. It will be on the disk and in the directory where you placed it.

13. Once that process is complete, you should sign off from your host computer. Using your favorite word processor, you should be able to bring up the text file which is on your disk and format it to your liking.

Congratulations! You have successfully used the File Transfer Protocol, or FTP, as the experts say.

Brief Review

1. We signed onto a remote computer which had a file which we wanted.

2. We found the directory in which the file was contained.

3. We used the **get** command to bring the file from the mainframe computer to our host computer.

4. We quit using FTP, and returned to our host prompt.

5. At the host prompt, we issued the command:

sx -a inet.services.txt

If we are sending ascii files using the XMODEM command, then the first part of this command (sx -a) will remain constant. The name of the file will change, as you will see in the following FTP sessions.

Here is our actual session:

NOTE: *Some of the screens will flash by before you can read them. You can stop this by limiting your* **dir** *command. Do this by typing* **dir inet*** *The * is a wild card character that works in much the same way as it does when you use DOS commands on your PC. After the screens flash by, try this method.*

```
host% ftp
ftp> open csd4.csd.uwm.edu
Connected to csd4.csd.uwm.edu.
220 csd4.csd.uwm.edu FTP server (ULTRIX Version 4.1 Tue Mar 19
00:38:17 EST 1991 ) ready.
Name (csd4.csd.uwm.edu:dsachs): anonymous
331 Guest login ok, send ident as password.
Password:
230 Guest login ok, access restrictions apply.
ftp> cd pub
250 CWD command successful.
ftp> pwd
257 "/pub" is current directory.
ftp> dir
200 PORT command successful.
150 Opening data connection for /bin/ls (192.74.137.5,1495) (0
bytes).
total 4193
-rwxr-xr-x  1  925   -2    7171   Sep  27   03:04   .cache
-rw-r-r-    1  925   -2   20107   Sep  26   23:17   .cache+
-rwxr-xr-x  1  4494  -2    4267   Jun  15    1992   .tclrc
drwxr-xr-x  2  2196  -2     512   Sep  19   18:34   8051
drwxr-xr-x  2  1302  -2     512   Aug  26   11:25   Behavior
                                                   Analysis
drwxr-xr-x  2  4502  -2     512   Sep  14   12:44   Custard
drwxr-xr-x  2  4502   1     512   Jun  15   13:30   Laptop
drwxr-xr-x  2  4502  -2     512   Apr  11   22:07   Milwaukee
drwxr-xr-x  2  4502  -2     512   Sep   4   22:14   Misc
drwxr-xr-x  2  4502  -2     512   Jun  15   13:31   Palmtop
drwxr-xr-x  5  4502  -2    5632   Sep  24   17:41   Portables
drwxr-xr-x  2  4502  -2     512   Jan  13    1993   Psion
drwxr-xr-x  4  1302  -2     512   Sep  21   16:47   Psychology
drwxrwxrwx  2  4053  -2     512   Aug  21   00:17   albion
-rw----     1  507   -2  162153   Jul   7   14:55   alice29.txt
drwxr-xr-x  2  1091  -2     512   Mar   1    1993   aragorn
drwxr-xr-x  4  4586  -2     512   May   6   13:26   bashar
drwxr-xr-x  2  2687  -2     512   Apr  12   12:49   berri
-rw-r-r-    1  501   -2  491551   May   5    1992   bjove.tar.Z
```

Getting Things

```
drwxr-xr-x  2 381  9    -2      512   Jun 30  11:59  carinhas
-rwxr-xr-x  1 4494      -2     8220   Sep  6  11:22  choosenews2
drwxr-xr-x  8 2196      -2      512   Sep 20  02:17  compilers
drwxr-xr-x  2 1555      -2      512   Oct  1   1992  ctk
drwxr-xr-x  2 1777      -2      512   Sep 24  07:34  ctumey
drwxr-xr-x  2 501       -2      512   Jul  7  11:25  dave
-rwxr-xr-x  1 4494      -2    11316   Jun 11  00:47  dotplan.c
-rwxr-xr-x  1 4494      -2     1817   Jun 11  00:47  dotplan.doc
drwxr-xr-x  2 1323      -2      512   Apr 22  17:25  eab
-rwxr-xr-x  1 4494      -2     5031   Sep  6  11:22  fingerinfo
-rw-r—r—    1 501       -2     7701   Nov  5   1991  ftphelp
drwxr-xr-x  4 4433      -2      512   Jun 30  14:33  gwc
drwxr-xr-x 24 5304 5304       3072   Sep 27  07:51  high-audio
-rw-r—r—    1 501       -2   779819   Feb  5   1993  hp2xx-
                                                     3.1.0.tar.Z
drwxr-xr-x  2 5304      -2     1024   Sep  9  09:43  ibm-diag
-rwxr-xr-x  1 4494      -2    46180   Sep 15  09:41  inet.ser-
                                                     vices.html
-rwxr-xr-x  1 4494      -2    34503   Sep 15  09:41  inet.ser-
                                                     vices.txt
-rwxr-xr-x  1 4494      -2    24768   Sep 15  09:37  internetwork-
                                                     mail-guide
```

and so on...

```
226 Transfer complete.
ftp> ascii
200 Type set to A.
ftp> get inet.services.txt
200 PORT command successful.
150 Opening data connection for inet.services.txt
(192.74.137.5,1700)
(34503 bytes).
226 Transfer complete.
35163 bytes received in 1.2 seconds (29 Kbytes/s)
ftp> quit
221 Goodbye.
host% sx -a inet.services.txt
Sending inet.services.txt, 269 blocks: Give your local XMODEM
receive command now.
host%
```

FTP PRACTICE #5

In this session, we will connect with the Open Computing Facility at the University of California at Berkeley. We will use their remote computer to enable us to retrieve some poetry.

Note that we will use the cd (change directory) command to enable us to go into a directory (pub), then into a sub-directory (library), then a sub-sub-directory (poetry), then a sub-sub-sub-directory (Frost) in order to find the actual poems we want.

If this makes you nervous, or if you get lost, you can always type **cd** (change directory) and it will take you back to the beginning. Remember that you can always use **pwd** (print working directory) to see where you are.

Here are the directions to follow:

1. Login to your host computer.

2. At the host prompt, type:

   ftp

3. At the ftp prompt, type:

   open ocf.berkeley.edu

   and press ENTER.

4. When you are prompted for a name, type:

   anonymous

5. Your password should be your fully qualified user ID, such as:

   dsachs@world.std.com

6. At the ftp prompt, change to the pub directory by typing:

   cd pub

7. Check where you are by typing:

   pwd (print working directory)

8. Typing **dir** will show you the set of files that are contained within **pub**.

We want to change to the directory called Library. Type:

cd Library

NOTE: *Make sure that you type a capital L at the beginning of the word Library, or you will be told that such a file or directory does not exist.*

9.   Type **pwd** to check where you are.

10. Now, let's change to the Poetry directory. Type:

cd Poetry (be sure to use a capital P)

11. Use the **dir** command to show all of the files and directories which are contained within this sub-sub-sub-directory.

12. Use **cd** once more to change to the Frost sub-sub-sub-sub-directory.

13. Use **pwd** to show you exactly where you are.

14. Use dir to show you the files which are contained in this sub-sub-sub-sub directory.

15. Since we will be getting an ascii (text) file, enter the command **ascii** now.

16. We will use the get command to enable us to send the Road Not Taken to our host computer. Type:

get frost.Road_Not_Taken

NOTE: *This must be typed exactly as is, with the underline symbol between each of the words, and, in this case, frost is NOT capitalized!*

17. Now, quit using ftp, and return to your host computer. Just type **quit** at the ftp prompt.

18. At your host prompt, type the following:

sx -a frost.Road_Not_Taken

Once again, you will be prompted to give your local XMODEM receive command. Do so now. Once the file has been successfully transferred, you should return to your host prompt.

You can now leave your Internet host and, using the word processor of your choice, you can format Frost's poem.

Here is what our session looked like:

```
host% ftp
ftp> open ocf.berkeley.edu
Connected to ocf.berkeley.edu.
220 typhoon FTP server (Version 4.28 (Apollo) Mon Nov 19
05:18:43 PST 1990) ready.
Name (ocf.berkeley.edu:dsachs): anonymous
331 Guest login ok, send ident as password.
Password:
230 Guest login ok, access restrictions apply.
ftp> cd pub
250 CWD command successful.
ftp> dir
200 PORT command successful.
150 Opening ASCII mode data connection for /bin/ls (0 bytes).
total 55
-rwxr-xr-x    1  gopher   ftp    972  Sep  27  11:01  .cache
-rw-r-r—      1  gopher   ftp   5042  Sep  27  10:43  .cache+
-rw-r-r—      1  root     ftp   1212  Jul  15  12:52  00README
drwxr-xrwx+   2  davmou   ftp   3072  Sep  24  10:45  AnimeB
drwxr-srwx+   3  root     ftp   1024  Sep  26  12:27  Apollo
drwxrwsrwx+   2  root     ftp   1024  Sep  23  13:34  Cal_Graphics
drwxr-xrwx+   4  goldfarb ftp   1024  Sep  23  21:29  Comics
dr-xrwsrwx+   2  root     ftp   1024  Sep  23  15:14  FTP_Sites
drwxrwxrwx+   3  root     ftp   1024  Sep  24  00:38  Kid_Dynamo
drwxr-srwx+  21  root     ftp   1024  Sep  23  12:29  Library
-rw-r-r—      1  root     ftp   9284  Apr  27  12:09  NFL_Draft
dr-xrwsrwx+   2  root     ftp   4096  Jul   1  07:43  RFCs
drwxr-xrwx+   5  gwh      ftp   1024  Sep  24  10:34  Space
drwxr-xrwx+   4  gwh      ftp   1024  Sep  26  16:43  Traveller
dr-xrwsrwx+   2  root     ftp   1024  Sep  24  18:24  Usenet_
                                                      Olympics
drwxr-xrwx+   2  mehlhaff ftp   1024  Sep  24  18:46  amiga
dr-xr-xrwx+   2  games    ftp   1024  Sep  24  10:35  games
drwxr-xrwx+   2  goldfarb ftp   1024  Sep  23  21:29  gunkldunk
d-wx-wsrwx+   2  root     ftp   1024  Jul  28  09:2   incoming
-rw-r-r—      1  alanc    ftp   6087  Aug  11  15:04  mac-speech-
                                                      demo.sit.hqx
drwxr-xrwx+   5  mehlhaff ftp   7168  Sep  24  22:47  netrek
drwxrwxrwx+   3  rsr      ftp   4096  Sep  24  07:48  purity
226 Transfer complete.
ftp> cd Library
250 CWD command successful.
ftp> pwd
```

257 "//typhoon/usr/local/ftp/pub/Library" is current
directory.
ftp> **cd Poetry**
250 CWD command successful.
ftp> **pwd**
257 "//typhoon/usr/local/ftp/pub/Library/Poetry" is current
directory.
ftp> **dir**
200 PORT command successful.
150 Opening ASCII mode data connection for /bin/ls (0 bytes).
total 104

```
-rwxr-xr-x   1  root    ftp  1352   Jul 27  1992   .cache
-rw-r—r—    1  gopher  ftp  8947   Sep 25  15:57  .cache+
-rw-r—r—    1  root    ftp  5271   Mar  8  1992   A_Visit_From_
                                                  St._Nicholas

drwxr-xr-x   2  root    ftp  1024   Apr 14  16:29  Aiken
-rw-r—r—    1  psb     ftp  1786   Feb 22  1990   An_die_Freude.
                                                  tex
drwxr-xr-x   2  root    ftp  1024   Apr 14  16:28  Auden
drwxr-xr-x   2  root    ftp  1024   Apr 14  16:30  Bronte
drwxr-xr-x   2  root    ftp  1024   Apr 14  16:42  Burns
drwxr-xr-x   2  root    ftp  1024   Apr 14  16:30  Byron
-rw-r—r—    1  root    ftp 32652   Mar  8  1992   Carroll.Hunting
                                                  _of_the_Snark
drwxr-xr-x   2  root    ftp  4096   Apr 20  23:56  EECummings
drwxr-xr-x   2  root    ftp  1024   Apr 14  16:26  Eliot
drwxr-xr-x   2  root    ftp  1024   Apr 14  16:31  Emerson
drwxr-xr-x   2  root    ftp  1024   Apr 14  16:30  Feng_Meng-lung
drwxr-xr-x   2  root    ftp  1024   Apr 14  16:29  Frost
drwxr-xr-x   2  root    ftp  4096   Apr 19  11:21  Graves
```

and so on. . . .

226 Transfer complete.
ftp> **cd Frost**
250 CWD command successful.
ftp> **pwd**
257 "//typhoon/usr/local/ftp/pub/Library/Poetry/Frost" is
current directory.
ftp> **dir**
200 PORT command successful.
150 Opening ASCII mode data connection for /bin/ls (0 bytes).
total 5

```
-rw-r—r—    1  lizi   ocf   277   Mar 13  1993   frost.Fire
                                                 _and_Ice
```

-rw-r—r—	1	psb	ftp	312	Feb 2	1990	frost.Iota _Subscript
-rw-r—r—	1	lizi	ocf	636	Apr 21	00:33	frost.Once_by _the_Pacific
-rw-r—r—	**1**	**psb**	**ftp**	**761**	**Oct 16**	**1989**	**frost.Road _Not_Taken**
-rw-r—r—	1	psb	ftp	589	Oct 16	1989	frost.Snowy _Evening

```
226 Transfer complete.
ftp> ascii
200 Type set to A.
ftp> get frost.Road_Not_Taken
200 PORT command successful.
150 Opening ASCII mode data connection for
frost.Road_Not_Taken (761 bytes). 226 Transfer complete.
788 bytes received in 0.05 seconds (15 Kbytes/s)
ftp> quit
221 Goodbye.
host% sx -a frost.Road_Not_Taken
Sending frost.Road_Not_Taken, 5 blocks: Give your local XMODEM
receive command
now.

host% exit
```

FTP PRACTICE #6

In this sixth FTP practice session, we will use FTP so that we may retrieve a copy of President Clinton's Inaugural Speech. As we mentioned in FTP Practice #2, there is something known as the Project Gutenberg archives at Illinois Benedictine College. In the process of retrieving this file, you will also have a chance to learn a bit more about Project Gutenberg, since that information precedes the actual text of the Inaugural Address.

We will follow the procedures which we have used in the preceding examples. Therefore, we will provide the directions to do this, without too much commentary. By now, you should be an old hand at this!

1. At your host prompt, type:

    ftp

    and press **ENTER.**

2. At the **ftp** prompt, type:

   open mrcnext.cso.uiuc.edu

3. When prompted for a name, type:

   anonymous

4. Type your user ID as the password (for example, dsachs@world.std.com)

5. Change to the pub directory, by typing:

   cd pub

6. Type **dir** to see the files and directories which are included in this directory.

7. Change to the **etext** directory by typing:

   cd etext

8. Type **dir** to see the files that are included in this sub-directory.

9. Change to the **etext93** directory by typing:

   cd etext93

10. Typing **pwd** will show you exactly where you are.

11. Now, type **dir** to see the files which are included in this sub-sub-directory

12. Since we will be getting an ascii (text) file, type:

    ascii

    at your ftp prompt.

13. We will get the file called **clinton3.txt** . Type:

    get clinton3.txt

    All 19,505 bytes of the inaugural speech, plus some information about Project Gutenberg, will be sent to your host computer in .64 seconds (!)

14. Leave ftp and return to your host prompt — type **quit** to do this.

15. At your host prompt, type the following to send the file your own computer:

    sx -a clinton3.txt

You will be prompted to give your local XMODEM receive command, as before.

Here is what resulted when we followed the above commands:

```
host% open mrcnext.cso.uiuc.edu
Connected to mrcnext.cso.uiuc.edu.
220 mrcnext.cso.uiuc.edu FTP server (Version 5.1 (NeXT 1.0)
Tue Jul 21, 1992)
ready.
Name (mrcnext.cso.uiuc.edu:dsachs): anonymous
331 Guest login ok, send ident as password.
Password:
230 Guest login ok, access restrictions apply.
Remote system type is UNIX.
Using binary mode to transfer files.
ftp> cd pub
250 CWD command successful.
ftp> dir
200 PORT command successful.
150 Opening ASCII mode data connection for /bin/ls.
total 7
drwxr-xr-x   2  root   wheel   1024  Jul 27 1999   .NeXT
drwxrwxrwt  63  root   wheel   2048  Mar 12 16:56  .NextTrash
drwxr-xr-x   8  187    wheel   1024  Aug  4 2001   cache
drwxr-xr-x   9  24     wheel   1024  Mar 31 09:03  etext
drwxr-x—     4  24     wheel   1024  Apr  2 2001   hart
drwxrwxr-x   8  root   wheel   1024  Nov 13 16:12  local
226 Transfer complete.
ftp> cd etext
250 CWD command successful.
ftp> dir
200 PORT command successful.
150 Opening ASCII mode data connection for /bin/ls.
total 53
-rw-r—r—    1  24  wheel  13777  Mar 31 09:03  0INDEX.GUT
-rw-r—r—    1  24  wheel    300  Sep 28 2000   ETEXT92
-rw-r—r—    1  24  wheel   9214  Jul 19 1998   LIST.COM
-rw-r—r—    1  24  wheel   4420  Jun  3 2000   NEWUSER.GUT
drwxr-xr-x   3  24  wheel   1024  Mar 23 17:58  articles
drwxr-xr-x   3  24  wheel   2048  Mar 30 14:40  etext91
drwxr-xr-x   3  24  wheel   2048  Mar 30 14:40  etext92
drwxr-xr-x   2  24  wheel   2048  Mar 28 18:10  etext93
drwxr-xr-x   2  24  wheel   1024  Feb  5 15:37  freenet
-rw-r—r—    1  24  wheel  14005  Sep  2 2001   gutmar3.3
```

```
drwx-wx—    2  24  wheel    1024  Sep 24  2000  incoming
drwxr-xr-x  2  24  wheel    1024  Apr 27  2000  usonly
226 Transfer complete.
ftp> cd etext93
250 CWD command successful.
ftp> pwd
257 "/pub/etext/etext93" is current directory.
ftp> dir
200 PORT command successful.
150 Opening ASCII mode data connection for /bin/ls.
total 29754
-rw-r-r—    1  24  wheel1166473  Sep  2  2001  2sqrt10.txt
-rw-r-r—    1  24  wheel 552131  Sep  2  2001  2sqrt10.zip
-rw-r-r—    1  24  wheel 247391  Dec 31 20:13  32pri10.txt
-rw-r-r—    1  24  wheel 124130  Dec 31 20:13  32pri10.zip
-rw-r-r—    1  24  wheel 637842  Mar  5 01:59  7gabl10.txt
-rw-r-r—    1  24  wheel 276240  Mar  5 02:00  7gabl10.zip
-rw-r-r—    1  24  wheel  38818  Oct  2 23:39  alad10.txt
-rw-r-r—    1  24  wheel  16197  Oct  2 23:05  alad10.zip
-rw-r-r—    1  24  wheel 275975  Jan  8 13:19  badge10.txt
-rw-r-r—    1  24  wheel 116147  Jan  8 13:19  badge10.zip
-rw-r-r—    1  24  wheel 494868  Dec  4 15:01  blexp10.txt
-rw-r-r—    1  24  wheel 197171  Dec  4 15:02  blexp10.zip
-rw-r-r—    1  24  wheel  61768  Jan  1 23:36  civil10.txt
-rw-r-r—    1  24  wheel  26407  Jan  1 23:37  civil10.zip
-rw-r-r—    1  24  wheel  19281  Jul 26  2001  clinton1.txt
-rw-r-r—    1  24  wheel  19897  Jul 26  2001  clinton2.txt
-rw-r-r—    1  24  wheel  19505  Jul 26  2001  clinton3.txt
-rw-r-r—    1  24  wheel 141533  Sep 30  2001  dcart10.txt
-rw-r-r—    1  24  wheel  55077  Sep 30  2001  dcart10.zip

and so on...

226 Transfer complete.
ftp> ascii
200 Type set to A.
ftp> get clinton3.txt
200 PORT Command successful
150 Opening BINARY mode data connection for clinton3.txt
(19505 bytes).
226 Transfer compete.
19505 bytes received in 0.64 seconds (30 Kbytes/s)
ftp> quit
221 Goodbye.
host% sx -a clinton3.txt
```

```
Sending clinton3.txt, 152 blocks: Give your local XMODEM
receive command now.

host% exit
host% logout
```

Additional Thoughts

Knowing how to use FTP comfortably is a particularly valuable component of using the Internet. In this session, we have attempted to provide you with a good "running start" in that direction.

However, you should be aware that there is a great deal which we did not cover here. Although transferring ASCII files is a relatively straight forward process, there is another type of file, known as BINARY (or IMAGE) which is somewhat more complicated to transfer. Typically, software programs are BINARY files; that is, they contain computer code which must be transferred exactly from one computer to another. They cannot be read by a word processor; in fact, should you try to do so, they will appear as gibberish on your screen.

In addition, they are specific to operating systems. That is, if they are for DOS, they will not run properly on MacIntosh computers.

In addition, and what makes this conversation so challenging, is that many BINARY files are extremely large. Consequently, people have figured out ways to compress them, so that they might be smaller, and so that they might be quicker to transfer from one computer to another. However, there are quite a few different ways to compress BINARY files, and it would take far more time and space than we have in this book to teach you how to do that effectively.

Should you wish to learn more about this topic, feel free to learn about it in some of the books which are listed in Appendix A. In particular, Chapter 8 of the Internet Passport, is quite helpful.

Finding FTP Sources

In Appendix A, we list a number of excellent books about the Internet.

Each lists many places that are (or were at the time of printing) open to "anonymous" FTP. An extremely wide range of resources is available, including documents, graphics, and software programs.

Getting Things

Warning: Be cautious of downloading programs. If you are going to do that, be sure that you are able to check them for viruses with a good (and current) virus checking program. Much of the software available by FTP is "as is, whereis" in terms of security.

Session Eight will provide you with some indications about additional places to look with FTP.

Happy Hunting!

■ ■ Session Seven Vocabulary and Command Summary

file transfer protocol .... the process that is used to transfer files from a mainframe computer to your host computer

ftp .... the abbreviation and commandfor file transfer protocol

"anonymous" file
transfer protocol .... the convention that permits Internet users to logon to remote host computers

pwd .... print working directory

cd .... change directory

dir .... the command that will list all of the files and directories

ascii .... the acronym that indicates that a file is a text file

binary .... the word that indicates that the file is, most likely, a program or a graphic

close .... the word that is used to end the connection with the remote host

quit .... the command that will take you out of FTP and back to your host prompt

more .... the command that will permit you to read one screen of an ascii (text) file at a time

readme .... often used as the name of a file that will provide the user with information about other files and directories on the system

pub .... often used as the name of the directory that contains files that are available to the public

cat .... the command that will "print" a file in a continuous stream onto your monitor — may be used in conjunction with the name of a program while your "capture" software is turned on

sx .... send file using XMODEM protocol

–a .... used to indicate an ASCII file

Getting Things

SESSION EIGHT

Finding Things

As you might imagine, with a resource as large as the Internet, just finding the information or software or resources you need can be quite challenging. Fortunately, a number of industrious souls have begun to develop a set of tools that will enable you to find what you are looking for in a relatively comfortable and productive way. We will focus on a number of these tools in this session.

In particular, we will focus on four tools:

1. **Gopher** – a utility that permits you to "go fer" information in lots of places;

2. **Archie** – a utility that permits you to find files that you can then "send" to your own computer;

3. **WAIS** – a Wide Area Information Server utility that will permit you to look for information on a variety of hosts without having to be concerned with where the information is located, or how to get to it;

4. **World Wide Web (W3)** – A system that is being developed to provide access to documents wherever they are located.

Each one of these serves a particular purpose. And mastery of all four of them, can directly enhance your ability to use the Internet more effectively. We will provide you with some sample sessions for each one, so that you might become familiar with them. More detailed information may be found in several of the sources which are listed in Appendix A.

Things change rapidly on the Internet. The following examples may not always work as we show them. If this happens, try to find what will allow you to proceed. You may need to contact your systems administrator.

Section I: What the Gopher Can Do For You

The Internet Gopher was designed to help you to find a variety of resources on the Internet without your having to learn where they are or how to retrieve them. The utility was developed by the Computer and Information Services Department of the University of Minnesota. Using a variety of "gopher servers" will enable you to have access to computer documentation, phone books, libraries, news, weather, humor, recipes, etc. Before trying to find anything in particular, let's just logon and see what this is all about.

GOPHER PRACTICE #1

Directions

1. Logon to your host computer.

2. Type the following command:

    gopher

If your host does not respond, it does not have a "gopher client." Contact your administrator.

Here is a sample screen to show you what happens when we first use gopher.

```
host% gopher

Retrieving Directory-/|\-/|\-/|\Internet Gopher+ Information
Client v1.2beta5

Root gopher server: gopher2.tc.umn.edu

   ->    1.     Information About Gopher/
         2.     Computer Information/
         3.     Internet file server (ftp) sites/
         4.     Fun & Games/
         5.     Libraries/
         6.     Mailing Lists/
         7.     News/
         8.     Other Gopher and Information Servers/
         9.     Phone Books/
         10.    Search Gopher Titles at the University of Minnesota
                 <?>
         11.    Search lots of places at the U of M <?>
```

```
12.    UofM Campus Information
Press ? for Help, q to Quit, u to go up a menu
Page:1/1
```

Commentary

Notice all of the various choices that you may make. To select any one of them, just use your up or down arrow keys to move the "pointer" up or down. Once you have found your desired selection, just press **ENTER**. Or you may just type the number of your selection and then press **ENTER**. At the moment, we wish to leave this menu. So,

1. Press **q** for Quit.

2. You should be back at your host prompt.

GOPHER PRACTICE #2

Overview

In this second Gopher Practice, we will use the Internet and Gopher to help us to acquire current information about travel abroad. It happens that one of the authors is planning to take a trip to India with several colleagues in the near future. Here is the information that Gopher is able to provide:

Directions

1. Logon to your host computer.

2. Type the following command:

   gopher

   You will see the same screens as in Gopher Session #1. However, this time we will make some choices:

3. Choose **5** for Libraries, and press **ENTER**.

NOTE: *Libraries may be at a different number on your system.*

4. Choose **7** for Reference Works, and press **ENTER**.

5. Choose **12** for US-State-Department-Travel-Advisories, and press **ENTER**.

6. Choose **2** for Current Advisories, and press **ENTER**.

7. Press the **SPACE BAR** four times, until you come to the screen with India (choice #88) on it.

8. Select **88**, and press **ENTER**.

Here is the first part of the information that we received, when we followed the directions above:

```
ReceivingInformation...     Receiving file/
STATE DEPARTMENT TRAVEL INFORMATION - India
============================================================
U.S. DEPARTMENT OF STATE
Office of the Assistant Secretary / Spokesman

For Immediate Release
March 31, 1993

STATEMENT BY RICHARD BOUCHER, SPOKESMAN

Cancellation of Public Announcement - India

        In a March 15 public announcement on India, the
Department of State encouraged U.S. citizens to temporarily
defer travel to New Delhi because of information that
suggested there was a heightened threat of terrorism. While it
is possible that terrorist events may occur for which the
Department has no forewarning, the Department no longer
believes it is necessary to defer travel to New Delhi. For
current information, travelers may refer to the Consular
Information Sheet on India by contacting the Citizens
Emergency Center in the Department of State at 202-647-5225.

-Less- (1%) [Press space bar to continue, q to quit]
------------------------------------------------------

STATE DEPARTMENT TRAVEL INFORMATION - India
============================================================
India - Consular Information Sheet
March 30, 1993

Country Description: India is a developing democratic
republic. Tourist facilities are widely available in the major
population centers and main tourist areas. Entry
```

```
Requirements: For entry into India for touring or business, a
passport and visa (which must be obtained in advance) are
required. Evidence of yellow fever immunization is needed if
the traveler is arriving from an infected area. For further
entry information, the traveler can contact the Embassy of
India at 2536 Massachusetts Avenue N.W., Washington, D.C.
20008, telephone (202) 939-9839 or 939-9850. There are Indian
consulates general in Chicago, New York and San Francisco.

-Less- (2%) [Press space bar to continue, q to quit]
```

Commentary

We could choose to continue to read this information on the screen. However, the file is quite long, and reading it all on the computer screen could take time and become quite tedious.

However, there is a way to have the entire file "mailed" to us. Here is how to do so:

1. Choose **q** for quit.

2. You will receive a prompt which says:

   Press <RETURN> to continue, <m> to mail:

3. Type **m** for mail.

4. Type your Internet mail id into the box which is labelled:

   Mail current document to:

5. Press **ENTER** when you are done.

6. The file will be mailed to your Internet address, where you may retrieve it at your convenience. (You might be interested to know that in this particular case, the file is 75,342 bytes of information!)

7. If you are done, press **q** to Quit Gopher.

GOPHER CONCLUSION

As you have already seen, the Internet contains a vast array of information. Gopher is a relatively quick, menu-driven way to find some of it. You can't make very many costly mistakes with it, the menu system is very straightforward, and time seems to fly very quickly when one uses Gopher. Enjoy!

Section II: Archie

Archie was developed at the McGill University School of Computer Science. This on-line file-finding utility can be of utmost value, once you know a little bit about how it works and what it can do for you. Typically, those who use it are interested in finding information about particular topics. More precisely, to use Archie effectively is a two-part process.

Part 1   –   Finding files of information about particular topics;

Part 2   –   Transporting those files from wherever they are onto your own computer.

You have learned about the transporting of files (also known as the File Transfer Protocol) in Session #7. Here, we will show you how to find the information that you might wish to transport. We will present this process in a series of small steps. Follow along!

ARCHIE PRACTICE #1

For our first Archie Practice, we would like to find out all of the computers that will provide us with the ability to use Archie. To do this, following the directions below:

Directions:

1.   At your host prompt, type the following:

archie -L   (Be sure to use a CAPITAL L)

Here is what you will see:

```
Known archie servers:
        archie.ans.net (USA [NY])
        archie.rutgers.edu (USA [NJ])
        archie.sura.net (USA [MD])
        archie.unl.edu (USA [NE])
        archie.mcgill.ca (Canada)
        archie.funet.fi (Finland/Mainland Europe)
        archie.au (Australia)
```

```
         archie.doc.ic.ac.uk (Great Britain/Ireland)
         archie.wide.ad.jp (Japan)
         archie.ncu.edu.tw (Taiwan)
  *archie.sura.net is the default Archie server.
  * For the most up-to-date list, write to an Archie server and
  give it the command 'servers'.
```

Now that we know where Archie "file servers" may be found, we can use this information for our next session. We would like to have Archie tell us more about itself. Here is how to do so:

ARCHIE PRACTICE #2

Directions

1. Type the following:

   telnet archie.ans.net

2. At the login prompt, type: **archie**

3. At the archie prompt, type: **help**

4. At the help prompt, type: **about**

Here is what should occur:

```
host% telnet archie.ans.net
Trying 147.225.1.10...
Connected to forum.ans.net.
Escape character is '^]'.

AIX telnet (forum.ans.net)

IBM AIX Version 3 for RISC System/6000
(C) Copyrights by IBM and by others 1982, 1991.
login: archie *-------------------------------------------*
  | — The default search method is set to "exact".          |
  | — Type "help set search" for more details.              |
  |                                                         |
  | Other Servers:                                          |
  | archie.unl.edu        129.93.1.14                       |
  | archie.sura.net       128.167.254.194                   |
  | archie.rutgers.edu    128.6.18.15                       |
```

```
|                                                       |
| archie.au          139.130.4.6                        |
| archie.funet.fi    128.214.6.100                      |
| archie.ncu.edu.tw  140.115.19.24                      |
| archie.doc.ic.ac.uk  146.169.11.3                     |
| archie.sogang.ac.kr  163.239.1.11                     |
|                                                       |
| o Questions/comments to archie-admin@ans.net, site    |
| add/ delete                                           |
| requests to archie-updates@bunyip.com                 |
|                                                       |
| Client software is available on ftp.ans.net:/pub/archie |
| / clients;                                            |
| documentation in /pub/archie/doc.                     |
*_____-----------------------------------*
# term set to vt100 24 80
```

archie> **help**   **NOTE: HERE IS WHERE WE TYPED help**

Help gives you information about various topics, including all the commands that are available and how to use them. Telling archie about your terminal type and size (via the "term" variable) and to use the pager (via the "pager" variable) is not necessary to use help, but provides a somewhat nicer interface.

Currently, the available help topics are:

```
    about    -   a blurb about archie
    bugs     -   known bugs and undesirable features
    bye      -   same as "quit"
    email    -   how to contact the archie email interface
    exit     -   same as "quit"
    help     -   this message
    list     -   list the sites in the archie database
    mail     -   mail output to a user
    nopager  -   *** use 'unset pager' instead
    prog     -   search the database for a file
    quit     -   exit archie
    set      -   set a variable
    show     -   display the value of a variable
    site     -   list the files at an archive site
    term     -   *** use 'set term ...' instead
    unset    -   unset a variable
    whatis   -   search for keyword in the software description
                 database
```

For information on one of these topics type:
  help <topic>

A '?' at the help prompt will list the available sub-topics.

Help topics available:
about	bugs	bye	email
list	mail	nopager	pager
prog	regex	set	show
site	term	unset	whatis

Help topic? **about**   **NOTE: HERE IS WHERE WE TYPED   about**

Archie: the McGill School of Computer Science Archive Server
Listing Service

Given the number of hosts being used as archive sites
nowadays, there can be great difficulty in finding needed
software in a distributed environment. You may know that the
software that you need is out there, but it can sometimes be
difficult to find. The School of Computer Science at McGill
University has one solution to the problem - "archie".
Archie is a pair of software tools: the first maintains a list
of about 600 Internet ftp archive sites. Each night software
executes an anonymous ftp to a subset of these sites and
fetches a recursive directory listing of each, which it stores
in a database. We hit about 1/30th of the list each time, so
each site gets updated about once a month, hopefully balancing
timely updates against unnecessary network load. The "raw"
listings are stored in compressed form on quiche.cs.mcgill.ca
(132.206.2.3), where they are made available via anonymous ftp
in the directory ~ftp/archie/listings. Listings can also be
obtained at ftp.ans.net (147.225.1.2) in the directory ~ftp/
pub/archie/listings.

Press return for more:

The second tool is the interesting one as far as the users are
concerned. It consists of a program running on a dummy user
code that allows outsiders to log onto the archive server host
to query the database. This is in fact the program we call
Archie.

Users can ask archie to search for specific name strings. For
example, "prog kcl" would find all occurrences of the string

"kcl" and tell you which hosts have entries with this string, the size of the program, its last modification date and where it can be found on the host along with some other useful information. In this example, you could thus find those archive sites that are storing Kyoto Common Lisp. With one central database for all the archive sites we know about, archie greatly speeds the task of finding a specific program on the net.

Complete anonymous ftp listings of the various sites that we keep in the database may be obtained via the 'site' command and for a list of the sites which we keep track of, see the 'list' command.

Archie also maintains a 'Software Description Database' which consists of the names and descriptions of various software packages, documents and datasets that are kept on anonymous ftp archive sites all around the Internet. The 'whatis' command allows you to search this database.

Send comments, bug reports etc to
        archie-group@cs.mcgill.ca

If you have a favourite anonymous ftp site that archie doesn't seem to maintain, or if you have additions or corrections to the Software Description database, send mail to

        archie-admin@cs.mcgill.ca
        archie-admin@ans.net

Archie was written and is maintained by Alan Emtage (bajan@cs.mcgill.ca) and Bill Heelan (wheelan@cs.mcgill.ca). Peter Deutsch (peterd@cc.mcgill.ca) provided (and continues to provide) ideas and inspiration.

Now that you know a bit about archie, let's see how it works.

ARCHIE PRACTICE #3

In this session, we would like to find out where files of lyrics for songs are stored. You will notice that there are 50 (!) computer sites that hold those files. Here are the directions and the beginning screen shot of what we found:

1.   Logon to your internet host.

2. At the host prompt, type the following:

   telnet archie.ans.net

3. At the login prompt, type: **archie**

4. At the archie prompt, type: **prog lyrics**
   (NOTE: The word prog just tells archie to use its search program.)

Here is the first part of what we found when we did the search:

```
archie> prog lyrics

# matches / % database searched: 0 /100%  1  2  3  4  5  6
      7  8  9  10  11  12  13  14  15  16  17  18 19 20 21 22 23
      24 25 26 27 28  29  30  31  32  33  34  35  36  37  38  39
      40  41  42  43  44  45  46  47  48  49  50  50 / 50 /100%

Host uxc.cso.uiuc.edu  (128.174.5.50)
Last updated 07:02 26 Jun 1993

    Location: /pub/KateBush
       DIRECTORY rwxr-xr-x      512 Jul  7 1989   lyrics

Host unix.hensa.ac.uk  (129.12.21.7)
Last updated 05:00 26 Jun 1993

    Location: /pub/uunet/usenet/rec.music.gaffa/kb
       DIRECTORY rwxr-xr-x     1024 Aug 19 1992   lyrics

Host stein2.u.washington.edu  (140.142.56.2)
Last updated 14:35 25 Jun 1993

    Location: /pub/user-supported/ICSC
       FILE      rw-r—r—   129811 Nov  5 1992   lyrics

Host syrinx.umd.edu  (129.2.8.114)
Last updated 07:37 23 Jun 1993

    Location: /rush
       DIRECTORY rwxrwxr-x      512 Apr  3 15:26   lyrics
    Location: /floyd
       DIRECTORY rwxr-xr-x     1024 Jan  9 15:20   lyrics

Host plaza.aarnet.edu.au  (139.130.4.6)
```

```
Last updated 17:36 21 Jun 1993

   Location: /graphics/gif/l
       FILE      r—r—r—    81735  Feb 10 02:43   lyrics

Host ftp.uu.net  (192.48.96.9)
Last updated 08:06  8 Jun 1993

   Location: /usenet/rec.music.gaffa/kb
       DIRECTORY rwxr-xr-x    1024  Aug 17  1992   lyrics
```

ARCHIE CONCLUSION

There is lots more to learn about Archie, as you might imagine. Additional information may be found in the sources which we have included in Appendix A. However, as a beginning Archie user, you now know enough to get started. The format will always be the same:

1. At your host prompt, sign onto Archie. We used the command

    telnet archie.ans.net

    You might prefer to use another Archie server.

2. Once you are at the "Archie prompt," enter the command prog (for program) followed by a space and the character string for which you are looking (for example, lyrics, education, or computers).

3. Save the information that appears, either on a disk or on paper, so that you might use file transfer protocol to retrieve the indicated files. (FTP was explained in Session Seven.)

Section III: Wide Area Information Server (WAIS)

WAIS (pronounced "ways") was developed by Thinking Machines Corp. of Cambridge, Massachusetts, in collaboration with Dow Jones & Co., Apple Computer, and KPMG Peat Marwick. Put simply, this software permits the user to search and retrieve information from databases that are located throughout the Internet. By using a single interface, the user has access to local and distant databases, while having to learn only one consistent method.

As you have seen earlier with Gopher, there will be one simple command to learn, and then from that point on your search will be menu driven. Here is how it works:

WAIS PRACTICE #1

Directions

1. Logon to your host computer.

2. At your Internet prompt, type the following:

     telnet quake.think.com

3. Login as **"wais"**

4. Enter your internet id (i.e. dsachs@world.std.com)

5. Press **ENTER** at TERM = (vt100)

In the following example, we decided to see what President Clinton has said about Bosnia. Here is what occurred:

```
host% telnet quake.think.com
Trying 192.31.181.1...
Connected to quake.think.com.
Escape character is '^]'.

SunOS UNIX (quake)

login: wais
Last login: Sat Jun 26 18:26:11 from world.std.com

SunOS Release 4.1.1 (QUAKE) #3: Tue Jul 7 11:09:01 PDT 1992

Welcome to swais.

Please type user identifier (optional, i.e. user@host):
dsachs@world.std.com

TERM = (vt100)

Starting swais (this may take a little while)...
```

Finding Things

```
SWAIS                           Source Selection

Sources: 452
```

NOTE: IN THIS SECTION, WE ARE GIVEN A LISTING OF AVAILABLE SOURCES

```
  #     Server                        Source
Cost
001:            [archie.au]   aarnet-resource-guide     Free
002:       [munin.ub2.lu.se]  academic_email_conf       Free
003: [wraith.cs.uow.edu.au]   acronyms                  Free
004:       [archive.orst.edu] aeronautics               Free
005: [ftp.cs.colorado.edu]    aftp-cs-colorado-edu      Free
006: [nostromo.oes.orst.ed]   agricultural-market-news  Free
007:       [archive.orst.edu] alt.drugs                 Free
008:       [wais.oit.unc.edu] alt.gopher                Free
009: [sun-wais.oit.unc.edu]   alt.sys.sun               Free
010:       [wais.oit.unc.edu] alt.wais                  Free
011: [alfred.ccs.carleton.]   amiga-slip                Free
012:       [munin.ub2.lu.se]  amiga_fish_contents       Free
013:   [coombs.anu.edu.au]    ANU Aboriginal-Studies    $0.00
014:   [coombs.anu.edu.au]    ANU-Asian-Religions       $0.00
015:   [coombs.anu.edu.au]    ANU-CAUT-Projects         $0.00
016:   [coombs.anu.edu.au]    ANU-Coombspapers-Index    $0.00
017:   [coombs.anu.edu.au]    ANU-Local-Waiservers      $0.00
018:   [coombs.anu.edu.au]    ANU-SSDA-Catalogues       $0.00

Keywords:

001:    [          archie.au] aarnet-resource-guide
Free<space> selects, w for keywords, arrows move, <return>
searches, q quits, or ?SWAIS   Source Selection Help Page: 1
```

NOTE: IN THIS SECTION, WHEN WE PRESSED ?, WE RECEIVED HELP

```
j, down arrow, ^N          Move Down one source
k, up arrow, ^P            Move Up one source
J, ^V, ^D                  Move Down one screen
K, <esc> v, ^U             Move Up one screen
###                        Position to source number ##
/sss                       Search for source sss
<space>, <period>          Select current source
=                          Deselect all sources
v, <comma>                 View current source info
<ret>                      Perform search
```

s	Select new sources (refresh sources list)
w	Select new keywords
X, -	Remove current source permanently
o	Set and show swais options
h, ?	Show this help display
H	Display program history
q	Leave this program

NOTE: USING THE DOWN ARROW KEY, WE MOVED THROUGH A SERIES OF SOURCES UNTIL WE CAME TO NUMBER 87, WHICH CONTAINS PRESIDENT CLINTON'S SPEECHES

079	wais.concert.net]	cert-advisories
080	wais.concert.net]	cert-clippings
081	wais.cic.net]	cica-win3
082	cicg-communication.g]	cicg.bibliotheque
083	wais.cic.net]	cicnet-directory-of servers
084		cicnet-resource-guide
085	wais.cic.net]	cicnet-wais-servers
086		cissites
087	sunsite	clinton-speeches
088	quake.think.com]	CM-applications
089	cmns-moon.think.com]	CM-fortran-manual

NOTE: AT THIS POINT, WE ENTERED THE KEYWORDS bosnia and Bosnia

Enter keywords with spaces between them; <return> to search; ^C to cancel Keywords:

Keywords: bosnia Bosnia

Searching clinton-speechess.src... Initializing connection...Found 27 items.
SWAIS   Search Results   Items: 27
  # Score Source   Title Lines
001: [1000] (clinton-speeche)   FOREIGN POLICY:Speech by Al Go 575
002: [389] (clinton-speeche)   BUSH-QUAYLE IRAQ POLICY: Analys 181
003: [333] (clinton-speeche)   IRAQ/IRAN : Speech-Oshkosh,WI 198
004: [305] (clinton-speeche)   IRAN/IRAQ: Statement -9/24/92 145
005: [291] (clinton-speeche)   IRAQ/IRAN:Press Release-10/1 78

```
006: [ 180] (clinton-speeche)    ARMS-FOR-HOSTAGES: Statement
                                  -56
007: [ 152] (clinton-speeche)    VP DEBATE ANALYSIS:
                                  Encyclopedi  697
008: [ 139] (clinton-speeche)    VARIOUS TOPICS: Analysis of
                                  VP    282
009: [ 139] (clinton-speeche)    FOREIGN AFFAIRS: Speech-Los A
                                  466
010: [ 125] (clinton-speeche)    CHARACTER : Press Release
                                  10/  83
011: [ 111] (clinton-speeche)    APRIL GLASPIE CABLES: Press
                                  Rel    52
012: [  97] (clinton-speeche)    STATEGATE: Press Release -10
                                  1   157
013: [  97] (clinton-speeche)    MILITARY/FOREIGN AFFAIRS:
                                  "New    696
014: [  97] (clinton-speeche)    FOREIGN POLICY: Speech
                                  Washin   691
015: [  97] (clinton-speeche)    ISRAEL: Position Paper 201
016: [  83] (clinton-speeche)    VARIOUS TOPICS: Talking
                                  Points     73
017: [  83] (clinton-speeche)    VARIOUS TOPICS: Analysis of
                                  Deb   183
018: [  83] (clinton-speeche)    DEBATE 2: Further Analysis
                                  10   272
019: [  69] (clinton-speeche)    NATIONAL SECURITY: Position
                                  Pap   507
020      6                       ISRAEL: Speech - Washington,
                                  DC   43
021      69                      AL GORE: Biography 57
022      69                      INTERNATIONAL AFFAIRS:
                                  Position   156
023      69                      FOREIGN AFFAIRS: Statement
                                  10    63
024      69                      DEBATE: Statement - 10/19/92
                                  40
025      69                      ISRAEL: Statement-8/12/92 49
026      6                       BOSNIA: Statement-7/26/92 98
027      6                       ARMS CONTROL: Position Paper
                                  115
```

NOTE: WE SELECTED NUMBER 26, AND RETRIEVED THE SPEECH ON BOSNIA FROM 7/26/92

```
Retrieving: BOSNIA: Statement - 7/26/92 Getting " BOSNIA:
Statement - 7/26/92" from clinton-speechess.src... BOSNIA:
```

```
Statement - 7/26/92

Statement by Governor Bill Clinton On the Crisis in Bosnia
July 26, 1992

    The continuing bloodshed in Bosnia and the former
Yugoslavia demands urgent international action.
    Tens of thousands of innocent civilians have been killed
and countless cities have been destroyed. Over two million
refugees have fled their homes, with vast numbers flooding
into neighboring countries — the largest displacement of
people in Europe since World War II. This human tragedy is not
merely a by-product of war; it is the result of a deliberate
effort: the Serbian policy of "ethnic cleansing," designed to
drive whole peoples from the lands of their parents and move
strangers into their vacant homes.
```

NOTE: THE SPEECH CONTINUES...

Wide Area Information Servers Conclusion

As the name implies, a wide variety of resources is available through the use of WAIS. The good news is that these resources are available rather quickly, and you do not need to know where they are located, how to get to them, or any difficult computer commands to enable you to find them. However, as has become obvious from this session, what you will find is not always predictable, the searching does take time, and sometimes what you find may not be exactly what you were looking for. With all those provisos in mind, WAIS is still a very powerful resource for Internet users.

Section IV: World Wide Web (WWW)

World Wide Web Introduction

The World Wide Web is another way to permit users to access information quickly without necessarily knowing where that information is located. In addition, the special aspect of this system is that it employs what is known as **hypertext**. This means that many of the terms that you will encounter are linked to other terms throughout the network. Since related documents are already linked together, your inquiry can go in many different but related directions relatively easily. Let's take a first look at World Wide Web and see how it works.

WORLD WIDE WEB PRACTICE #1

In this first session, we will just sign onto WWW and look at the opening screens. Here are the directions to do so:

1. Login to your host computer.

2. At your host prompt, type the following:

    telnet info.cern.ch

Here is what you should see:

```
host% telnet info.cern.ch
Trying 128.141.201.74...
Connected to nxoc01.cern.ch.
Escape character is '^]'.

CERN Information Service
(ttyp4 on nxoc01)

Overview of the Web (27/28)
GENERAL OVERVIEW

There is no "top" to the World-Wide Web. You can look at it
from many points of view. If you have no other bias, here are
some places to start:

by Subject[1]    A classification by subject of interest.
                 Incomplete but easiest to use.

by Type[2]       Looking by type of service (access protocol,
                 etc) may allow to find things if you know
                 what you are looking  for.

About WWW[3]     About the World-Wide Web global information
                 sharing project

Starting somewhere else

To use a different default page, perhaps one representing your
field of interest, see "customizing your home page"[4].

What happened to CERN?
```

1-6, Up, <RETURN> for more, Quit, or Help:

NOTE: HERE WE PRESSED RETURN

This default page used to be the CERN-specific but
inappropriate for users world-wide. However, the CERN[5] and
HEP[6] lists are still there! So if you are at CERN, set your
environment variable, logical name, etc., WWW_HOME to "http://
info.cern.ch/" to get the CERN home page back!   [End]

1-6, Up, Quit, or Help:

NOTE: HERE WE SELECTED 3 AND PRESSED RETURN

The World Wide Web project
WORLD WIDE WEB

The WorldWideWeb (W3) is a wide-area hypermedia[1] information
retrieval initiative aiming to give universal access to a
large universe of documents.

Everything there is online about W3 is linked directly or
indirectly to this document, including an executive summary[2]
of the project, an illustrated talk[3], Mailing lists[4] ,
Policy[5] and Conditions[6] , May's W3 news[7] , Frequently
Asked Questions[8] .

What's out there?[9]	Pointers to the world's online information, subjects[10] , W3 servers[11] , etc.
Software Products[12]	What there is and how to get it: clients, servers and tools.
Technical[13]	Details of protocols, formats, program internals etc
Bibliography[14]	Paper documentation on W3 and references. Also: manuals[15] .
People[16]	A list of some people involved in the project.

1-20, Back, Up, <RETURN> for more, Quit, or Help:

World Wide Web Practice #1 Commentary

This session is typical of what you will find when using the World Wide Web and serves to provide an interesting example of what is meant by hypertext. Notice that throughout the text, numbers are embedded in square brackets. Each one of those numbers represents a link to another file that will provide you with information.

Let's look at the first screen together:

1. Several of the terms (Subject, Type, WWW) are followed by square brackets with numbers in them.

2. At the bottom of the first screen, on the left hand side, we are told that we may choose any number from 1 through 6.

3. We chose the number 3, which was contained in square brackets after the term WWW.

4. This took us to additional information about World Wide Web (WWW).

5. This screen contains more terms that are followed by square brackets with numbers in them, and we are told at the bottom that we may select from 1 to 20.

You get the picture.

Basically, that is how World Wide Web will work. You will have an infinite number of choices to make, which will lead you in whatever direction you would prefer. You will always have the opportunity to go **back**, or **up** a screen, should you change your mind.

WORLD WIDE WEB PRACTICE #2

In this second practice, we will explore World Wide Web in greater depth. We will begin the practice the same way as the first one, but then we will make some additional choices. If you follow along, you will learn more about how World Wide Web works, and also more about World Wide Web's amazing array of information. Here goes:

Directions

1. Login to your host computer.

2. At your host prompt, type the following:

   telnet info.cern.ch

3. At the end of the first screen, select:

   About WWW [3]

   by pressing the number **3**, and then **ENTER**.

4. At the end of the next screen, choose

   An illustrated talk [3]

   by pressing the number **3**, and then **ENTER**.

5. At the end of the next screen, select:

   What is WWW? [4]

   by pressing the number **4**, and then **ENTER**.

6. Finally, we will select:

   The Universe of Online Information [4]

   by pressing the number **4**, and then **ENTER**.

Here is what happened when we did that:

```
Overview of the Web
GENERAL OVERVIEW

There is no "top" to the World-Wide Web. You can look at it
from many points of view. If you have no other bias, here are
some places to start:

by Subject[1]    A classification by subject of interest.
                 Incomplete but easiest to use.

by Type[2]       Looking by type of service (access protocol,
                 etc) may allow to find things if you know
                 what you are looking for.

About WWW[3]     About the World-Wide Web global information
                 sharing project
```

Starting somewhere else

To use a different default page, perhaps one representing your field of interest, see "customizing your home page"[4].

What happened to CERN?

1-6, Up, <RETURN> for more, Quit, or Help: **3**
The World Wide Web project
WORLD WIDE WEB

The WorldWideWeb (W3) is a wide-area hypermedia[1] information retrieval initiative aiming to give universal access to a large universe of documents.

Everything there is online about W3 is linked directly or indirectly to this document, including an executive summary[2] of the project, an illustrated talk[3], Mailing lists[4] , Policy[5] and Conditions[6], May's W3 news[7], Frequently Asked Questions[8].

What's out there?[9]	Pointers to the world's online information, subjects[10], W3 servers[11] , etc.
Software Products[12]	What there is and how to get it: clients, servers and tools.
Technical[13]	Details of protocols, formats, program internals etc
Bibliography[14]	Paper documentation on W3 and references. Also:manuals[15] .
People[16]	A list of some people involved in the project.

1-20, Back, Up, <RETURN> for more, Quit, or Help: **3**

World-Wide Web: An Illustrated Seminar
WORLDWIDE WEB SEMINAR
                                    Tim Berners-Lee CERN

Welcome to this online seminar on the World-Wide Web (W3). Will give first an overview of W3[1] for those to whom it is new, a review of the current status, and our plans for the future. (On giving this talk[2])

Overview in pictures

TShirt[3]   Welcome.

What is WWW?[4]

Basic hypertext[5]   Terminology: Links, anchors

Indexes as hypertext[6]
                           How searches fit into the model

Easy for users[7]   The seamlessly consistent user
                           interface

Architecture[8]   An overview of the client-server
                           gateway architecture .

1-23, Back, Up, <RETURN> for more, Quit, or Help: **4**

WHAT IS WWW? and how do I pronounce it?

     A concept[1]
     A set of protocols[2]
     A collection of software[3]
     The universe of online information[4]
     [End]

1-4, Back, Up, Quit, or Help: **4**

The World-Wide Web Virtual Library: Subject Catalogue
INFORMATION BY SUBJECT

See also arrangement by service type[1]. Mail www
request@info.cern.ch if you know of online information not in
this list.

Aeronautics   Mailing list archive index[2] .
Agriculture[3]   Separate list, see also Almanac mail
                           servers[4].
Astronomy and Astrophysics
                           Abstract Indexes[5] at NASA,
                           Astrophysics work at FNAL[6] and
                           Princeton's[7] Sloane Digital Sky
                           Survey. See also: space[8] .
Bio Sciences[9]   Separate list .
Computing[10]   Separate list.

Engineering[11]   Separate list.
Environment[12]   Separate list

1-44, Back, Up, <RETURN> for more, Quit, or Help:

The World-Wide Web Virtual Library: Subject Catalogue (45/69)

Geography   World maps[13]. CIA World Fact
                       Book[14], India: Miscellaneous
                       information[15], Thai-Yunnan: Davis
                       collection[16],
History   See Literature & Art[17], Newsgroup
                       soc.history[18]
Law[19]   US Copyright law[20]., Uniform
                       Commercial Code[21], etc
Libraries[22]   Lists of online catalogues etc.
Literature & Art[23]   Separate list.
Mathematics   CIRM library[24] (french). The
                       International Journal of Analytical
                       and Experimental Modal Analysis[25]
Meteorology   US weather[26], state by state. Also
                       WAIS weather[27] (around MIT :-).
Music   MIDI interfacing[28], Song lyrics[29]
                       (apparently disabled for copyright
                       reasons)

1-44, Back, Up, <RETURN> for more, Quit, or Help:

The World-Wide Web Virtual Library: Subject Catalogue (68/69)

Philosophy   American Philosophical
                       Association[30]
Psychology   " Psychology[31] " electronic journal.
Physics   High Energy Physics[32], Space
                       Science[33]. See also:
                       astrophysics[34].
Politics and Economics US politics[35].
Reference   Roget's Thesaurus[36]. Experimental
                       English dictionary[37].
Religion   The Bible[38] (King James version),
                       The Book of Mormon[39], The Holy
                       Qur'an[40]
Social Sciences   Coombs papers archive[41]. Journals of
                       the scholarly communications
                       project[42].
Other virtual libraries:

```
The UU-NNA metalibrary[43], the O'Reilly Whole Internet
Resource
1-44, Back, Up, Quit, or Help:
```

WORLD WIDE WEB CONCLUSION

The World Wide Web is an amazingly user-friendly system. Chock-full of information, it is intended to provide you with an interface that is both intriguing in its simplicity and awesome in its power. Think about it:

1. You can go anywhere that you want to go using the World Wide Web.

2. You can't get lost.

3. You can go in any direction, at any time, depending upon your mood or inclination.

4. It is getting bigger, and better, all the time!

As you can tell, your authors are quite impressed!

Conclusion

This session has been filled with many wonderful tools. All of them are intended to provide you with a better, more powerful way to access the resources of the Internet. As might be expected, they each have their own strengths and weaknesses. Most importantly, you begin to be aware that such resources exist and know how to use them. In all likelihood, as the Internet user community continues to expand, so too will the number of resources such as these. In time, we would also imagine that their ease of use and power will increase as well.

Finding Things

■ ■ Session Eight Vocabulary and Command Summary

telnet .... the command used to logon to another host computer

gopher .... the command that will enable us to search for specific information

archie -L .... the command used to provide us with a list of Archie servers

prog .... the word that begins the search program on an Archie server

wais .... wide area information server

world wide web .... a wide-area hypermedia information retrieval initiative aiming to give universal access to a large universe of documents

hypertext .... a method by which related documents are linked together

ESSION NINE

Quick Reference

This final session is intended to provide you with a chance to review all that you have learned. In addition, we hope it will provide you with a "quick reference" to turn to as you continue with your Internet sessions.

Session One – Logging In

Summary

In the first session, you learned about:

1. Accounts

2. Hosts

3. Loginnames

4. Logging in

5. Looking around

6. Getting out

Vocabulary and Commands Used In This Session

login .... signing onto a host computer

loginname .... the name that you use on that computer

password .... the special word that you use to identify yourself

pwd .... print working directory to tell where you are

cd .... the command used to change directories

ls .... list files in the directory more .... the command that permits you to read one screen at a time

cat .... the command that lists things one after another, with no break

man .... the command used to provide you with the manual for a given command — for example, man pwd

who .... the command used to tell you who else is currently logged onto your host system

w | more .... the command that is used to tell you what everyone else is doing and that will permit you to view screens, one screen at a time

whatis .... permits you to get a brief amount of information — for example, whatis pwd

logout .... to leave your Internet host account

Session Two – Electronic Mail

Summary

In the second session, you learned about:

1. Sending mail

2. Receiving mail

3. Forwarding mail

4. Email addresses

5. Finding addresses

6. Advertising your address

7. Moving mail to and from your PC

Vocabulary and Commands Used In This Session

mail .... the command used to begin the mail program

mail loginname@host .... the command used to send a particular individual an email message

t1 .... type (meaning display on the screen) the first message

p1 .... print (meaning display on the screen) the first message

q .... used to quit the mail session

new .... the word that is used to keep holding a message as a new one

reply .... the word that permits you to respond to an email message

save1 .... the command that is used to save the first message

mbox .... your "personal" mail box

more mbox .... the command that will permit you to view what is in your mail box, one screen at a time

delete 1 .... the command used to delete the first message

upload .... sending text or a file from your personal computer "up" to the mainframe host computer

download .... moving files or messages from the host "down" to your personal computer

man mail | more .... the command used to send the manual for the mail command to your screen, one screen at a time

man mail | cat .... the command used to send the entire mail manual to your screen, so that you might "capture it" onto a disk

Session Three – The News

Summary

In this third session, you learned about:

1. Usenet

2. Newsgroup categories

3. Moderated groups

4. Threads and newsreaders

5. Using the nn newsreader

6. news.announce.newusers

7. Finding what's out there

8. Setting up your own .newsrc file

9. New newsgroups and unsubscribing

Vocabulary and Commands Used In This Session

Usenet .... The set of people who exchange articles tagged with one or more universally recognized labels, called "newsgroups"

news.announce.newusers .. a newsgroup particularly designed for new users

nn .... a "newsreader" program that is used to begin a newsgroup session

rm .... remove a file; that is, delete it

.newsrc .... the special file that contains the names of the newsgroups you would like to read when you login to nn (literally, the news run command program)

.newsrc.bak .... the backup file for the .newsrc file

SPACEBAR .... used to move forward through the index of articles that are presented by nn
also used for displaying news articles once they have been selected

BACKSPACE key .... used to move back up a page through articles

? .... used to provide one page help screens

Q .... used to stop (Quit) the nn program and to take you back to the host prompt

thread .... a string of articles with the same subject

vi .... the editor you use to create your own .newsrc file

vi .newsrc .... the command used to begin the creation of a .newsrc file

I .... the command used to set up the file for entry

Esc key and :q! .... the sequence to type if you make a serious mistake while creating your .newsrc file

Esc key and ZZ .... the sequence to type when you are done creating your .newsrc file

nn -x the.group.name .... the sequence to type if you wish to read a particular newsgroup file, but do NOT wish to change the .newsrc file. For example,
nn -x news.announce.newusers will permit you to read this file without changing your .newsrc file

Quick Reference

Session Four – Contributing to Usenet

Summary

In the fourth session, you learned about:

1. The Usenet rules

2. Test groups

3. Practice posting

4. :post

5. Replying by email

6. Followup postings

7. Flames and flame wars

8. Signatures

Vocabulary and Commands Used In This Session

nn -x test.group.name .... the command used to "test" out your usenet abilities - be sure to substitute the name of the test group located nearest to you

vi .... the text editor that may be used to write messages

A (capital a) .... the key to be pressed so that you might append your message

Esc key and ZZ .... the sequence used to end your vi session

R (capital r) .... the key to be pressed so that you might reply to your test message

F (capital f) .... the key to be pressed so that you might follow up to a message

.signature .... the file that you can create that will automatically be added to the end of each message which you post

Session Five – Mailing Lists

Summary

In the fifth session, you learned about:

1. Mailing lists

2. Subscribing to mailing lists

3. Unsubscribing to mailing lists

4. Contributing to mailing list

5. Sample lists

6. Complete lists

Vocabulary and Commands Used In This Session

-request .... the word that is added to the part before an @ symbol when you wish to subscribe or unsubscribe to a list — for example, bicycles-request@BBN.COM

subscribe .... the word that is used in the body of an email message, when you wish to subscribe to the mailing list

unsubscribe .... the word that is used in the body of an email message, when you wish to unsubscribe to the mailing list

Session Six – Other Hosts - Telnet

Summary

In the sixth session, you learned about:

1. Telnet basics

2. Weather Underground

3. Cleveland Freenet

4. NYSERNET

5. University of Maryland INFO

6. The National Space Science Data Center

7. NASA Spacelink

8. Geographic Name Server

Vocabulary and Commands Used In This Session

telnet .... the command that enables you to logon to other
mainframe computers

Session Seven – Getting Things: File Transfer Protocol

Summary

In the seventh session, you learned about:

1. File transfer protocol

2. "Anonymous" FTP

3. Finding your way around

4. ASCII and BINARY files

5. Getting files

6. The Internet Society

7. The Gutenberg Project

8. The Electronic Frontiers Foundation

9. Getting files to your PC

10. Finding FTP sources

Vocabulary and Commands Used In This Session

file transfer protocol .... the process used to transfer files from a mainframe
computer to your host computer

ftp .... the abbreviation and command for file transfer
protocol

"anonymous" file
transfer protocol .... the convention that permits Internet users to
logon to remote host computers

pwd .... print working directory cd .... change directory

dir .... the command that will list all of the files and directories

ascii .... the acronym that indicates that a file is a text file

binary .... the word that indicates that the file is, most likely, a program or a graphic

close .... the word that is used to end the connection with the remote host

quit .... the command that will take you out of FTP and back to your host prompt

more .... the command that will permit you to read one screen of an ascii (text) file at a time

readme .... often used as the name of a file that will provide the user with information about other files and directories on the system

pub .... often used as the name of the directory that contains files that are available to the public

cat .... the command that will "print" a file in a continuous stream onto your monitor — may be used in conjunction with the name of a program while your "capture" software is turned on

Session Eight – Finding Things

Summary

In the eighth session, you learned about:

1. Internet tools

2. Gopher

3. Archie

4. WAIS

Quick Reference

5. World Wide Web

Vocabulary and Commands Used In This Session

telnet .... the command used to logon to another host computer

gopher .... the command that will enable us to search for specific information

archie -L .... the command used to provide us with a list of Archie servers

prog .... the word that begins the search program on an Archie server

wais .... wide area information server

world wide web .... a wide-area hypermedia information retrieval initiative aiming to give universal access to a large universe of documents

hypertext .... a method by which related documents are linked together

Now It's Up To You

We hope that you have learned a great deal while reading this book and trying out exercises on the Internet. With luck, you should have a fairly good idea about what the Internet is all about and how to access some of its many resources.

Here are some suggestions about what to do next:

1. If you have gone through this book on your own, in a linear fashion (meaning from Session One through Session Nine), you might wish to go back through it again. For new users, there is an enormous amount of information that is best absorbed only on the second or third pass through it.

2. Pick one section of the book that you found most interesting (email, newsgroups, telnet, ftp, archie, gopher, etc.) and spend some time just perfecting your skills in that area. We have found that repeated practice, especially in some of the areas, makes a significant difference in one's comfort level.

3. Read through one or more of the resources that are listed in Appendix A. We have tried to list books that will add to the understanding that you now should have. Be forewarned that some of them are more "user friendly" than others, and several of them include a fair amount of Unix commands as part of their discussions.

APPENDIX A

Where to Learn More

New books on the Internet, including this one, are coming out in a steady stream. After you have mastered the basics with our book, you may want to read further and learn more. As we write, the books listed below are the most current.

Books may be obtained from the publishers or from a nearby book store.

Books

The Internet Companion by Tracy LaQuey with Jeanne C. Ryer, published in paperback by Addison-Wesley. ISBN 0-201-62224-6, 196 pages

Zen and the Art of the Internet by Brendan P. Kehoe, published in paperback by PTR Prentice Hall. ISBN 0-13-010778-6, 112 pages

INTERNET: Getting Started by April Marine, et al, published in paperback by Prentice Hall. ISBN 0-13-327933-2, 360 pages

INTERNET: Mailing Lists by Edward T. L. Hardie and Vivian Neou, published in paperback by Prentice Hall. ISBN 0-13-327941-3, 356 pages

The Whole Internet User's Guide & Catalog by Ed Krol, published by O'Reilly & Associates, Inc. ISBN 1-56592-025-2, 376 pages

NorthWestNet's Guide to our World Online by Jonathan Kochmer and NorthWestNet, published in paperback by NorthWestNet and NorthWestNet Academic Consortium, Inc. ISBN 0-9635281-0-6, 515 pages

!%@:: A Directory of Electronic Mail, Addressing & Networks by Donnalyn Frey and Rick Adams, published in paperback by O'Reilly & Associates, Inc. ISBN 0-937175-15-3, 420 pages

RFCs and FYIs

These "Electronic" documents are available from several sources by anonymous FTP (see Session Seven). You may obtain any of these by using FTP.

The RFCs are, for the most part, very technical documents concerning the actual workings of the Internet and the various "protocols" needed to make everything communicate. The new user will rarely need to get into this depth.

Of greater interest to new users are the FYIs. These For Your Information (FYI) files, listed below, are a marvelous source of additional information. You can obtain the FYIs by using FTP as described in the index text below.

Here is the index of FYIs as we write. You will want to get the latest index by FTP to be sure you are current. The index, as noted below, is in reverse numeric order to show you the most recent FYI first. You should probably start with FYI #4, and go on to FYIs #10 and #7.

FYI Index

This file contains citations for all FYIs in reverse numerical order. FYI citations appear in this format:

Title of FYI. Author 1.; Author 2.; Author 3.   Issue date; ## p. (Format: PS=xxx TXT=zzz bytes) (Also RFC ##)
    (Obsoletes xxx; Obsoleted by xxx; Updates xxx; Updated by xxx)

Key to Citations:

is the FYI number; ## p. is the total number of pages.

The format and byte information follow the page information in parentheses. The format, either ASCII text (TXT) or PostScript (PS) or both, is noted, followed by an equal sign and the number of bytes for that version. (PostScript is a registered trademark of Adobe Systems Incorporated.) The example (Format: PS=xxx TXT=zzz bytes) shows that the PostScript version of the FYI is xxx bytes and the ASCII text version is zzz bytes.

The (Also RFC ####) phrase gives the equivalent RFC number for each FYI document. Each FYI is also an RFC.

"Obsoletes RFC xxx" refers to other FYIs that this one replaces; "Obsoleted by RFC xxx" refers to FYIs that have replaced this one. "Updates RFC xxx" refers to other FYIs that this one merely updates (but does not replace); "Updated by RFC xxx" refers to FYIs that have been updated by this one (but not replaced). Only immediately succeeding and/or preceding FYIs are indicated, not the entire history of each related earlier or later FYI in a related series.

For example:

1. F.Y.I. on F.Y.I.: Introduction to the F.Y.I. notes. Malkin, G.S.;   Reynolds, J.K. 1990 March; 4 p. (Format: TXT=7867 bytes) (Also RFC   1150)

Paper copies of all FYIs are available from SRI, either individually or as part of an RFC subscription service (for more information contact nisc@nisc.sri.com or call 1-415-859-6387). Online copies are available for anonymous FTP from ftp.nisc.sri.com as fyi/fyi##.txt or fyi/fyi##.ps (## is the FYI number without leading zeroes).

Additionally, FYIs may be requested through electronic mail from SRI's automated mail server by sending a message to mail-server@nisc.sri.com. In the body of the message, write "send fyi##" for text versions or "send fyi##.ps" for PostScript versions. To obtain the FYI index, your message should read "send fyi-index".

FYI Index

18 Internet Users' Glossary. Malkin, G.S.; Parker, T.L., eds. 1993 January; 53 p. (Format: TXT=104624 bytes) (Also RFC 1392)

17 The Tao of IETF: A Guide for New Attendees of the Internet Engineering Task Force. Malkin, G.S. 1993 January; 19 p. (Format: TXT=23569 bytes) (Also RFC 1391)

16 Connecting to the Internet: What connecting institutions should anticipate. ACM SIGUCCS Networking Task Force 1992 August; 25 p. (Format: TXT=53449 bytes) (Also RFC 1359)

15 Privacy and accuracy issues in network information center databases. Curran, J.; Marine, A.N. 1992 August; 4 p. (Format: TXT=8858 bytes) (Also RFC 1355)

14 Technical overview of directory services using the X.500 protocol. Weider, C.; Reynolds, J.K.; Heker, S. 1992 March; 16 p. (Format: TXT=35694 bytes) (Also RFC 1309)

13 Executive introduction to directory services using the X.500 protocol. Weider, C.; Reynolds, J.K. 1992 March; 4 p. (Format: TXT=9392 bytes) (Also RFC 1308)

12 Building a network information services infrastructure. Sitzler, D.D.; Smith, P.G.; Marine, A.N. 1992 February; 13 p. (Format: TXT=29135 bytes) (Also RFC 1302)

11 Catalog of Available X.500 Implementations. Lang, R.; Wright, R. 1991 December; 103 p. (Format: TXT=129468 bytes) (Also RFC 1292)

10 There's Gold in them thar Networks! or Searching for Treasure in all the Wrong Places. Martin, J. 1993 January; 39 p. (Format: TXT=71176 bytes) (Also RFC 1402)   (Obsoletes RFC 1290)

9 Who's who in the Internet: Biographies of IAB, IESG and IRSG members. Malkin, G.S. 1992 May; 33 p. (Format: TXT=92119 bytes) (Also RFC 1336) (Obsoletes RFC 1251)

8 Site Security Handbook. Holbrook, J.P.; Reynolds, J.K., eds. 1991 July; 101 p. (Format: TXT=259129 bytes) (Also RFC 1244)

7 FYI on Questions and Answers: Answers to commonly asked "experienced Internet user" questions. Malkin, G.S.; Marine, A.N.; Reynolds, J.K. 1991 February; 15 p. (Format: TXT=33385 bytes) (Also RFC 1207)

6 FYI on the X window system. Scheifler, R.W. 1991 January; 3 p. (Format: TXT=3629 bytes) (Also RFC 1198)

5 Choosing a name for your computer. Libes, D. 1990 August; 8 p. (Format: TXT=18472 bytes) (Also RFC 1178)

4 FYI on questions and answers: Answers to commonly asked "new Internet user" questions. Malkin, G.S.; Marine, A.N. 1992 May; 42 p. (Format: TXT=91884 bytes) (Also RFC 1325)   (Obsoletes RFC 1206)

3 FYI on where to start: A bibliography of internetworking information. Bowers, K.L.; LaQuey, T.L.; Reynolds, J.K.; Roubicek, K.; Stahl, M.K.; Yuan, A. 1990 August; 42 p. (Format: TXT=67330 bytes) (Also RFC 1175)

2 FYI on a network management tool catalog: Tools for monitoring and debugging TCP/IP internets and interconnected devices. Stine, R.H., ed. 1990 April; 126 p. (Format: TXT=336906, PS=555225 bytes) (Also RFC 1147)

1 F.Y.I. on F.Y.I.: Introduction to the F.Y.I. notes. Malkin, G.S.; Reynolds, J.K. 1990 March; 4 p. (Format: TXT=7867 bytes) (Also RFC 1150)

APPENDIX B

PC Communications and The Disk

Communicating from your PC

You may be one of the many PC users who is using a PC to communicate with others. If you already have a modem and a general communications program, then you should skip ahead to the section at the end of this Appendix entitled Configuring your Modem and Program.

If you already have a modem, but have a specialized communications program such as Prodigy, you will need a more general communications program. We have included with this book a fully functional demonstration version of one called Telix Lite. You may wish to skip ahead to Communications Programs or you may wish to review the background material below.

If you are new to the whole area of communicating from your PC and need to get a modem, we will show you how to go about acquiring one. Below is a quick overview of what you may want to know about the process.

What You Need

To communicate effectively from your PC, you need three items that are used exclusively for PC communications. First, a telephone line that is located not too far from the PC. Second, a modem and a cable to your PC. And third, a PC program that will be used to "talk" to the modem and the telephone line. We describe each in order.

The Telephone Line

Usually this will be your regular voice telephone line. However, it is important to remember that while you are communicating with your PC, you can't use the line to make regular voice telephone calls. Also, if you have telephone features such as Call Waiting, you need to disable them while you are using the modem.

Beeps and clicks from these features will disrupt what you will see on your PC screen.

If, after you have been using the Internet for a while, you find that you are tying up your main voice telephone line for long periods, you may want to consider getting a second line just for the modem. If you are thinking of getting a FAX, the modem and the FAX can easily share the line. There are also devices that you can buy at telephone stores that will permit you to share one line among all these devices. However, the key point remains that only one device can use the line at a time.

You will want to make sure that a telephone jack is not too far from your PC so that you and others do not trip over the telephone wire to the modem. Most telephone connections that have been set up in the last 10 years have the little clear plastic plugs and wall jacks about the size of the tip of your little finger. If you don't have this type of telephone connection, you may want to ask your local hardware store how to install one. If you hesitate to do this yourself, an electrician or your telephone company will do it for a charge.

Finally, you will need a telephone wire from the jack to where you will put the modem. It's just a regular telephone wire with the little jacks on the ends. It is the same type that you would use to connect another telephone, but it is different from the cord between the telephone set and the handset. These wires can now be found at all hardware and home supply stores.

The Modem

The modem (short for MODulator DEModulator) is just a device to convert the digital data from your PC to specialized tones or hisses that will pass over the voice telephone network to another modem. Almost all modems today support what is called the "Hayes AT Command" set. We are going to assume that you have a Hayes AT compatible modem. Check your PC and its manuals carefully. Many computers today come with modems, sometimes called FAX/modems. You may already have a modem installed in your computer.

If you do, you will find that it has a jack for the little clear plastic telephone plug. If it has two jacks, one will usually be labeled "line" and the other will be labeled "phone" or "telephone." If you wish, you can connect the modem between the wall jack and a telephone set by connecting the wall jack to the "line" and your telephone set to the other. You will need two telephone connecting wires.

If you need to buy a modem, the key to price will be the modem's speed. Speed on a modem is talked about in bits per second or bps. Speeds for modems today range from 2400 bps to 4800 bps to 9600 bps to 14,400 bps. You will soon be able to buy modems at 19,200 bps, but you might want to wait until the standards for those are really complete.

The price you pay will depend on how fast the modem runs. We wouldn't recommend a modem slower than 2400 bps. Many modems at that speed are available for less than $100. Sometimes, they are included in promotional offers. The faster modems will range above $500 and may include FAX features.

You will also have two choices other than speed. You can purchase an "internal" modem that has to be installed inside your computer. If you are used to doing this with other cards and you have empty slots (of the right kind), you may save a few dollars and some space with an internal modem.

If you don't want to go inside your PC, you can purchase an "external" modem and a cable to connect it to a "serial" connector on your PC. The manual that comes with the modem will show you how to do this. Remember to buy a cable when you purchase the modem and ask the store for help in picking it out. This cable needs to be just long enough to reach the serial connector on your PC.

Now you are ready to select a communications program.

Communications Programs

If you have been using computer bulletin boards or services, you may already have a communications program. If you have been using Prodigy, CompuServe's CIS, or any specialized graphics interface program, you will need to use a more general communications program.

We have included a disk with this book that contains a fully functional demonstration version of a general communications program. The full program is called Telix; the one which is included with this book is called Telix Lite. Before we describe Telix Lite, you should review the following list of programs. Each one of them has a communications program that you can also use "built in." If you already are using one of them, you may prefer to continue to do so for your communications needs. After we show you how to set up and use Telix Lite, we will describe how each of the programs below can be setup to dial Internet services.

Lotus Works
Microsoft Windows
Microsoft Works

If you already have one or more of these programs, you can choose which to use. We suggest that you install our demonstration Telix Lite disk and then compare them. If you have another communications program that you currently use, you can skip ahead to Configuring Your Modem and Program near the end of this appendix.

The Telix Lite Disk

Through the courtesy of deltaComm Development, Inc., we are able to include a fully functional demonstration version of their communications program Telix Lite. If you find this program useful, we suggest that you contact deltaComm Development, Inc. and upgrade to a fully featured version. You will find an order form in the back of this appendix.

Getting Started

We will assume that you have a hard disk and a 3 1/2 inch "A" drive on your PC. If you have only a 5 1/4 inch "A" drive, you will need to have someone copy the five files from our 3 1/2 inch disk to a 5 1/4 inch floppy. Be sure that all five files are copied.

1. To install Telix Lite on your PC, insert the diskette in your PC's floppy drive and change the prompt to that drive. In most cases that will be an A> prompt.

    Telix Lite has a complete setup program that will create or modify your existing configuration to work best with your modem, and will modify your modem settings to work best with Telix.

2. To run the configuration program, from the DOS prompt of the floppy drive containing the install disk, type:

    INSTALL

    and press ENTER

3. After copying the necessary files to the directory of your choice, a box will appear showing the progress of the installation as the files are "exploded" from their compressed form.

4. When this is complete, you will be asked if you wish to have your AUTOEXEC.BAT file changed.

   We recommend that you DO NOT allow INSTALL to do this.

   In general this will not affect your use of Telix Lite. Later, after you have reviewed the documentation file, you may make these changes yourself.

5. Next, a menu will be shown from which you should select the model of your modem. If your modem is not listed as one of the options, select one of the following that most closely describes your modem. Many modems are described as "Hayes Compatibles" and you may then select from the first two in our list based on the speed of your modem in bits per second.

   > Hayes Smartmodem 1200 External
   > Hayes Smartmodem 2400
   > 1200 bps without switches
   > 1200 bps with switches
   > 2400 bps without switches
   > 2400 bps with switches

6. You may be shown a list of the settings for the modem itself, including any switch settings, if known. Please write down the switch settings as you will need them later.

7. You may also be asked if you wish to configure your modem. If so, answer by pressing the 'Y' key.

8. INSTALL will ask you for your comm port as well. The comm port will have a name like COM1 or COM2. You will need to know what comm port you modem uses. Please refer to your modem and computer manuals for this information.

NOTE: *If you cannot find what port is used, try COM1 if the modem is outside your PC and COM2 if it is inside.*

If all goes well, a successful configuration message will be shown. If there is a problem, be sure that the proper comm port has been specified and try again. If the problem persists, contact your modem manufacturer.

9. The exit screen of INSTALL contains final instructions on how to make best use out of the setup that has been written for you. Please make a note of these for later referral.

After the INSTALL program is complete, you will be left at the prompt of the directory you specified for Telix. This should look something like:

C:\TELIX>

When you have finished the installation, you will find a number of files on your disk. Included is a user manual called TELIX.DOC. You may choose to read this file on your screen or to print it using your favorite word processor. If you decide to print it, you should know that it contains about 80 pages of text.

Put the distribution disk away in a safe place. If you change modems, you will need to re-install Telix Lite and will need to use the disk again.

How to Set Up Telix Lite

Setup for Telix Lite is fast and easy. First, you will need to know the telephone number of the service you wish to call. The number will have to be in the same form you would use if you were to dial it manually.

Second, you should also know what "parameters" the service uses. However, you can change these later. Usually, there are only two choices, called 7E1 or 8N1. We will have you select 8N1. This is the default setting for Telix Lite. If you get weird characters on your screen, you can change the setting to 7E1. Don't worry, you can't break things with the wrong settings. (In Telix's setup, they appear as E-7-1 or N-8-1.)

1. Start Telix Lite by changing to its directory and typing Telix. This might look like:

cd /telix   (Press ENTER)

telix   (Press ENTER)

You will be shown an initial logo screen followed shortly (and automatically) by the following screen.

```
Telix Copyright (C) 1986-93 deltaComm Development, Inc.
Version 1.21/Lite, released 02-04-93

Press ALT-Z for help on special keys.

AT E1Q0V1X4&C1&D2 S7=55 S11=60 S0=0
OK



Alt-Z for Help | ANSI    |  2400 N81 FDX |   |  |        |
Offline
```

Notice the "Status Bar" along the bottom.

2. Press down the ALT key and press the letter D (for dial). The status bar changes to ask:

    Entries to dial: Press <Enter> for Directory

3. Press the ENTER key to see the Dialing Directory. Notice the list of functions at the bottom of the screen.

4. Press E to Edit the highlighted first (and only) entry.

    Now you can type in the name of the service so you can remember what the number 1 stands for.

5. Press ENTER and you will be asked for a number. This is the complete telephone number of the service you will be dialing (for example, 1-800-123-4567).

6. Press ENTER and you will be asked for your baud rate (modem speed).

    Use the cursor keys until your modem speed is highlighted, and then press ENTER.

7. Now press ENTER for each of the "Parity", the "Data Bits" and the "Stop Bits" selections. This will select N81, also known as 8N1.

8. Press ENTER for the "Linked Script" selection.

9. Now you will be asked for your choice of "Terminal Emulation." Use the cursor to highlight VT102 and press ENTER.

10. Now press ENTER until you complete "Save this Entry?" Notice that your new data for entry number 1 appears in the directory. If you wish to add other lines, press A , move the highlight to number 2 and press E to edit this new line.

Now Let's See If It All Works.

1. Make sure that your modem is connected to your PC and to the telephone line and that it is turned on.

NOTE: *You may want to take the telephone wire from the modem "line" jack and plug it into a telephone to be sure that you are getting "dial tone" to the modem. Remember to put the wire back into the modem "line" jack.*

2. From the DIALING Directory screen, move the highlight to your entry and press D for Dial.

    You should hear your modem get dial tone and begin dialing.

    IMPORTANT: You can stop the dialing process by hitting the ESC key.

3. You should now see the login prompt or welcome screen of your Internet service. You may need to press ENTER once or twice to begin the service.

    If you get strange looking characters on your screen instead of the login prompt, you may need to change to the E71 setting. You may need to call the people at your Internet service provider to help.

4. When you are done, you should be sure to hang up. To hang up the telephone line, hold the ALT key and press the H (hang up) key.

    To clear the screen, hold ALT and press the C key.

    To get a screen of all of the ALT key meanings, hold the ALT key and press the Z key.

    You can use ALT-X to leave Telix Lite.

Problem Solving

If you don't hear your modem dialing, you may either have the modem speaker volume set too low or you may be connected to the wrong serial "port."

Hold down ALT and press the P key and you will be shown a menu of line settings. Your current settings will be shown at the top of the box. The last parameter is your serial "COM" port.

If you are not getting the modem to dial, try changing COM1 to COM2. Press 2 and ENTER to save the changes and try dialing again.

If this doesn't work, try COM3 and then COM4.

If you are still having problems, review your modem setup with the modem manual.

At this point, you should be able to dialup an Internet service provider. Remember to use ALT-H to hang up the phone line after you are through with each session and use ALT-X to leave Telix Lite.

Other Communications Programs

A number of popular programs have communications functions built into them. Three of them are LotusWorks, Microsoft Windows, and Microsoft Works. Here is a brief description of how to find the communications sections in these programs.

Lotus Works

1. From the LotusWorks main screen, select "Setup" with either the TAB and Enter keys or with the mouse.

2. Select Modem from the menu bar and choose your communications settings. You will need to set the speed of your modem and the serial "port" for your modem. Lotus Works uses the word Baud for speed; you should enter the bits per second speed for your modem.

3. You should set the Terminal to VT100 and the Parity, Data Bits and Stop Bits to N, 8 and 1 respectively.

4. You may also wish to turn on Audible Dialing so you can hear both the dial tone and the dialing.

This will set up the "defaults" to be used each time you communicate.

5. When you are done, click on Accept and return to the main Lotus Works screen. You have now set your defaults for communications.

6. From the main Lotus Works screen, select Communications and dial your service. You may use any of Lotus Works' several options to preserve the phone number.

Microsoft Windows

In Microsoft Windows (3.0 and 3.1), the communications program is called "Terminal." Terminal can be found in the Accessories Window.

1. To setup this program, double click on the Terminal Icon and select Settings. Then you need to set the Phone Number and Communications areas.

2. In Communications, you will find that 8N1 and COM1 are already set, but you will need to select the correct speed for your modem.

3. To connect to your service, just click on Phone and Dial. Terminal will do the rest.

   If you have trouble getting dial tone, go back to Settings and Communications and select COM2 (or COM3 or COM4).

   After this, you can follow the directions in the Windows Manual under the chapter on Terminal for all of the various options available.

Microsoft Works

1. From the main Microsoft Works screen, select File and Create a New File.

2. In the dialog box that appears, select Communications and click on OK.

3. Then select Options from the menu bar and click on Terminal.

4. Change the setting to ANSI and click on OK.

5. Again select Options and click on Communications.

6. In this dialog box, set Parity to None and select your modem speed. Then click on OK.

7. Now select Options and Phone and type in the number of your service. Again click on OK.

8. Now click on Connect and you should hear dial tone and dialing.

9. After you are finished with your session, choose File Close. When asked if it is OK to disconnect, answer OK.

   Refer to your Microsoft Works manuals to extend your abilities with the communications functions of Works.

Configuring your Modem and Program

We have recommended consistent settings for Telix Lite, Windows, Lotus Works and Microsoft Works in the text above. If you are using other communications programs, we will recap the settings here and suggest where changes might have to be made for particular services. All communications programs allow you to have different settings for different services. As you work with each service provider, you will learn what settings are preferred.

You will need to use some judgment on the modem speed setting. Some commercial services charge different rates for different speeds and you may not want to pay for the fastest speeds while you are typing or reading mail. If, however, you are downloading large files, you may want to use the highest speed your modem and service offer.

Here are the "default" settings we recommend:

Terminal Emulation	**VT102, VT100 or ANSI**
Parity	**None**
Data Bits	**8**
Stop Bits	**1**
Flow Control	**Xon/Xoff**

Consult the administrator for your service and the manuals for your modem and your communications programs to determine the best settings for your use of each service.

Happy Communicating!

Telix Ordering/Registration Information

This copy of Telix Lite is fully licensed and requires no additional purchase or remuneration. The commercial versionof Telix allows you to use many features not present inTelix Lite. Registered Telix users get the current version of Telix on disk along with their own serial number, an optional printed manual, mailed notification of major Telix updates, and priority when calling the Telix Software support BBS.

Users of Telix Lite may purchase Telix 3.xx registration for $29 US / $37 CDN. Such a purchase includes a licensed copy of Telix 3.xx on disk. A printed manual is available for $12 US / $15 CDN. An evaluation disk with the current shareware version of Telix on it is also available for $10 US / $12 CDN. This is to be used to try out Telix, and does not include registration (the right to use Telix after the evaluation period). The fee covers the cost of diskette(s) and handling.

Payment may be in the form of check, money order, or with a VISA card or Mastercard. All US dollar checks must be drawn on a US bank, and all Canadian dollar checks must be drawn on a Canadian bank. Note that we quote equivalent prices in both $US and $CDN, but as we are a US company all credit card orders will be billed in $US, and your card statement will show any conversion between currencies.

Shipping is $2 per copy to addresses in North America, and $3 per copy to other countries. On orders with printed manuals, add $3 additional shipping per copy, $5 outside of North America.

To place an order, please use the order form on the following page, or call us toll free from North America at (800) TLX-8000, with your VISA card or Mastercard ready.

Telix Upgrade from Telix Lite   #930930-121

Remit to: deltaComm Development, PO Box 1185, Cary NC 27512

Quantity	Item	US/CDN	Price
_____	Telix 3.xx Registration	@ $29/$37 ea	$_____
	(includes serial #, registration + program and manual on disk)		
_____	Telix evaluation disk	@ $10/$12 ea	$_____
	(includes program and manual on disk, but not registration)		
_____	Printed Manual	@ $12/$15 ea	$_____
	(includes Telix, Script, Host docs)		

Disk media: 5.25" [   ]   3.5" [   ]   Low Density [   ]

Shipping/Handling is: Shipping $_____

     North America: $2 (plus $3 for manuals)
     Overseas: $3 (plus $5 for manuals)
                                       Subtotal $_____

North Carolina orders please add Sales Tax (6%) $_____

                                           TOTAL $_____

Payment by: [   ] Check or MO   [   ]VISA   [   ] Mastercard

Name   _____

Company   _____

Address   _____

                   _____

Visa/MC orders will be charged in US currency.
The following information is needed for card payments

     Phone (_____)_____ Other (_____)_____

     Card #_____ Expiry _____

Name of cardholder _____

Signature   _____

(VISA/MC orders may also call voice: 800-TLX-8000)

APPENDIX C

Dial-Up Internet Services

There are a number of service providers who offer dial-up connectivity to the Internet. You may also be affiliated with a business or campus system that offers dial-up access to hosts connected to the Internet. You will have to contact the administrators of these systems to get the details on how to dial-up.

If you don't have access to a business or campus system, there is a growing number of "commercial" Internet service providers. Some provide a full range of services based on the UNIX operating system and others provide menu screens of many of the most common Internet services described in this book. Some services offer you a choice of UNIX shells or menus.

Through the courtesy of three of these services, we have included introductory coupons for your use. We have included the "info" files from these three services. The files are current as we write, but you may wish contact the services for more recent information. You can use email as shown in Session Two. Send your email to:

> **help@cerf.net   OR   info@holonet.net   OR   office@world.std.com**

If you do not yet have an account, you can also telephone them. Their numbers, as we write, are:

> **cerf.net   800-876-2373 or 619-455-3900**
> **holonet.net   510-704-0160**
> **world.std.com   617-739-0202**

In addition, there are current lists of public dial access Internet providers which can be obtained using e-mail. After you have finished our session on email, you may wish to get one of these lists.

To obtain a copy of this list, send email to:

> **info-deli-server@netcom.com**

> Use the Subject: Send PDIAL

You don't need to have any message in the body of your email note, as you are actually sending mail to a computer that will automatically respond to the subject line of your message.

The server machine will return a copy of a file called PDIAL to you. The format of the list you will receive is self-explanatory, showing the name of the service as well as various data about each service. This should allow you to find a nearby host. Note that the dial-up number is a modem accessible number and indicates what loginname (such as "guest") you should type to use (and register) with the service.

DIAL n' CERF: General Information

This service provides Dial-up Internet Access to qualified users. DIAL n' CERF caters chiefly to:

Organizations/Individuals with legitimate but low start up needs to access the Internet.

Organizations/Individuals with legitimate but short term needs to access the Internet.

To "roamers", who already have access to the Internet in their parent organizations, but who need this access when traveling.

DIAL n' CERF offers: Terminal Service (telnet, rlogin)
        SLIP
        USENet News
        Internet Mailboxes
DIAL n' CERF modems support all standard speeds up to 19.2 Kbps.

DIAL n' CERF USA and selected locations support the V.32bis standard at 14.4 Kbps

Please refer all questions to help@cerf.net or call (619) 455-3900. You may fax a copy of agreements to (619) 455-3990 and follow up by sending originals by mail.

DIAL n' CERF LOCATIONS

[This document is available by anonymous FTP from NIC.CERF.NET in the file cerfnet/cerfnet_sales/dial-up_info/dial-n-cerf-locations.txt]

WHO QUALIFIES

You are required to sign and abide by the cerfnet-acceptable-use-policy

DIAL n' CERF SUBSCRIPTION AGREEMENT

[This document is available by anonymous ftp from NIC.CERF.NET in the file cerfnet/cerfnet_sales/dial-up_info/dial-n-cerf-agreement.txt]

HoloNet: An Easy-to-Use Internet Access BBS.

HoloNet is based on custom BBS software that provides an easy-to-use menu driven interface. HoloNet is ideal for those looking for an easy way to use Internet services. HoloNet does not currently provide UNIX shell access.

Services include:

1. Convenient access

    Currently, more than 170 access numbers in cities nationwide.

2. Online publications include *USA Today, Decisionline, Newsbytes, Datanet Computer News, Eeeekbits,* and *Boardwatch Magazine.*

3. Usenet averages over 30MB of USENET news per day. The following news readers are available: NN, TIN, and RN.

4. Internet email

    Members have an Internet email address similar to: member@holonet.net

5. Internet access

    Access to telnet, talk, finger, IRC, and FTP. (Note: you must comply with the policies of any networks you use.)

6. Single and multiplayer games

    Board, card, fantasy, and puzzle games.

How to try HoloNet for FREE:

Telnet: holonet.net

Modem: 510-704-1058 (Berkeley, CA) at 1200, 2400, 9600, or 14400bps   There are free demo numbers nationwide, send email, with any content, to holonet-access@holonet.net for a list of numbers.

How to get more information:

E-mail: info@holonet.net

Modem: 510-704-1058 at 1200, 2400, 9600, or 14400bps

Voice: 510-704-0160

Fax: 510-704-8019

HoloNet is a service mark of Information Access Technologies, Inc. Copyright (c) 1992 Information Access Technologies, Inc. All Rights Reserved.

This file is available by sending e-mail to:
info@holonet.mailer.net

H O L O N E T (sm)

HoloNet(sm) is composed of a wide variety of networking services provided by Information Access Technologies, Inc. HoloNet has access nationwide and provides access at both individual and corporate levels.

If you would like information mailed or faxed to you, or if you have any questions, please contact our offices: 510-704-0160/voice

```
========
```
Services
```
========
```

HoloNet BBS -   Individual Access to the Internet. This service provides users with an Internet e-mail address and access to interactive Internet services like telnet and FTP.

For more information, e-mail: holonet-bbs@holonet.mailer.net

HoloMailer - Provides automated mail information distribution.

Allows the distribution of information via a "mailer.net" address.

For more information, e-mail: holomailer@holonet.mailer.net

HoloQM -   Links CE Software QuickMail systems to the Internet.

For more information, e-mail: holoqm@holonet.mailer.net

HoloUUCP -   Links Office E-mail, BBSes, and computers to the
              Internet.

              This service provides an easy way for offices
              to expand the scope of their LAN e-mail to the
              Internet.

              For more information, e-mail:
              holouucp@holonet.mailer.net

```
===================
```
General Information
```
===================
```

Terms & Conditions - HoloNet users must agree to certain terms
              and conditions.

                   For a copy of the current terms, send e-mail
                   to: terms@holonet.mailer.net

                   Access By Minors - For minors to use HoloNet we
                   must have a letter on file.

                   Minors must have a parent or guardian sign a
                   letter of consent to access HoloNet. For a copy
                   of the current letter, send e-mail to:
                   minor@holonet.mailer.net

Access Numbers - Dial-up access numbers for HoloNet for North
              America

                   Through our dial-up access numbers, HoloNet is a
                   local call in over 850 cities nationwide. Our
                   dial-up access numbers are continually being
                   expanded and upgraded. For a copy of the current
                   numbers with access instructions, send e-mail
                   to: access@holonet.mailer.net

Rates -   HoloNet charges hourly rates for basic services.
              These services include HoloNet BBS, HoloUUCP,
              and access through various dial-up networks. For
              current rate information, send e-mail to:
              rates@holonet.mailer.net

Billing -   HoloNet offers a variety of billing options.

Credit card, deposit, and purchase order billing
are available. For information on these options,
send e-mail to: billing@holonet.mailer.net

====================
Contact Information
====================

Information Access Technologies, Inc.
46 Shattuck Square, Suite 11
Berkeley, CA 94704-1152
Voice: 510-704-0160
Fax: 510-704-8019
BBS: 510-704-1058
E-mail: support@holonet.net

HoloNet is a service mark of Information Access Technologies,
Inc.
Copyright (c) 1992 Information Access Technologies, Inc.
All Rights Reserved.

Software Tool & Die
   presents

T H E   W O R L D

The World is the premier online service for dial-up access to
the Internet. Since November, 1989, The World has been
offering a myriad of Internet services which include
electronic mail, USENET, telnet, ftp, irc, gopher, library
catalogs, and much more. Using ordinary terminal emulation
software, customers of The World have access to a UNIX-based
computer that supports all the software and utilities for
Internet access. Software Tool & Die is committed to providing
cost effective, reliable network services for dial-up
customers in the Internet community.

INTERNET

The Internet is collaboration of computer networks that allows
the instantaneous transfer of information between computers
located all over the globe. Within the information society,
Internet is the fastest growing and most widely available
computer based communications network. The international
Internet community encompasses a wide variety of people
including university professors, students and staff; employees
of for-profit businesses and not-for-profit organizations;
members of Fortune 500 companies as well as individual family-
owned businesses; government employees such as the President;
and individual computer owners.

COMPUTER AND NETWORK RESOURCES

The World is a Solbourne 5E/900 5 CPU SPARC server with 256MB
of main memory and over 9GB of local disk storage. The World
is connected to the Internet via multiple high speed links to
the Alternet commercial access network. On the dial-up side,
the World offers modems supporting the v.32bis, v.32, v.42bis,
v.42, and MNP5 protocols. Modem settings are 8 bit, no parity,
and 1 stop bit. A vt100 terminal emulation is recommended for
optimal communications.

RATES

The World offers two billing plans with rates that are uniform
24hours per day at all connection speeds. The Basic Rate plan
includesa $5 monthly account fee plus a $2 per hour usage fee.

Basic Rate accounts include a 5MB of private disk space. The 20/20 Plan is a volume usage rate where $20 paid in advance buys 20 hours of online time during a calendar month. The 20/20 Plan includes the $5 monthly account fee and 20/20 Plan accounts receive an increased disk space of 2MB. Any 20/20 Plan account used for more than 20 hours during the month is billed at the rate of $1 per hour.

The World offers payment options via MasterCard or Visa, postal invoice, or email invoice. Additional billing plans are available for members of the Boston Computer Society, the BMUG organization and for corporate customers. Send email to "info@world.std.com" for details.

SIGNUP PROCEDURE

To sign up for World access, dial 617-739-WRLD (617-739-9753) or telnet to the hostname, world.std.com (192.74.137.5). At The World's login prompt, use the login "new" to access the account request program. You will be asked several questions necessary to create your account. The World will allow you to select your own loginname which will also be your email address. Most people select their name, their initials, or a combination of both. Your initial password will be provided by the account creation software. All customers must contact our office for account activation after making the account request. Every World account is eligible for a one hour trial period (see details below).

THE WORLD'S STAFF

The World is managed by a professional full-time staff, all of whom have UNIX and international networking experience. We are committed to providing our customers with reliable, cost effective Internet services. In order that our customers can exploit the power of today's electronic community, our primary occupation is the support of The World and its resources.

ONE HOUR TRIAL

All accounts are eligible for a one hour trial period. This provides an opportunity to explore The World and its resources without incurring any obligation. Simply complete the account request procedure and take a sixty minute tour of The World.

OVERVIEW OF SERVICES OFFERED BY THE WORLD

Customer Support

Software Tool & Die believes that customer support is the primary service which our staff offers. Our customer support members have extensive knowledge of UNIX, Internet, and computer based communications. We encourage our customers to contact us when they have questions, problems, or comments.

A comprehensive online help utility is maintained by our staff and provides up to the minute details on Internet services. All information within the help utility is available for customer access.

A detailed tutorial style user guide is available both in electronic form and in a printed manual. This is designed for customers who have never before used the UNIX environment and provides concise step-by-step instructions on the essential World services.

Additionally, customer support is provided by telephone at 617-739-0202, by email through the address staff@world.std.com and in a public spirited format on the USENET newsgroup wstd.help.

Electronic Mail

Electronic mail is the most ubiquitous service of the World and of the Internet. From a World account your electronic messages are delivered direct to any other Internet member at any location around the globe. In addition to access to all Internet mailboxes, The World can be used to send electronic mail to other mailbox services such as CompuServe, Applelink, MCImail, BIX, Fidonet and UUCP sites.

The World offers all popular UNIX mail programs including mail, pine, elm, mh, mush, GNU's RMAIL, dmail and mm.

An added feature of Internet mail is the ability to join a mailing list. These mailing lists are collections of kindred souls devoted to a specialized topic. World customers may also select to create and manage their own mailing lists.
USENET Newsgroups

The international public forum called USENET is the most

extensive bulletin board system in the world. This collection
of over 4700 newsgroups ranging in topics from technical and
scientific discussions to recreational conversations unites
people in an electronic community. The World distributes all
available USENET newsgroups including many groups from foreign
countries in their native languages.

The newsreaders available on World are rn, nn, trn, tass, and
GNUS.

Electronic Newspapers

The World offers two electronic newspaper services which
provide direct access to the newswire services from AP,
Reuters, and others. From Clarinet communications, World
receives the UPI wire service; syndicated columnists, such as
Dave Barry; daily closing prices for the stock markets; and
Newsbytes, a service specializing in hightech related news.
From MSEN, the Reuters newswire is available. Both of
these electronic newspapers are delivered in the USENET
newsgroup formats.

Gopher, WAIS, and WWW

These three services, Gopher, WAIS, and WWW provide different
ways of accessing large collections of information. Gopher is
an Internet navigation utility providing a menu based format
for roaming the Internet. Wide Area Information Server (WAIS)
is a tool for searching an indexed database by making English-
like queries. After locating the information, WAIS allows for
retrieving of the entire document. World Wide Web (WWW) is
another database access tool based on a hypertext design.

Internet Relay Chat

The Internet Relay Chat allows for World customers to join a
live, interactive discussion in a format much like talk radio.
Each channel is devoted to a specified topic and has
participants from any of the Internet hosts. After joining a
channel, your messages are immediately delivered to listeners
around the globe. IRC even has channels in various languages.

Information Archives

The Internet has many extensive archives of information which
are freely accessible. These archives include shareware

software, public domain software, product catalogs, newsletters, etc. The program called FTP is used to access these archives and retrieve the information. An FTP index is available via the program called, archie.

Online Book Initiative

The purpose of the OBI is to create a publicly accessible repository for freely redistributable collections of textual information, a net-worker's library. The OBI project was started by Barry Shein, who is also founder and president of The World. The complete OBI collection is available to World customers.

Corporate Services

Businesses, small and large, are the fastest growing segment of the Internet community. World offers several special services for corporate customers. The corporate mailbox service allows a business to register an Internet domain name and receive email address to their Internet address. FTP and gopher archive areas can be established for distribution of information about your business and products. Discounted rates are offered for corporate customers with multiple World accounts. Onsite Internet training sessions are available.

Unix Software

An extensive compilation of the utilities and programs which have become an integral part of the UNIX environment are available. The unix command shells include sh, csh, ksh, bash, tcsh, zsh and rc.

GNU Software

The Free Software Foundation is a Cambridge based organization providing free software. Their primary project is called GNU and intends to distribute a complete set of UNIX utilities and software for no charge. Many of the available GNU components, such as EMACS, GCC, G++, GDB, GAS, BASH, GAWK, are installed. This collection is particularly useful for customers who are interested in software development.

Games

Many games common to the UNIX environment are available. These include hack, moria, nethack, adventure, omega, robots, and

tetris. The MUD (Multiple User Dungeon) games offer access to
real-time interactive program where the players explore a
virtual space in a role-playing manner.

COST EFFECTIVE LONG DISTANCE ACCESS

At the present time, Boston is the only place where direct
dial Worldmmodems exist. For access from the greater-Boston
area, call 1-800-555-5000 for New England Telephone rates.
Various non-measured services are offered for flat monthly
fees. From outside Massachusetts, first check your long
distance service provider. Many companies offer affordable
rates for direct dial service particularly when you dial
frequently to the same number or area code. MCI will provide
additional discounts for World customers who list STD on their
Friends and Family Plan.

Lower cost local dial modems throughout the USA are available
with CompuServe's Packet Network (an additional $5.60/hr added
to your World bill, no CompuServe Information Service account
is required - call 800-848-8980 for your local number) or PC-
Pursuit (as low as $1/hr; available evenings, weekends and
holidays only - call 800-736-1130). World is not affiliated
with any of these modem network service providers.

****

This document was last modified on June 30, 1993.
For the latest update, check the ftp archive at world.std.com
or send your request via email to info@world.std.com

Software Tool & Die 1330 Beacon Street Brookline MA 02146
617-739-0202 office@world.std.com

Coupon: CERFnet

$50

CERFnet

Internet access for individuals:

- **Nationwide 800 number dial-up service**
- **Email, Usenet, FTP, Telnet, Gopher**
- **Shell or SLIP accounts**

This coupon entitles you to $50 off your first month's subscription. Call for details.

+1 800 876-CERF

**CALIFORNIA EDUCATION AND RESEARCH FEDERATION NETWORK
P.O. BOX 85608, SAN DIEGO, CA 92186-9784
help@cerf.net
Limit one per customer. Offer expires 12/31/94**

Coupon: HoloNet

HoloNet connects you to the Internet for less!

- Local call in over 850 cities nationwide
- Internet E-mail
- USENET NEWS
- Archie

- Internet Relay Chat
- FTP & Telnet
- Personal File Area
- User Friendly
- Gopher

Now get 50% off your first year of HoloNet membership. To qualify for this offer you must send in this coupon with your HoloNet member name on it within 30 days of signing up for HoloNet Service.
Good for new members only.

HoloNet Member Name_____

$30.00 Value

Limit one coupon per customer. Offer expires 12/31/94

HoloNet^{SM}

From Information Access Technologies, Inc.

HoloNet is a service mark of Information Access Technologies, Inc. • 46 Shattuck Square, Suite 11 • Berkeley, CA 94704
voice 510-704-0160 • © 1993 Information Access Technologies, Inc.

Coupon: The World

This coupon good for 20 hours on first month's subscription

THE WORLD

Public access unix
Electronic mail
FTP/Telnet
Usenet

Online Book Initiative
Internet relay chat
Software archives
Clarinet

A Public Information Utility
617-739-WRLD

Software Tool & Die • 1330 Beacon St., Brookline MA 02146
617-739-0202 office@world.std.com

APPENDIX D

The Internet Society

Okay. You have read the book and have your Internet driving license. What now?

You can enhance your skills and personal networking potential by joining the Internet Society. By joining the Internet Society, you can increase your involvement in the Internet revolution. Further, as a member of the Internet Society you will benefit from discounts on publications about the Internet and services offered by companies that can connect PC users to the Internet.

The Internet Society is a new international professional membership organization to promote the use of the Internet for research and scholarly communication and collaboration.

The Society provides a forum for government, industry, educators, and users to debate and recommend technical standards and procedures for the global Internet and private internets.

The Society seeks to advance open scholarship in all countries.

Membership

The Internet Society is a professional membership organization with individual voting members and institutional non-voting members. There are several classes of institutional members. The society publishes a newsletter on a regular basis and holds an annual meeting to which all members and other interested parties are invited. The topics of the annual meeting vary, but focus on current research in networking, Internet functionality and growth, and other interests of the Society constituency.

Charter

The Society is a nonprofit organization and is operated for academic, educational, charitable and scientific purposes, among which are:

1. To facilitate and support the technical evolution of the Internet as a research and education infrastructure and to stimulate the involvement of the academic, scientific, and engineering communities, among others in the evolution of the Internet.

2. To educate the academic and scientific communities and the public concerning the technology, use, and application of the Internet.

3. To promote scientific and educational applications of Internet technology for the benefit of educational institutions at all grade levels, industry, and the public at large.

4. To provide a forum for exploration of new Internet applications and to foster collaboration among organizations in their operation and use of the Internet.

What Now?

Copy the application form on the following page and FAX or mail it to the Internet Society. If you already have your Internet connection, then you can apply by email.

Howard Funk, Acting Executive Director
Internet Society
Reston, Virginia

September 1, 1993

APPLICATION FOR MEMBERSHIP

Internet Society

To: Internet Society

Please enroll me as a member of the Internet Society. I understand that membership entitles me to receive the quarterly Internet Society News, reduced fees for attendance at Internet Society conferences, and other benefits. Membership privileges will be for twelve months from the receipt of payment. I am applying for

_____   regular membership at $70
_____   student membership at $25 (please *include* proof of status)

NAME: (Mr/Mrs/Ms) _____

POSTAL ADDRESS: _____

_____

PHONE: _____   **FACSIMILE:** _____

INTERNET ADDRESS: _____

Payment Information: Payment of Internet Society annual dues may be made via check, money order, credit card or wire transfer. File headers will be accepted as signatures for e-mail transactions.

_____   Please bill me.

_____   Payment is included with this application as below.

For credit card payments:

_____AMEX _____VISA _____MC _____DINERS

_____CARTE BLANCHE

Card Number: _____

Expiration Date: _____

Signature: _____

Send **wire transfers** to:

Bank: Riggs Bank of Virginia
Merrifield Office
8315 Lee Highway
Fairfax, VA 22116 USA

Bank ABA Number: 056001260

Account Number: Internet Society
14838710

Internet Society
Suite 100
1895 Preston White Drive
Reston, VA 22091-5434 USA

Tel: +1 703 648 9888
Fax: +1 703 620 0913
e-mail: isoc@isoc.org

Index

Coupon: ⊞Hayes®

It's All Here. It's All Hayes.

- Proven Hayes reliability for your home, small office, or home office
- Low cost V.32/9600 bps standalone PC data modem + 9600 bps FAX
- V.42bis data compression for 38,400 bps throughput
- No worries about data accuracy with V.42 error-control
- No doubts about communicating with older modems with MNP 2-5
- Group 3 send/receive FAX - 9600-2400 bps
- Free modem-to-computer cable and Smartcom™ data and FAX software

Special Offer !

Use this coupon to buy a Hayes Accura 96 + FAX96 modem at $70.00 (U.S.) off suggested retail price. Limit one per customer. Allow 6-8 weeks for delivery. Shipping and handling charges are extra. To order please call:

Hayes Microcomputer Products, Inc.
Attn: Customer Service
(404) 441-1617

Offer good through 12/31/94